Hammer Goes to Hell

For Bill and Brian

Hammer Goes to Hell

The House of Horror's
Unmade Films

Kieran Foster

EDINBURGH
University Press

Edinburgh University Press is one of the leading university presses in the UK. We publish academic books and journals in our selected subject areas across the humanities and social sciences, combining cutting-edge scholarship with high editorial and production values to produce academic works of lasting importance. For more information visit our website: edinburghuniversitypress.com

© Kieran Foster, 2024

Grateful acknowledgement is made to the sources listed in the List of Illustrations for permission to reproduce material previously published elsewhere. Every effort has been made to trace the copyright holders, but if any have been inadvertently overlooked, the publisher will be pleased to make the necessary arrangements at the first opportunity.

Edinburgh University Press Ltd
13 Infirmary Street
Edinburgh EH1 1LT

First published in hardback by Edinburgh University Press 2024

Typeset in Arno and Myriad
by Manila Typesetting Company

A CIP record for this book is available from the British Library

ISBN 978 1 4744 9665 0 (hardback)
ISBN 978 1 4744 9666 7 (paperback)
ISBN 978 1 4744 9667 4 (webready PDF)
ISBN 978 1 4744 9668 1 (epub)

The right of Kieran Foster to be identified as the author of this work has been asserted in accordance with the Copyright, Designs and Patents Act 1988, and the Copyright and Related Rights Regulations 2003 (SI No. 2498).

Contents

List of figures	vii
Notes on text	viii
Acknowledgements	ix
Foreword, by Jonathan Rigby	xii
Introduction	**1**
Structure	9
Chapter 1: Frankenstein unmade	**13**
Enter *Frankenstein*: Subotsky and Hammer Films	18
Hammer in America: *Tales of Frankenstein*	25
Conclusion	34
Chapter 2: *The Night Creatures* and the censor	**37**
Contextualising *The Night Creatures*	40
Censoring *The Night Creatures*	48
The collapse of American finance	57
Chapter 3: The curse of *Dracula*	**61**
Reviving Dracula: the reinvention of Hammer's *Dracula* series	63
Kali Devil Bride of Dracula	71
Conclusion	84
Chapter 4: Grave encounters: *Vampirella* and *Vlad the Impaler*	**87**
Carreras's *Vlad the Impaler*: 1974–9	88

Hammer's *Star Wars?* Michael Carreras and *Vampirella*   92
Conclusion   104

Chapter 5: International waters: *Nessie* and overseas finance   107
Toho, Columbia and the financial complexity of *Nessie*   111
Calling Columbia: *Nessie* and American finance   118
Conclusion   125

Chapter 6: *Nessie* in dry dock   127
Nessie sinks   139
Conclusion   141

Chapter 7: High stakes: the Roy Skeggs years   146
Vlad the Impaler 1980–90   148
Hammer International: *Vlad the Impaler* 1990–2000   157
Conclusion   166

Conclusion   171
Vampirella: a live script reading and future study   174
Conclusion   180

Bibliography   183
Filmography   197
Appendix: Hammer Films – *The Quatermass Xperiment* to 1979   203
Index   206

Figures

I.1	The one piece of archival material held in the Hammer Archive on *Zeppelins v Pterodactyls*	6
1.1	The copy of Subotsky's *Frankenstein* screenplay, mistitled *The Curse of Frankenstein*	20
2.1	The cover page to Matheson's self-adaptation *The Night Creatures*	49
3.1	Houghton's 'historical notes', which precedes his synopsis	75
4.1	An example of a page of Wicking's *Vampirella* screenplay, which features comic-accurate artwork	96
6.1	The title page of the screenplay *Nessie*. Credited solely to Bryan Forbes, despite alterations by Michael Carreras	136
7.1	The title page of Jonas McCord's *Vlad the Impaler* screenplay, which gives an address for Hammer's American office near the Warner Bros. lot	161
C.1	The *Vampirella*: the live script reading poster designed by Graham Humphreys	179

Notes on text

Where the website boxofficemojo.com is referred to for box office figures, this is indicated in text by only the website name for brevity and presentation purposes. Full URL references can be found in the bibliography. British spelling is used throughout, with the exception of quotations which feature American spelling. When quotations utilise capitalisation or italics (or conversely do not), this is replicated in text.

Parts of Chapter 4 have been published as 'Repurposing the Archive: Unmade Films, *Vampirella* and Adaptation' in the *Journal of British Cinema and Television* (2022), 19(4): 518–35. Parts of Chapter 5 have been published as 'Nessie Has Risen from the Grave' in Hackett and Harrington's *Beasts of the Deep: Sea Creatures and Popular Culture* (2018), pp. 214–31. Parts of Chapter 6 have been published as 'Dracula Unseen: The Death and Afterlife of Hammer's *Vlad the Impaler*' in *Journal of Adaptation in Film & Performance* (2017), 10(3): 203–15.

Acknowledgements

All being well, this book will be released eight years after I started my PhD. The thesis which started this journey would not have seen the light of day without the funding provided by Midlands 4 Cities. I will always be extremely thankful to them and everyone at De Montfort University who supported me through the whole PhD process.

The only time I ever miss the PhD is when I think about the people I no longer share an office with. Huge love to Jen Voss, Frances Galt, Kieran Sellars, Sophie Swoffer and Becky Jones for your friendship and guidance.

I am immensely grateful to Gillian Leslie, Sam Johnson and everyone at Edinburgh University Press. Their professionalism and kindness have helped this daunting process feel a little less scary, and I feel privileged to be amongst such incredible horror scholarship. Thanks as well to my peer reviewers for their constructive comments which have undoubtedly improved the book. Special thanks also to Dave 'Mute' Huntley, for the incredible book cover.

I have also been lucky enough to get to know a range of phenomenal academics who have been extremely kind and supportive. With special thanks due to Laura Mee, Johnny Walker, Sabrina Moro, Shellie McMurdo, Iain Robert Smith, Elizabeth Evans, Gianluca Sergi, Helen W. Kennedy, Sue Vice, Hannah Hamad, Roberta Pearson and Justin Smith. James Fenwick deserves a special shoutout, mainly for being a terrific scholar and extremely patient with the tired dad energy I now bring to our (now numerous!) collaborations.

On special shout outs, Cassie Brummitt has been a therapist, proofreader and great friend for years now, and her support keeping my head above water and helping to get this manuscript whipped into shape has been greatly received. Thanks mate. Likewise Craig Ian Mann has been on hand nearly 24/7 (I go to bed at 10pm so maybe it just feels like that) to offer specific guidance with the manuscript, talk horror movies or just chat rubbish, all three of which I'm incredibly grateful for.

The vital help of the staff at the BFI Archive, BBFC Archive, Warner Bros. Archive, British Library and the Margaret Herrick Library is also hugely appreciated, and their help and guidance made doing research for the book far less intimidating. Hammer Films have also been incredibly helpful in responding and solving any queries I had about Hammer's historical projects, for which I am grateful. I'd also like to thank Jonathan Rigby, Marcus Hearn, Sarah Appleton, Richard Klemenson, Arthur Ellis and the fantastic 'Hammer Lovers' Facebook group for their helpful insights into Hammer throughout the years. Sadly, two people who were really supportive with their time and insights have passed away since my PhD in 2019. I say thank you to Denis Meikle and Tim Beddows for their kindness and generosity.

Outside of academia Charlie Moorcroft, Abi Heath, Nathan Leverton, Will Simpson, Shaun Butcher, Sam Osborne, Tom Bruccoleri, Alex Michael, Megan Edwards, Liz Calow, Amy Beresford, Graeme Woodcock, Lew Woodrow and Noah Goodliffe have been tremendous pillars of support. I count myself very lucky to have friends like them.

I have been surrounded by the love and encouragement of my family throughout the writing of this book. I am fortunate enough to have such a large family that to express thanks to them all separately could result in a list as long as the book itself, but I am extremely grateful for all their help throughout the last decade (and the two before that as well to be fair).

A running joke between me, my mum, dad and sister is that none of them really have a clue what I do for a living. Despite there absolutely being some truth to this, it has never stopped them offering their endless love and encouragement. All three of them have been lifelines throughout the research process, and I am incredibly lucky to have them. Now please read the book.

One big change between the thesis submission and finishing this book was the birth of my son Dylan in May 2021. Through these eighteen-plus months he has always been a bottomless pit of love, affection and Quavers. If anytime the book felt overwhelming or life and death, he was always on hand to make sure I knew what was really important (and probably to ask for a snack as well).

Finally, I would like to thank my wife Bryony who still, after over twelve years, surprises me with her kindness and generosity. I am confident that this book (and me probably) wouldn't exist without her. Thank you doesn't really cover it.

Foreword
By Jonathan Rigby

For long-time enthusiasts of Hammer Film Productions, there are numerous niggling little questions that pop into our minds at the oddest moments. For this particular long-time Hammer enthusiast, one of those questions relates to what might loosely be termed 'the Bryan Forbes situation'.

Here was an actor who, in the late 1950s, was cast in two particularly striking Hammer pictures, both of them directed by Val Guest: *Quatermass 2* and *Yesterday's Enemy*. By 1969, Forbes had established himself as a distinguished writer-director, with such titles as *Whistle Down the Wind*, *King Rat* and *The Whisperers* to his credit, and had become production head of EMI Films. Putting together an ambitious programme at Elstree, he was frustrated by the amount of studio space he had to give over to such garish, new-style Hammer pictures as *The Vampire Lovers* and *Scars of Dracula*, attributing this imposition to the incestuous 'you scratch my back' relationship between his boss, Bernard Delfont, and Hammer's clubbable managing director, James Carreras. Forbes's programme, touted in the press as a heroic attempt to shore up the British film industry, folded after a mere two years, and by 1976 the industry was in terminal decline. It was at this point that Forbes, as writer and mooted director, became involved with an extravagant and ultimately doomed Hammer project called *Nessie*. Given his rather fractious relationship with Hammer in the recent past, I sometimes used to wonder: how exactly did this 'strange bedfellows' arrangement work? And how did it go?

Well, I need wonder no more, because Kieran Foster, in his apocalyptically titled *Hammer Goes to Hell*, has provided the answer in unprecedented detail. Now, faced with that question 'How did it go?', I can confidently reply: 'Not well.'

The author's thesis is a stimulating one, starting with the proposition that books like his will soon, he hopes, become obsolete. This, he argues, is because historical analyses of film companies can never be complete without a detailed account – not just of the films that made it into production, the ones we're used to reading about already – but of unrealised projects too. Once this view is widely accepted, he's confident that *Hammer Goes to Hell* and its like will become superfluous as standalone works. Until that happens, however, the book makes its case cogently and persuasively, and I for one find it hard to argue with.

Winding back fifty years, the first Hammer book was a slim volume called *The House of Horror: The Story of Hammer Films*. Edited by Allen Eyles, Robert Adkinson and Nicholas Fry, it was issued by Lorrimer Publishing in 1973 and proved an invaluable primer to young fans, no matter how flimsy its content may appear today. In the middle were eight pages of colour plates collectively entitled 'Hammer Posters' – and the striking thing about them, apart from their eye-popping luridness, was that only three of the eight were for films that were actually made.

Pre-production posters for *Dr Jekyll & Sister Hyde*, *Dracula A.D. 1972* and *Frankenstein and the Monster from Hell*? Fine; lovely to see them. But what on earth were these others? *Zeppelins v Pterodactyls*, *Payment in Fear*, *When the Earth Cracked Open*, *Mistress of the Seas*, *Victim of His Imagination* . . . Whatever they were, they were enticing in the extreme. And as students of the company looked further into its history, they could add yet more mysterious titles of this sort – *The Rape of Sabena*, *The Bride of Newgate Jail* (aka *The Reluctant Virgin*), *Blood of the Foreign Legion*, *Chaka Zulu*, *The Savage Jackboot*, *Kali Devil Bride of Dracula*, to name just a few.

Hammer Goes to Hell doesn't detain us with exhaustive detail on *all* these enigmatic projects. The book would become absurdly unwieldy if it did. It focuses instead on a few selected case histories, from the fascinating moment in 1957 when Hammer booked Richard Matheson into a comfortable London hotel and asked him to write a screen adaptation of his ground-breaking novel *I Am Legend*, to the company's curious preoccupation, some fifteen years later, with *Dracula* 'origin' stories. The first of these, focusing on Bram Stoker's autocratic employer Henry Irving, was the *Victim of His Imagination* project referred to above. The second, *Vlad the Impaler*, was based on an origin theory that to me is much less persuasive, but nevertheless it rumbled on at Hammer for close to three decades.

Hammer Goes to Hell culminates with the convoluted saga of *Nessie*, but on the way to it we examine another project that has long intrigued Hammer fans, largely because of another striking piece of advertising art – *Vampirella*. This one I find especially fascinating because it involved me in an ambitious attempt, as Kieran Foster puts it, 'to foreground the company's unmade films in innovative ways'. Having narrated a live script reading of *The Unquenchable Thirst of Dracula* at Nottingham's Mayhem Film Festival in October 2015, I was asked to direct a similar enterprise at London's Regent Street Cinema. This one – produced by Kieran and staged, oddly enough, four years to the day after the *Unquenchable* event – was devoted to Christopher Wicking's script for *Vampirella*. Dated 27 October 1975, this was just one of several drafts commissioned by Hammer, but with a projected start date of 5 January 1976, plus Barbara Leigh and Peter Cushing engaged to star, it was almost certainly the one that came closest to being produced.

In the past, I'd tended to look on Hammer's unrealised plans for *Vampirella* with a degree of trepidation. In the absence of a script, it seemed to me a subject that, had it been made, could have easily defaulted to salaciousness – either that or, effects-wise, it would have been an example of Hammer's reach visibly exceeding its grasp. (In the same way, *Nessie* might have turned out to be little more than a cash-strapped 1970s update of the 1960 film *Gorgo*.) It was fascinating, then, to finally get hold of Wicking's *Vampirella* script and to marvel at its scope, its thoroughly bonkers plot, and its relative dearth of salaciousness.

Wicking generally signed his name to rather intricate, sometimes even impenetrable, horror scripts, but in adapting a famous comic-book he clearly realised he was dealing with 'pulp – glorious pulp'. The script fires off in every scattershot direction imaginable; to put it diplomatically, it clearly needed further work. But the section that really sells it for me is a twenty-minute trip to the Mirabelle Mansion, described by Wicking as 'a gloomy Gothic building that looks like the Old Dark House Mark II' – last refuge of a pair of octogenarian music-hall sisters, target of a home invasion by rioting Hells Angels, and finally a party venue for waltzing Edwardian zombies. This stupendous and beautifully written scene mashes together *Sunset Blvd., What Ever Happened to Baby Jane?, A Clockwork Orange, The Wild Angels, Night of the Living Dead, The Phantom of the Opera*, *The Masque of the Red Death* and on and on – and to have seen Hammer realise it would have justified the film's existence all by itself.

For staging purposes, the script was adapted by me, a process entailing some very minor dialogue trims, the creation of a brief voiceover prologue and a few newly written lines to cover awkward transitions, and the excision of a couple of inconsequential scenes. None of these changes did any damage to the basic fabric, nor to any of the important details. The event itself is discussed in more depth in the concluding section of this book, but the bottom line is that it turned out to be a very palpable hit. The question of whether or not a finished film based on Wicking's script would have been any good faded into the background; for one evening the script, with all its wonkiness and its absurdities, was given life, just as Wicking's Edwardian zombies are at the Mirabelle Mansion. Like Frankenstein, everyone present, on stage and off, could stagger back and cry, 'It's alive!'

Not only did the *Vampirella* event give an intriguing insight into what might have been, it also indicated that unmade scripts needn't just be dusty old artefacts mouldering in filing cabinets. They can be infused, decades later, with the life they never had, just as the study of them can lend renewed vitality to film history. And that really is what *Hammer Goes to Hell* is all about.

There have been many – let's be frank, probably too many – books about Hammer. But this one comes at the story from a different angle. It's crammed with new information, paints a vivid portrait of a company struggling quixotically for existence, and I suspect it will revitalise quite a few hardened Hammer pundits who thought they knew it all.

JONATHAN RIGBY is the author of the genre histories *English Gothic,* *American Gothic* **and** *Euro Gothic,* **together with** *Studies in Terror, Christopher Lee: The Authorised Screen History* **and** *Roxy Music: Both Ends Burning.*

Introduction

On 23 November 2021, *Variety* reported that the production company Hammer Films had teamed with Network Distributing to form a new company called Hammer Studios. Simon Oakes, CEO of Hammer, noted that the new partnership with Network 'will be able to build on the legacy of Britain's most iconic film brand, one that started in 1934 and is alive and kicking in 2021' (in Ramachandran 2021). The formation of this company represented a new chapter in the legacy of Hammer, the story of which has been extensively documented over its near ninety-year history. Hammer Films is 'one of the British film industry's greatest success stories' (Kinsey 2002: 6), that with the release of the X-rated science fiction film *The Quatermass Xperiment* (Guest, 1955) and until its closure in 1979, revitalized the horror genre in Britain and left a lasting filmic legacy on the international stage.

This book looks to examine this legacy through a production study of Hammer Films which foregrounds the company's unmade projects as key texts often underrepresented in most studies of Hammer (and, for that matter, wider film and television history). This is not a book that looks to index or catalogue an exhaustive list of Hammer's unmade films, or provide a comprehensive account of all of these unmade projects' stories and synopses. This is a chronological history of Hammer Films, focusing primarily on the period between 1957 – when its first gothic horror, Terence Fisher's *The Curse of Frankenstein*, was released – until its takeover by a consortium led by Charles Saatchi in 2000. This monograph is one in a long line to focus on Hammer, from books that, like this one, are dedicated to a chronological examination of the company's history (Hearn and Barnes 2007; Meikle 2009; Hearn 2011; Kinsey 2002, 2007);

to those that have studied the company through the prism of the British gothic tradition (Forshaw 2013; Rigby 2002; Hutchings 1993; Pirie 1973); and those which have used it as a key case study in broader works on British cinema and genre (Walker 2016; Harper and Porter 2003).

Yet what makes this book distinct is its integration and foregrounding of Hammer's most notable unmade projects into this history, offering new perspectives and insights into this well-documented company. To comprehend why these unmade projects are so crucial to understanding the economic and creative labour undertaken at Hammer, one needs to consider its output over a thirty year period. Between 1950 and 1959, it produced sixty-one feature films; the 1960s saw Hammer produce fifty-four; and between 1970 and 1979, this figure fell dramatically to thirty-three. Yet more telling is the fact that thirty-one of these films were produced before 1975, with only *To The Devil a Daughter* (Sykes, 1976) and *The Lady Vanishes* (Page, 1979) produced between 1975 and 1979. Despite this stark decline in production in the mid to late 1970s, none of the existing studies of the company alter their methodologies when discussing this period to look closely at the films Hammer was expending an enormous amount of effort trying to make in this fallow period. Also, although Hammer's unmade projects are often at least mentioned in other studies of the company, they are often removed from any chronological examination of its fortunes. For example, in *The Hammer Vault*, Marcus Hearn (2011) presents a film-by-film chronological account of Hammer, but its unmade films appear grouped together in a six-page spread on pages 160 to 165, and the projects mentioned range from the year 1958 to 1979. As a result, these unmade projects are removed from their production context and ultimately put in a vacuum, with no contextualised analysis of how they affected Hammer at the time they were proposed, or what position Hammer were in at the time of their development.

Like the previously mentioned studies of Hammer, this book's research parameters focus primarily on the company's horror output. This is so that the key difference foregrounded in this alternate history of Hammer is the significance of unmade case studies, although I acknowledge that there is a comparative dearth of research focusing on Hammer's work outside the horror genre. However, by focusing on the horror genre, this book will highlight how important the consideration of Hammer's unmade works is to understanding the impact and workings of the company, and illustrate that a comprehensive history of a production company as prolific as this one will never be complete without considering the films it did not make alongside those it did. The book will draw extensively on previously unseen archival materials relating to the company's unmade projects with the intention of demonstrating that the production histories of unmade films not only raises new methodological questions about the nature of film production, but also provides important contextual evidence that sheds new light on existing works.

With unmade films being the key focus of this book, it is important to map the terrain of existing work in the field of unmade film studies. In regards to the industry itself, the ubiquity of failed, uncompleted or lost productions cannot be overstated. Clashes of personalities, changing executives, logistical hurdles and financial disasters are par for the course in film production, and a film successfully making it through the production process is, to quote *Top Gun: Maverick* (2022) director Joseph Kosinski, 'a miracle' (BBC Online 2013). In fact, Peter Krämer notes that it is unmade projects that 'have absorbed much of the creativity and a substantial proportion of the financial investments of the American film industry' (2016: 381). But if this is true of the film industry itself, it is certainly not the case within film studies. While there has undoubtedly been excellent work within the field of unmade film studies inside and outside of academia, work on this subject is largely discounted outside of this small, emergent field. As such, one of the primary motivations of this book is to take up Krämer's call, in relation to unmade film and television, for 'film academics to do some catching up' (2018: 71).

In each chapter of this chronological study of Hammer Films, the case studies examined will be unmade projects developed at the company between the 1950s and the late 1990s. The Hammer Script Archive at De Montfort University (DMU) is the central resource upon which the study is based, being the source of the majority of the primary documentation (such as screenplays, financial documents, correspondence). The archive has been held in the Cinema and Television History Institute (CATHI) since 2012 and received a second delivery of material from Hammer in April 2016. This book represents the first sustained research project that has utilised the Hammer Script Archive and its materials as a primary resource, with almost no academic work having been done on the unmade films of Hammer, with the key exception being Peter Hutchings's chapter on Hammer's unmade vampire adaptation *The Night Creatures* in *Sight Unseen* (2008: 53–71), a project also discussed by Stacey Abbott in her monograph *Undead Apocalypse: Vampires and Zombies in the 21st Century* (2016).

While unmade film studies is a relatively neglected area of study, a growing field exists nonetheless. The few publications that have emerged from it have come from diverse quarters, often being singular case studies of a film or filmmaker and with no consistent methodological approach emerging in relation to the study of an unmade film. In a collection I co-edited entitled *Shadow Cinema: The Historical and Production Context of Unmade Films* (Fenwick et al. 2020), we frame unmade film studies as a:

> revisionist approach to film history [that] can be based on textual readings and interpretations from a variety of contexts: adaptation, political history and censorship, industrial relations, social history, critical media industry, biographical, feminist, queer, postcolonial criticism, production studies and many more besides. (7)

However, while the study of unmade films can be incredibly diverse, undoubtedly one of the more dominant methodological practices has been situating an unmade project in the canonical work of a director and 'building up a picture of their subject's triumphs and failures' (North 2008: 1). Within these works, unmade films are often used as case studies to cement thematic preoccupations already noted in the director's established works, or instead to situate these unmade projects historically in the director's filmography (Armstrong 2008: 105–20; Carringer 1985: 1–16; Castle 2009; Cobb 2014; Waldman 1991). Beyond this approach, work in producer studies, specifically by Andrew Spicer and A. T. McKenna, has also engaged with unmade case studies to emphasise the 'intermediary' (Spicer 2010: 299) nature of the producer's role across all aspects of film production (Spicer 2008: 87–105; 2011: 71–88; 2020: 57–71; Spicer and McKenna 2013). As well as this focus on the individual's role in film production, there has also been work on unproduced adaptations, and how they successfully circumvent debates on fidelity due to there being no completed film text available for comparative analysis (Hutchings 2008: 53–71; Krämer 2016: 372–82; Murray 2008: 5–23).

While these works present valid and fascinating insights into the film and television industries, one of the key focuses of this monograph will be the collaborative nature of film production. The roles of screenwriters, producers, distributors, financiers and directors are all foregrounded in this book and underline the temperamental balancing act of film production. By focusing on the unmade films of one company and noting the changing nature of wider industrial factors as well as key internal relationships, this study will underline just how crucial unmade films are to production histories and will, in part, challenge the view that production history is determined only by completed films.

Indeed, its central argument is that any comprehensive industry study needs to take account of those projects that did not come to fruition, as well as those that did. So how do we define an unmade film? After all, a film in development can be anything from a brief outline or a two-page treatment; it can have undergone several script iterations; it might have gotten as far through pre-production as to have been budgeted, cast and crewed. Sometimes it has close relations to other projects that were completed; sometimes it stands alone as a long-forgotten ambition. Whatever an unmade film may be, it is defined, for the purposes of this book, by the evidence left behind in the archive.

The prioritising of contextual materials over the films themselves means that the research featured within this book is heavily reliant on archival sources. This is not uncommon in production histories, with 'the central importance of primary sources' being put forward as a key feature of 'New Film History' (Chapman et al. 2007: 7). However, what is slightly less common is the centrality of one key archive to an entire study, and as such it is worth concentrating more on the Hammer Script Archive and its importance. The materials held within the Hammer Script Archive are extensive but inconsistent, and the availability of certain resources within the archive has undoubtedly dictated some of the case studies used within this research. While the case studies have been carefully chosen to foreground the key arguments of each chapter, there are well-known unmade Hammer projects that are not prominently featured. For example, one of the most striking posters produced for Hammer is for their unmade project *Zeppelins v Pterodactyls*. The unmade film's poster, drawn by Tom Chantrell, lives up to the exciting promise of its title, and the combination of both title and poster has seen the film discussed regularly in Hammer fan circles. This led to a live script reading of the project in Nottingham in October 2017 at the Broadway Cinema's Mayhem Film Festival, which demonstrated the popularity of the project and will be discussed in this book's conclusion. However, despite the unmade project's notoriety among Hammer fandom, very little primary material on the proposed film exists. The Hammer Script Archive only holds one treatment on the project, which was subsequently adapted by screenwriter and Mayhem Festival co-organiser Steven Shiel into a full screenplay for the live reading. With only one piece of archival material available, it is extremely difficult to gauge its development and impact on Hammer, and as such it acts as a pertinent reminder that basing one's research primarily on one specific archive undoubtedly leaves the researcher at the mercy of omissions and inconsistencies.

One of the ways of combatting the unreliability of some of these documents is through cross-referencing sources from other archives. Although the Hammer Script Archive is central to this study, I have also visited and utilised materials from the British Board of Film Classification (BBFC), the British Film Institute (BFI), the Margaret Herrick Library and the University of Southern California's (USC) Warner Bros. Archive. Materials found in the BFI and BBFC on projects such as the unmade Hammer

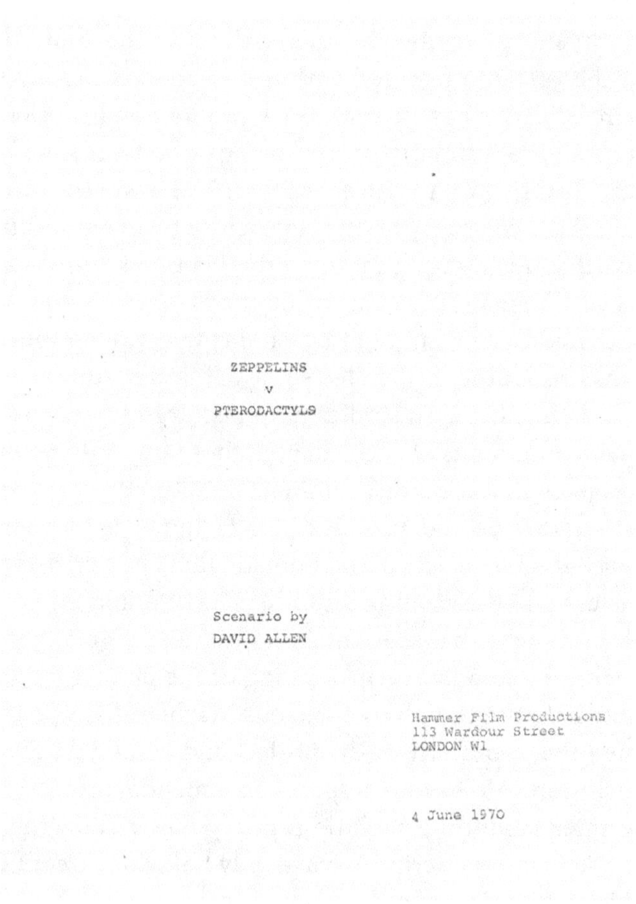

```
                    ZEPPELINS
                        v
                   PTERODACTYLS




                  Scenario by
                  DAVID ALLEN


                              Hammer Film Productions
                              113 Wardour Street
                              LONDON W1

                              4 June 1970
```

Figure I.1 The one piece of archival material held in the Hammer Archive on *Zeppelins v Pterodactyls*

television show *Tales of Frankenstein* and *The Night Creatures* form a great deal of the primary documentation utilised in Chapters 1 and 2.

These archives have given the research a far greater scope. However, archival research is only one (albeit crucial) resource for a study on Hammer's unmade films, and others must be utilised to gain a greater understanding of the topic. With one of the key aspects of this book being the adoption of new approaches to the study of a well-established production company, the question as to why Hammer is so extensively documented comes to the fore. I would argue Hammer has remained so significant within discussions of British cinema not only through academic accounts of the company, but through an engaged and still sizeable fanbase. While increasing access to various film archives across the world plays an incalculable role in the preservation of unmade scripts and their related documents, the role of the fan and fan communities as custodians of both information and primary materials on unmade films should not be understated.

Fan magazines such as *The House of Hammer* (1976–8) and *Little Shoppe of Horrors* (1972–) provide crucial contemporaneous accounts of Hammer from when it was active under Michael Carreras, with interviews and articles vital in examining the development of key projects. Today, fans of Hammer Films are still extremely active, particularly on social media forums. Groups such as the Facebook page 'The Hammer Lovers' (which as of July 2022 has over 10,000 members) share photos, videos and posts on classic Hammer films, as well as events and conventions related to the group. As Krämer notes, 'cinephiles have long shown an interest in such unrealised projects' (2018: 70), and the critical attention fans give to marginalised or forgotten texts holds many key similarities to academia. Interviews were also a useful method in the study, with Hammer experts such as Denis Meikle and Marcus Hearn offering crucial context and documentation not held within the archive. I also interviewed British screenwriter Arthur Ellis, who worked on *Vlad the Impaler* in the early 1980s for Hammer; he provided a number of fascinating insights into the project which is discussed in detail in Chapter 7.

This book is the first chronological company study which utilises unmade films as its primary case studies and the resources I have discussed, be they archival materials, interviews, academic books or non-academic/fan resources, will all help provide details on these unmade projects which, until now, have not been explored. As such, the broader methodological implications of its central focus are also of note. For example, foregrounding unmade texts frustrates a characteristic recourse in many studies of Hammer, which is the textual and aesthetic analysis of their most notable films. Using unmade texts necessitates a shift away from an analysis of Hammer's visual style and instead onto an examination of the methods of production, and the creative roles of the managing director, producer and screenwriter specifically. This study, which uses primary sources on a project's pre-production but has no finished film to textually analyse, necessarily employs a methodology which focuses instead on the development process itself, as opposed to the finished film. Through examining the pre-production of a film as opposed to its production or release, key production roles that are often unrecognised or invisible within academic film studies gain more attention. By studying film development, we may achieve a more comprehensive account of its collaborative labours. For example, since many of the unmade projects discussed in the book reached screenplay stage (sometimes through several script versions), screenwriters are one vital component of the study. Chapters 3 and 6 in particular focus on screenwriters (Don Houghton and Bryan Forbes respectively) and their relationships with the managing director of Hammer, Michael Carreras.

Michael Carreras's role at Hammer is the most comprehensively examined within the study. Carreras had several different roles at Hammer, from writer and director to producer and managing director. Carreras's autocracy often caused tensions during his tenure as head of the company. For example, Chapter 6 details Forbes writing a furious letter to Carreras on finding out he had partially rewritten Forbes's script, with Carreras's instincts as a writer obscuring the long-term repercussions this may have had for him as managing director. Throughout the book, we see key creative decisions Carreras made in the role of managing director and producer, and the impact they had for the company in the face of a rapidly changing international market. How he responded to these changes highlights the various internal relationships between the managing director and screenwriter, or managing director and producer, as well as external relationships Hammer had with financiers, be it independent investors or major production companies such as Columbia (see Chapter 5).

A detailed study of these unmade projects does not only look to answer the question of why the proposed project did not get produced, but also foregrounds often neglected roles within the production process. A director is of course vital to any film, but as many of these case studies will demonstrate, they can often arrive late in the production process, with financing secured and a script already firmly in place. The conception of a film, and the intricacies involved in its development and funding, can often be overlooked in pursuit of the finished product. But where the researcher's pay-off in tracing the creative struggles during a production can often be the marks left on the film itself, unmade films tell untold stories about production cultures. While I have already noted some of the ways unmade films have been used within existing works, one consistent aspect throughout is that prioritising the unmade film as a case study frustrates existing methodologies and as result, offers new methods for analysing the production process that underpins all films – those that are completed, and those that never see the light of day. As this book looks to demonstrate, any comprehensive production history needs to account for both.

Structure

Chapter 1 of this book begins a chronological study of Hammer's unmade projects, offering key historical context on its pre-1950s history, before focusing on the late 1950s and early 1960s: a time when the company began to establish its reputation as an expert in the field of horror. How Hammer crafted this reputation, and the precariousness of it in these formative years, will be studied through the use of two unmade Hammer projects. Both projects relate to one of Hammer's most notable franchises, *Frankenstein* (1957–73). This chapter will examine the production contexts of the original *Frankenstein* project that was brought to Hammer by the American producer Eliot Hyman. This specific adaptation of Mary Shelley's 1818 gothic horror novel was written by American producer Milton Subotsky and is entirely different from the screenplay which became *The Curse of Frankenstein*. After examining this unmade project's turbulent production process, this chapter will then look at how Hammer tried to parlay the incredible success of *The Curse of Frankenstein* into television as well. Almost immediately after the success of *The Curse of Frankenstein*, Hammer entered into a co-production deal with Columbia who, under their television production company Screen Gems, looked to produce a series with Hammer called *Tales of Frankenstein* for American television. However, only the pilot was produced, as Hammer struggled to acclimatise to producing a network television show for American audiences.

Chapter 2 will continue the analysis of this period and will examine Hammer's attempts at consolidating its success in the horror genre through an examination of Richard Matheson's self-adaptation of his novel *I Am Legend* – *The Night Creatures*. *The Night Creatures* is an anomalous addition to Hammer's slate of horror films at this time, which primarily looked to expand on the gothic horror trappings of *The Curse of Frankenstein*. The project ultimately failed to get past the British censor, and I argue that this proved a crucial learning curve for Hammer in regard to the types of horror material the censor was willing to tolerate. The chapter not only examines Hammer's relationship with the British censor, but also the Motion Picture Association of America's reaction to the script, which proved notably divergent from that of the BBFC. This chapter will also go on to contextualise the 1960s at Hammer as a relatively stable period for the company, concurring with Hearn's assessment that 'it is a measure of Hammer's reputation and success that almost every subject they pitched to distributors from the mid-1950s to the late 1960s found finance' (2011: 160). However, this chapter will go on to note the seismic shifts that happened within the British film industry more broadly at the advent of the 1970s, which effectively saw the wholesale withdrawal of American finance from the British industry, a crucial element of Hammer's entire finance and distribution strategy.

Chapter 3 will examine exactly how these changes in the industry affected the company. Hammer moved production studios from Bray to Elstree, lost its most influential producer in Anthony Hinds when he retired in 1970 and formally changed hands in 1973, with James Carreras selling the company to his son Michael. In order to track this instability at Hammer, the chapter will focus on their most illustrious franchise: *Dracula*. Contextualising notable unmade *Dracula* projects in the canon of Hammer's produced *Dracula* series (1958–74), the chapter will look at how Hammer tried to reinvigorate the franchise in the face of declining interest from American production and distribution companies. The key case study will be *Kali Devil Bride of Dracula*, a project developed in 1974 by Don Houghton, which would have seen Dracula travel to India to marry the goddess Kali. *Kali Devil Bride of Dracula* demonstrates Hammer's concerted efforts to revitalize an ailing franchise, but also shows Hammer struggling to find viable production deals without the full backing of American financiers. The chapter will posit that the failure of *Kali Devil Bride of Dracula* and the end of the Dracula franchise at Hammer, signalled a huge change in Hammer's production strategy.

This book is also the first work on Hammer to note that the two unmade Hammer projects that featured the character of Dracula in India – *The Unquenchable Thirst of Dracula* and *Kali Devil Bride of Dracula* – are not redrafted versions of the same script but two distinct projects, with separate stories and production histories. These histories will be the key focus of Chapter 3.

Chapter 4 will examine what I will argue is a key tension at Hammer in the mid-1970s. Aware that Hammer needed to move away from its past focus on gothic horror, Carreras instead began to focus on large budget ventures that he felt would maximise Hammer's chances of procuring international finance. However, by examining two of these projects, *Vlad the Impaler* and *Vampirella* (which began development in 1974 and 1975 respectively), it is clear Carreras was reluctant to move away entirely from the gothic horror formula. *Vlad the Impaler* acts as a big budget origin story of one of Hammer's most established characters and Christopher Wicking's *Vampirella* screenplay features numerous references to former Hammer films. This chapter will examine the production histories of these projects in detail, before arguing that this tension between the old Hammer and the new hindered the already weakened company, and forced Carreras to become more radical in his approach to these new big budget projects.

Chapter 5 will then examine this more radical strategy in detail, through the prism of Hammer's most ambitious unmade film: *Nessie*. *Nessie*'s impact on Hammer is so significant that it will be split across two chapters, with the first focusing specifically on Hammer's attempt to court international finance. Wishing to move away from an over-reliance on American money by financing projects through a number of different backers, this chapter will look at this new strategy in detail, using detailed financial records and correspondence to outline Hammer's working relationship with Toho in Japan and Columbia in the United States. Ultimately, the chapter looks to determine if Hammer's eventual failure to produce the film was due to their own internal failings or through the broader machinations of the film industry itself. Chapter 6 will look at the other side of this debate, examining Hammer's internal workings in relation to the development of *Nessie*. As well as detailing the plot of the proposed film, one of the key focuses of this chapter will be Carreras's relationship with *Nessie* screenwriter Bryan Forbes, and how the once amicable relationship became acrimonious as mounting financial and creative pressures took their toll. The final part of this chapter will examine the failure of *Nessie* and the fallout of Hammer's new big-budget strategy more broadly (namely Carreras's resignation and the company's forced closure by its creditors in 1979).

Chapter 7 will focus on a period of Hammer almost never documented, the revival of Hammer by two former board members, Roy Skeggs and Brian Lawrence, in 1980. Lawrence retired in 1985, but Skeggs stayed as the managing director of Hammer until 2000, though no theatrical films were produced during his tenure. In order to cover Skeggs's time as managing director, this chapter will look at the revival of *Vlad the Impaler* under Skeggs and its near thirty-year production history at Hammer. After Carreras's resignation, the project languished in almost constant development during Skeggs's two decades in charge, and the project's history will be used to draw conclusions as to whether Skeggs's tenure at Hammer could truly be considered a new phase for the company.

The concluding chapter will draw on the methodological practices used within the book and the case studies mounted to offer a revisionist history of Hammer's changing production culture that provides new insights into this well-documented company. It will also reflect on the way unmade films are utilised in the book for a sustained chronological study of one production company over a fifty-year period, and the potential benefits for film history that this original approach demonstrates. Finally, the conclusion will propose the next steps for unmade film studies, and how it may be further developed as a key practice within film studies and beyond.

1

Frankenstein unmade

Exclusive Films was formed by Enrique Carreras and William Hinds in May 1935. Individually, Carreras and Hinds brought a good deal of experience to the venture. Carreras had formerly run a successful chain of cinemas until 1935, and William Hinds, after a background in vaudeville and theatre (under the stage name Will Hammer), had registered his own film company, Hammer Films, in 1934. Both were savvy businessmen (with Hinds also being the owner of jewellers W. Hinds) but in 1937, only two years after the partnership, a slump in the British film industry saw Hammer Films go into liquidation.

Exclusive survived, and 1938 and 1939 saw the hiring of Enrique's son James and William's son Tony. James Carreras and Tony Hinds would go on to be essential to Hammer's success, and will be key figures throughout the book. However, their duties at Hammer were put on hold due to the advent of the Second World War, in which both served. In 1947 Hammer Films was revived as a production arm of Exclusive, as Exclusive began to focus on low budget 'quota quickie' productions. By 1949 Hammer was an officially registered company, with Enrique and James Carreras, and William and Tony Hinds as joint directors, while James Carreras took overall charge of the fledging production arm. Enrique Carreras died on 15 October 1950, after which point William Hinds would take a less active role in the company, leaving James Carreras and Tony Hinds to mould this new iteration of Hammer. This chapter will primarily examine the period of 1956–63, as Hammer, under the stewardship of James Carreras and Tony Hinds, became renowned as specialists in the gothic horror genre. This term, gothic horror, is a broad term with its own vast history. In the context of this book, the term is used as a descriptor of Hammer's most distinctive type of horror film. To quote Peter Hutchings:

> Both the settings and the style of Hammer horror function to accommodate and highlight a sense of... physicality. The castles, pubs and drawing rooms which comprise Hammer's characteristic Victorian or Edwardian milieux provide a suitably ordered backdrop against which various acts of violence are rendered even more striking than they would be otherwise. (1993: 58)

This combination of iconography and the lingering threat of these 'various acts of violence' define, for the purpose of this book, the Hammer gothic horror. Hutchings also notes that this gothic horror style was enshrined at Hammer through the repeated use of personnel. Not only the actors in front of the camera such as Peter Cushing and Christopher Lee, but those behind it such as director Terence Fisher, producer Tony Hinds, writer Jimmy Sangster, art director Bernard Robinson, director of photography Jack Asher and Michael Reed, and composer James Bernard (59). As this chapter charts the success of Hammer's gothic horrors, it differs considerably from the later chapters, which primarily focus on how Hammer tried to reverse the decline brought on by an ailing national film industry in the 1970s.

In order to gain insights into Hammer's success in the late 1950s and the ensuing decade, it is crucial to have an understanding of the company's relationship with the American film industry. As each chapter of this book will attest, Hammer's production strategies, from the late 1940s to 2000, all centre around American distribution and finance. It is therefore prudent at this stage to outline the industrial context of Anglo-American relations, and how Hammer operated in the period leading up to the late 1950s.

The immediate post-war period in Britain was marked by 'intense activity in UK film policy' (Magor and Schlesinger 2009: 302). The British government, in an attempt to 'vastly increase exports and reduce imports, used increased import taxes on American films as one of a number of such measures' (Kerrigan 2010: 66). This was known as the 'Dalton Duty' (after then Chancellor of the Exchequer Hugh Dalton), and would prove disastrous for Anglo-American industry relations, with Hollywood boycotting the British market (Kerrigan 2010: 66; Harper and Porter 2003: 114; Stubbs 2009: 2). The industry suffered, with Sarah Street noting that this crisis 'underlined the British film industry's structural weaknesses and vulnerable position in world markets' (Street 2002: 92). In 1950, this intense activity came to an end with the establishment of the British Film Fund, known as the Eady Levy. The Eady Levy required exhibitors to retain a proportion of the ticket price and give half of this sum to fund British film production (Fenwick 2017: 192; Magor and Schlesinger 2009: 302). Introduced as a voluntary scheme, the Eady Levy 'became compulsory under the 1957 Cinematograph Film Act and was administered by the British Film Fund Agency (BFFA) set up in that year' (Magor and Schlesinger 2009: 302). However, of note is the definition of a British film:

> [...] the scheme made no distinction between the wholly British companies and the British subsidies which the Hollywood companies had previously established to repatriate their blocked currency, and so British-registered runaway productions were able to qualify as British films. (Stubbs 2009: 5)

These runaway productions came 'to dominate the production fund' (Stubbs 2009: 7), and as a result it became increasingly difficult to maintain a clear distinction between American runaway productions and 'indigenous' British film-making (Stubbs 2009: 1). The levy was not the only reason American production emigrated to Britain, with the exchange rate of the dollar meaning it was still cheaper to shoot in the UK (Fenwick 2017: 193; Magor and Schlesinger 2009: 302). However, it was undeniably crucial to the British film industry at the time.

While it was the Eady Levy in 1950 that heralded the resurgence of Anglo-American industrial relations, Hammer Films had secured a transatlantic partnership two years prior. In the late 1940s, Hammer were making finance and distribution deals on a film-by-film basis, and James Carreras looked to 'muster more reliable financial support' (Harper and Porter 2003: 141). This led to a deal between Hammer and the American production company Robert Lippert Productions in 1948, to produce B-pictures for the American market. This shift away from radio adaptations such as the *Dick Barton* trilogy (1948–1950) and towards transnational B-movies was taken because Hammer 'could supply at reasonable cost the kind of modest B-picture that was fast dying out in Hollywood due to rising costs and a shrinking market' (Eyles et al. 1994: 29). The relative success of the arrangement saw Lippert and Hammer sign a new five-year deal in 1950 (Harper and Porter 2003: 141).

Through this deal, Hammer and Lippert utilised the Eady Levy, producing 'unremarkable second-feature fillers... featur[ing] fading American stars such as Richard Carlson, Zachary Scott, Cesar Romero, Dan Duryea, Dane Clark, Richard Conte and John Ireland' (Springhall 2009: 15). The Lippert deal also meant that Hammer distributed twelve films to American cinemas a year, but perhaps more crucially ensured that Lippert 'would give substantial help in fine-tuning them for that market' (Harper and Porter 2003: 141). This help primarily came in post-production, with American editors ensuring the films appealed to American markets. Specifically, Harper and Porter note one instance where the editor Leon Basha was employed to make one of these co-productions – *Whispering Smith Hits London* (Searle, 1952) – 'less Britishy' (Harper and Porter 2003: 142). The actual benefits of this 'fine-tuning' are impossible to measure, but this early guidance in how best to break through into the lucrative American market was undoubtedly advantageous for Hammer, and was arguably a fundamental element in Hammer's later transatlantic success.

As the 1950s progressed, the company had been bolstered by the commercial reception (Meikle 2009: 24) of its first X-rated film, *The Quatermass Xperiment* (Guest, 1955) an adaptation of Nigel Kneale's seminal BBC television series *The Quatermass Experiment* (Kneale, 1953). Released in black and white, the film broke new ground for Hammer not just with its X-certificate, but as arguably the company's first foray into the horror genre. This is suggested by Denis Meikle, who notes that with the release of *The Quatermass Xperiment*, 'Hammer Horror also arrived on the scene' (2009: 20). In the following section of this chapter, I will briefly contextualise *The Quatermass Xperiment* as part of a fledging British horror cycle. However, with its narrative focused on space exploration and an extra-terrestrial disease, the film is arguably more indebted to the science fiction genre. This is telling as, in the wake of the film's success, Hammer initially looked to emphasise elements of science fiction in its upcoming X-rated films. Hammer produced *X the Unknown* (Norman, 1956), a black and white science fiction film notable for being the writing debut of Jimmy Sangster (who will be discussed in detail later in this chapter), and a direct sequel to *The Quatermass Xperiment*, *Quatermass 2* (Guest), was released in May 1957. It was a relative success, but was overshadowed by another Hammer release in May 1957, *The Curse of Frankenstein* (Fisher).

The Curse of Frankenstein was Hammer's first colour gothic horror, and the beginning of a longstanding cycle of such films. Its outstanding success would see Hammer produce six further instalments in the *Frankenstein* series (1957–73). The success of *The Curse of Frankenstein* would have a monumental effect on the company as they looked to immediately capitalise on its reception with an adaptation of Bram Stoker's *Dracula* (1897) in 1958, which produced eight sequels (1960–74). *The Quatermass Xperiment* may have been crucial in gaining Hammer international success (and notoriety), but it was *The Curse of Frankenstein* that provided the template for the majority of Hammer's later gothic horror films.

However, while their production slate may indicate that Hammer transitioned naturally into the gothic horror cycle, one of the key notions put forward in this chapter is how crucial the pre-production and immediate aftermath of *The Curse of Frankenstein* was for Hammer. Using materials held at the Hammer Script Archive, the Warner Bros. Archive at the University of Southern California (USC) and the British Film Institute (BFI) Archive, this chapter will primarily use two key unmade projects at Hammer to demonstrate how different Hammer's trajectory during the production and immediately after the release of *The Curse of Frankenstein* could have been.

The first project that will be examined is American producer Milton Subotsky's *Frankenstein* screenplay, written independently and offered to Hammer in 1956 by producer Eliot Hyman. While Hammer's *The Curse of Frankenstein* was eventually written by Jimmy Sangster, Subotsky (through Hyman) was the first to approach Hammer with a project relating to *Frankenstein*. As a precursor to Hammer's most important project, Subotsky's *Frankenstein* was vital to *The Curse of Frankenstein*'s eventual production, and this chapter will analyse its development primarily using Subotsky's screenplay, which is held in the Warner Bros. Archive, as well as through correspondence between Hammer and Eliot Hyman held in the British Film Institute's (BFI) Special Collections. Secondly, the chapter will examine Hammer's first attempt at a television series – *Tales of Frankenstein*, developed primarily in 1957/8, in the wake of *The Curse of Frankenstein*'s success. The series was intended to be an American co-production with Screen Gems (the television subsidiary of Columbia), but ultimately failed to make it into production as a series, with only the pilot being produced (but never released). The series is important not only as Hammer's first attempted television venture, but as an attempt to consolidate their recent success in the gothic horror genre as well. The show was a rare misstep for Hammer at the time, and shows them having to quickly come to terms with increased American interest. In order to discuss *Tales of Frankenstein* in detail, archival material held at the BFI Special Collections will be used. Specifically, internal correspondence between Michael Carreras and Jimmy Sangster, a document dated 28 February 1958 titled 'General information for Writers', and five synopses for potential episodes, each with producer's notes also attached. The produced pilot will also be discussed, and the analysis will be supplemented with materials from trade magazines written at the time of the show's production.

Enter *Frankenstein*: Subotsky and Hammer Films

1956 is arguably the most important year in Hammer's history. It saw the conclusion of a brief cycle of films, with *Quatermass 2* beginning shooting on the 21 May (Kinsey 2002: 49) heralding the end of Hammer's short-lived black and white, X-rated science fiction cycle. It also saw the end of Hammer's longstanding deal with Robert Lippert Productions. Although the expiration of the Lippert deal in 1956 could be seen as a potential crisis point for Hammer, its end actually proved to be remarkably beneficial to the company's later success. With the Lippert deal ending, James Carreras began looking for new partners, a task which seemingly complemented his management style. In his memoir, Hammer director Freddie Francis notes that:

> Jimmy loved the business side, the wheeler-dealing and the glamor. He was a socialite and more interested in that and running The Variety Club of Great Britain than he was in film production. We rarely saw him during filming because I suspect he didn't really care what we were doing. As far as he was concerned, we could have been making furniture. (Francis with Dalton 2013: 115)

The charitable organisations of the Variety Club of Great Britain and its international branch gave Carreras access to a huge number of society's most wealthy patrons, and he held a number of prominent positions in both branches, eventually serving for two terms as president of the Variety Club International from 1961 (Meikle 2009: 14). Carreras utilised his connection to the Variety Club to secure Hammer's next partnership. Through their mutual association of the club (Pirie 2008: 57; Kinsey 2002: 50), Carreras struck a deal with Eliot Hyman and Associated

Artists Pictures. This deal benefitted Hammer almost immediately. When Hyman was pitched a new version of *Frankenstein* by the relatively inexperienced duo of Milton Subotsky and Max Rosenberg, he knew exactly which company to call.

James Carreras agreed to enter into a partnership with Hyman on *Frankenstein*, and by March 1956, 'James and Michael Carreras had begun negotiations based on a working draft of the screenplay' (Meikle 2009: 31). The Warner Bros. Archive holds a copy of Subotsky's script dated 1956. The Hammer Script Archive also holds an undated and untitled scanned copy of a script which, when cross-referenced with the one held at the Warner Bros. Archive, is confirmed to be a duplicate of Subotsky's script. Though the script did not necessarily have a direct textual influence on Sangster's screenplay for *The Curse of Frankenstein*, it was the genesis of the *Frankenstein* project at Hammer, and as such was fundamental to Hammer's later success within the gothic horror genre.

Subotsky's screenplay differs almost entirely from Sangster's eventually produced script and is a more faithful adaptation of Mary Shelley's original novel. It is also keenly influenced by Universal's earlier adaptations directed by James Whale, *Frankenstein* (1931) and *Bride of Frankenstein* (1935). It starts with a prologue startlingly similar to that of *Bride of Frankenstein*. Opening 'in the summer of 1818' (Subotsky 1956: 1), it begins on the night that Mary Shelley conceives the novel *Frankenstein*. No dialogue is spoken, but the narrator notes how this night birthed 'the greatest horror story of all time' (Subotsky 1956: 3). Unlike Sangster's *The Curse of Frankenstein*, which, despite a brief flashback on a young Victor, focuses entirely on Frankenstein as an adult, Subotsky's script is mainly focused on a young Frankenstein beginning his experiments at university. Like Whale's adaptations before it, Subotsky's script emphasises the Creature over his creator, an important distinction to make when regarding Sangster's later adaptation, which focuses far more on Peter Cushing's Baron. Both Whale and Subotsky have several sequences that see the Monster/Creature having escaped Frankenstein's laboratory and exploring the world on his own. For example, in a sequence roughly halfway through the screenplay, the Creature comes upon a child who has fallen in the lake and rescues her. However, her father and a group of villagers arrive to see the Creature standing over her and attack it, forcing it to flee. This leads directly into another loosely adapted sequence from the novel and *Bride of Frankenstein*, as the Creature is taken in by a blind man who takes pity on him and offers him food and shelter. However, when the blind man's family return, it is revealed to be the family of the girl who attacked the Creature. These sequences, despite having precedent in the novel, are strongly reminiscent of Whale's previous films, a factor that would go on to be a concern for Hammer later in its production.

Subotsky's script also features a clear reference to Jack Pierce's iconic design of the Monster in Whale's *Frankenstein* films. Although giving no actual description of the Creature, Subotsky specifies the 'electrodes on the Creature's head' (Subotsky 1956: 34). Removed from context, these homages to Whale's earlier films would not be particularly notable. Adaptations of the same novel are bound to have similarities, and Subotsky's nod to Whale's films could be interpreted as a deferential acknowledgment of *Frankenstein* and *Bride of Frankenstein*'s permeation of popular culture. However, these sequences and homages became one of the fundamental reasons Subotsky's script was eventually deemed unsuitable at Hammer. The ubiquity of Universal's *Frankenstein* series (1931–48) meant that

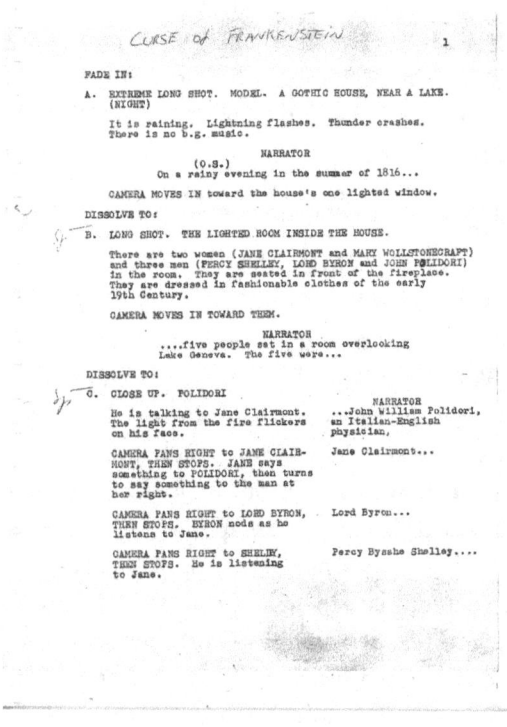

Figure 1.1 The copy of Subotsky's *Frankenstein* screenplay, mistitled *The Curse of Frankenstein*

Universal did not take Hammer's decision to produce their own version lightly. With a sense of ownership over the property, Universal looked to curtail Hammer at every turn, raising 'the prospect of a lawsuit against the company should their picture contain any elements, textual or otherwise, unique to their movies' (Hearn and Barnes 2007: 22). On 23 August 1956, James Carreras wrote to Hyman, breaking down into five points Hammer's strategy to deal with Universal's attempts to stop the production. The first three deal with the fact that Mary Shelley's novel was in fact in the public domain, and therefore, in the words of James Carreras 'if our screenplay is based on the book "FRANKENSTEIN" nobody on earth can do anything about it' (Carreras to Hyman: 23 August 1956). Carreras had been informed of this on the same day that he wrote to Hyman (23), as a letter contained in the BFI Archive and dated 24 August from an unknown source reads:

> With reference to our conversation over the telephone yesterday, I have made investigations and find that the work entitled 'FRANKENSTEIN' . . . is in the public domain and you are entitled to make a film based thereon together with such alterations and additions thereto as you may desire. (Anon. to Carreras: 24 August 1956)

Although this seemed to present a clear justification for Hammer to adapt the novel itself, Carreras also highlighted a key issue this gave the production: 'If we use any ideas in the Universal International pictures on "FRANKENSTEIN", then we are headed for trouble' (Carreras to Hyman: 23 August 1956). Universal's attempts to hinder Hammer's adaptation of *Frankenstein* plagued the production, and continued throughout its development, even after Subotsky's script had been discarded. Two days into the filming of the picture, Carreras sent a memo to Hyman dated 21 November 1956, noting that 'Universal International have objected to the registration of the title "THE CURSE OF FRANKENSTEIN"' and urged his American partner to 'fight this with everything you've got, because we are advised here that being in the public domain anybody can call a film "Frankenstein"' (Carreras to Hyman: 21 November 1956). This extreme pressure by Universal put Hammer in an extraordinarily difficult position. It immediately scuppered Hammer's first plan for the production, which was to potentially produce the picture in black and white and enlist Boris Karloff to star (Rigby 2002: 43; Hearn and Barnes 2007: 23).

Universal's copyright concerns also immediately ruled out the prologue to Subotsky's script, and the brief note he gave on the Creature's design.

These two examples are particularly overt, but the vagueness of the wording in Universal's threat to Hammer – 'textual or otherwise' – made it difficult for the company to discern what material would keep them on the right side of Universal's lawyers. Even Subotsky's adaptation of some of Shelley's scenes could potentially cause issue. One of the most striking sequences in Whale's *Frankenstein* sees an inversion of Shelley's scene at the lake, where the Monster, in a tragic misunderstanding, drowns a child he had briefly befriended. This also could be said for the Creature's visit to the blind man, which appears in the book, but is also a key sequence in Whale's *Bride of Frankenstein*. These sequences, despite initially featuring in some form in Shelley's novel, have elements that at least echo Universal's own films.

Despite Subotsky's script referencing Shelley's novel far more than Whale's earlier films, even producers at Hammer saw the script as merely a lesser version of Universal's adaptations. Tony Hinds, who was brought onto the project as a producer later in development, noted that one of the key reasons he eventually brought in Sangster was that Subotsky's script 'was a complete steal' (cited in Meikle 2009: 35). In a detailed letter to Subotsky from Michael Carreras, one of Carreras's main concerns was the script's similarities to Universal's *Frankenstein*. He wrote:

> [it] must very carefully be checked that there is no parallel to the original film (Universal 1931). It is not sufficient to take the book and write an original from it; if this is done you will find that at least 80% of the good ideas were used in the original. (Cited in Kinsey 2002: 50)

Despite the script not being particularly well received by Michael Carreras (and later Hinds), Hammer was clearly still considering using the script. The company sent it to the BBFC to get their advice on what potential rating the film would receive. The BBFC Archive notes that the script was sent back on 22 June with some minor cuts noted but relatively little resistance from the censor. By this time, Hinds had come on board as a producer and was less enthusiastic about the script than Michael Carreras. With this in mind, Hinds noted to James Carreras that, due to the novel being in the public domain, Hammer were not necessarily beholden to Subotsky's script and could develop its own (Meikle 2009: 36; Rigby 2002: 43).

Subotsky's script was rejected, but he would return to the British horror scene in 1962 where, along with his partner Max Rosenberg, he founded Amicus Productions, the outfit which utilised many original Hammer stars (such as Peter Cushing and Christopher Lee) and became known for their portmanteau horror films.

Jimmy Sangster, who had been a production manager at Hammer since 1954 and had recently written his first feature film, *X the Unknown*, was offered *The Curse of Frankenstein* by Hinds after Subotsky's script was shelved. In his memoir *Inside Hammer* (2001), Sangster recounts that Hinds 'asked me to start from scratch and write my version based on the original book' (Sangster 2001: 27). Sangster also notes that 'I had no idea at the time that there was a script already in existence, and to this day I've never read it' (Sangster 2001: 27). Given Sangster's position as a production manager at the company, one would think that Sangster was at least aware of the ongoing pre-production of *Frankenstein*. However, there is no contradictory evidence to Sangster's claim of having never seen Subotsky's script, though it does share one overt similarity to his own. Both find Frankenstein in prison at the beginning of the story, with a visit causing him to recount his misadventures. The flashbacks then form the main crux of the film. This does not occur in the book and is either a coincidental use of a framing device, or Sangster utilising a small element of Subotsky's former script.

Sangster avoids the pitfalls of Subotsky's script by producing an extremely loose adaptation of Shelley's novel. Furthermore, Sangster puts some distance between his screenplay and the Universal films not only by altering key parts of the narrative, but by drastically altering the characterisation of Frankenstein himself. Sangster notes that 'the first major change I made was to make Baron Frankenstein the villain, as opposed to the monster' (Sangster 2001: 28). Colin Clive's portrayal of the monster's creator in *Frankenstein* and *Bride of Frankenstein* was of a driven and often obsessive man compelled to push the boundaries of science for the greater good of mankind. However, he was by no means the primary focus of the films, which 'centred on the Monster rather than Frankenstein himself' (Hutchings 1993: 101). In contrast, Sangster's Baron is an arrogant, unsympathetic and murderous figure. While Sangster's script is undoubtedly more overt and provocative in its horror material, one interesting thing to note is Subotsky's much more ambiguous ending. Sangster's script ends with the Creature destroyed, and the characters Elizabeth and Krempe leaving the Baron as he is led to the guillotine to pay for his crimes. This ending effectively sets the template for future Hammer gothic horrors, with good ultimately triumphing over evil. Subotsky's ending is arguably much darker. The Monster is shot as it throws Elizabeth to her death, and then the film ends with Frankenstein begging Krempe (who in Subotsky's draft never sees the Monster) to believe his story. The final shot then reveals the Monster survived, as it stumbles towards the camera with its arms reaching out for the viewer. However even with this ending considered, it is inarguable that both the narrative and characterisation were dramatically altered in Sangster's draft, putting crucial distance between Universal's films series and Hammer's upcoming gothic horror.

Not only did these changes shift Hammer's *The Curse of Frankenstein* away from Universal's earlier films, but just by merely hiring Sangster, the perception of the project markedly changed. Subotsky and Rosenberg's involvement with the project, instigated by Eliot Hyman, highlighted the transatlantic partnership between Hammer and Hyman. However, despite Hyman still being a critical part of the project's financing (Barnett 2014: 233–7), the project's cast, director, producers and writer were all now British. Therefore Hammer, by bringing in Sangster instead of Subotsky, created another degree of separation by crafting what is essentially an entirely British production.

The film's release and subsequent international success laid the groundwork for Hammer's later gothic horrors. However, this examination of Subotsky's script and the production context of *The Curse of Frankenstein* more broadly demonstrates how some of the key components of Hammer's gothic horror formula were dictated by circumstance rather than long-term strategizing. Subotsky's script would have undoubtedly presented a more conventional take on the material, but despite clear misgivings from Hammer producers such as Tony Hinds, Hammer did initially seem content enough to send the script for approval to the BBFC, with the intent to seemingly produce the picture in black and white. It was Universal's insistence that the production differ entirely from their own which caused Hammer to seriously reconsider the project again. Subotsky's script featured many key sequences and characters from Shelley's novel, and as such featured enough similar material to the Universal films to worry Hammer. Hinds's decision to hire Sangster to produce his own *Frankenstein* script was prudent not only due to Sangster's desire to radically alter the characters and events of the novel, but also due to his status as a former production manager. In an interview with Wayne Kinsey, Sangster notes that one of the first questions he asked Hinds on being offered the assignment was 'how much are we going to spend on the picture' (in Kinsey 2010: 97)? Sangster's experience in managing a production, and his knowledge of Hammer's frugal budgets, made him a more than adept replacement for Subotsky. Sangster's ideas would ignite Hinds's enthusiasm for the project, leading to its eventual shooting in colour. Almost every memorable component of what would become Hammer's gothic horror formula would be visible in *The Curse of Frankenstein*, yet as the above clearly demonstrates, many of its most enduring facets, such as its focus on an antagonistic Baron Frankenstein over the Creature and startlingly original creature design, came about through the lessons learned in the troubled production process of Subotsky's *Frankenstein*.

Hammer in America: *Tales of Frankenstein*

Hammer was quick to capitalise on the monumental success (Barnett 2014: 236–7) of *The Curse of Frankenstein*. In October 1957, Hammer submitted Sangster's screenplay for *Dracula* to the BBFC, and in November that same year, the sequel to *The Curse of Frankenstein*, *The Revenge of Frankenstein*, was also submitted to the BBFC. Hammer was quick to respond to audiences' desire for more gothic horror films, but also looked to bring this success to television as well.

Two crucial deals in the months of June and September 1957 facilitated what was to be Hammer's first foray into television. The first was between Universal and Screen Gems, Columbia's television production subsidiary, with *Billboard* noting 'the acquisition of 550 Universal features' (Strong 1957: 18) in its 17 June 1957 issue. This deal saw Screen Gems acquire a substantial portion of Universal's pre-1948 horror product, which was packaged as *Shock!* or *Shock Theater*. This was the first package of horror films on the television market, and within little more than a week, nine television stations had 'shelled out some $2,500,000 for Screen Gem's new "Shock" package of 52 chillers' (Anon. 1957a: 28, 40). Horror on television was clearly immensely profitable for Screen Gems, and laid the groundwork for a more ambitious venture further down the line.

The second deal came in September 1957 and was between Hammer and Columbia. Despite *The Curse of Frankenstein* proving to be a huge success for Hammer and Eliot Hyman, the financial partnership had proven extremely testing. This is notable in a piece of correspondence held at the BFI from James Carreras to Hyman sent in December 1956 during production of the film. Carreras began the letter clearly referencing an accusation levelled at him by Hyman: 'Hysterical you suggest. After looking through our correspondence it's a wonder I'm not biting lumps out of the carpet' (Carreras to Hyman: December 1956). Carreras also underlined the key issue between Hammer and Hyman: 'No pre-production cash from you and your share twelve days after the shooting starts – What sort of 50/50 partnership is that?' (ibid.).

Eager to move on from this, Hammer secured a three-picture deal with Columbia in September 1957. The 11 September 1957 issue of *Variety* notes that the three films produced under the deal were to be *The Snorkel* (Green, 1958), *The Camp on Blood Island* (Guest, 1958) and *The Blood of Frankenstein*, which was the sequel that would later be renamed *The Revenge of Frankenstein*. The deal secured Hammer worldwide distribution for all three pictures, and 50 per cent financing for *The Snorkel* and *The Camp on Blood Island* (with Hammer fully financing *The Revenge of Frankenstein*) (Myers 1957: 7, 12). Crucially, this deal also gave Hammer access to Columbia's Screen Gems, and less than two weeks later, Screen Gems announced their own television show *Tales of Frankenstein*. Interestingly, Hammer is not mentioned in the article, and the series was touted as having Boris Karloff set to 'host and occasionally star' (Anon. 1957b: 31). By late October, however, Hammer's involvement as co-producers on the show was made clear and the nature of the deal was further explained. In the 23 October issue of *Variety*, the trade noted that ABC (the American Broadcasting Company), had agreed to co-produce the venture (Anon. 1957c: 50). The same article outlined that 'production on the show will be split between Hollywood and England, with Bryan Foy producing shows on the Coast and James Carreras . . . in England' (Anon. 1957c: 50). The article also went on to note that *Tales of Frankenstein* will be an anthology series, and that Boris Karloff 'is now out of the picture' (Anon. 1957c: 50).

The BFI Archive holds materials which detail internal correspondence at Hammer and demonstrate that Hammer was taking the opportunity of American syndication very seriously. The first and seemingly earliest letter is from Jimmy Sangster and was undated, but the archive also holds what is clearly Michael Carreras's reply, dated 15 October 1957. Sangster's original letter (presumably written a week or less before this), detailed eight potential avenues in which he would take the Frankenstein character. These various escapades include (but are not limited to) the Baron dabbling in 'voodoo' and 'black magic', having a 'set to with Zombies' and trying to comprehend 'how much pain can a human being stand'

(Sangster to Carreras). Carreras writes back to Sangster asking if he 'would be available to write six thirty-minute stories for this series' (Carreras to Sangster: 15 October 1957). Tony Hinds is designated to oversee production for Hammer in America (Hearn and Barnes 2007: 36), which makes it clear that Hammer was looking to closely replicate the success of *The Curse of Frankenstein* by utilising the same creative team.

An article in *Broadcasting* notes that the series was to have thirty-nine episodes, with twenty produced in the United States under producer Bryan Foy, while James Carreras would produce nineteen in the United Kingdom (Anon. 1957d: 90). The article also reports that the series was looking to be shown in the 1958/9 season on American television. The pilot for *Tales of Frankenstein* (Siodmak) was produced in January 1958, with German actor Anton Diffring in the title role. This immediately shows an increase in Hammer's relationship with American studios, with this project not only relying on American financiers and distributors, but actually planning on filming half of the episodes in America as well, handing over control of these episode to Foy.

However, before examining the pilot (ultimately the only produced episode of the series), it is worth noting Hammer's long-term plan for the series as a whole, which were set out in a document dated 28 February 1958, and titled 'General information for Writers'. Held at the BFI Archive, this detailed document was to act as a bible for writers drafted in to work on the show, covering the length of each episode, recurring sets and characters (and character profiles), and notes to producers on how to select and engage writers for the series. The document noted that the series will be twenty-six episodes (down from the originally mooted thirty-nine), with thirteen made in the United Kingdom. Surprisingly, the document also revealed that only eight of these 'will actually include the character of Baron Frankenstein' (Anon. 1958a). The BFI Archive also holds five treatments for potential episodes dated between March and April 1958 (Rawlinson 1958, Woodhouse 1958, Kersh 1958, Dryhurst 1958, Bryan 1958). These synopses are by five separate writers and do not seem to be based on any of Sangster's brief story outlines in his correspondence. Some of the writers drafted in for the project, however, were extremely experienced. For example, A. R. Rawlinson (writer of *The Man Who Knew Too Much* (Hitchcock, 1934)) had been a prolific writer for nearly four decades when he was drafted in to write the first synopsis.

Rawlinson's synopsis is of note not just due to his pedigree as a writer, but for the many story elements that are seemingly incorporated within later Hammer *Frankenstein* films. The story outline sees a man named Peter visiting Frankenstein's home village, and falling for a woman called Lisa, whom he meets outside Frankenstein's castle. They talk, but Peter notices a peculiar relationship between the Baron and Lisa. After Peter demands that the Baron let her leave the castle with him, the Baron says he will if Peter can persuade Lisa to leave. As Peter declares his love for her, Lisa stabs him in the shoulder. The Baron and Peter eventually try to subdue Lisa, but she falls from the stairs and is killed. The Baron reveals to Peter that Lisa was one of his creations, born with no heart or soul, and due to this, had slowly become evil. At the end of the episode, Peter leaves the castle as the Baron goes back to his laboratory. Producer Tony Hinds wrote of the synopsis: 'I feel that the story is acceptable up to paragraph 24. From there on, it should be improved. It might be an idea to keep the girl alive and to use her in say, story number 2' (Hinds to Rawlinson: 26 March 1958). Despite a relatively lukewarm response to the synopsis from Hinds, elements of Rawlinson's story can be identified in *Frankenstein Created Woman* (Fisher, 1967), which sees the doomed romance of two villagers result in the creation of a female monster by Frankenstein. Produced nearly a decade later, *Frankenstein Created Woman* has parallels with Rawlinson's plot synopsis, and interestingly, is written by Hinds under his pseudonym John Elder.

Another treatment held at the BFI also seemingly influences a later film. The fifth treatment was written by Peter Bryan and begins with Frankenstein approaching a successful hypnotist named Khotan for help waking his new creature. Frankenstein has successfully transferred a brain into a new host, but the Creature is effectively brain-dead. Frankenstein hopes that Khotan (who is in fact a disgraced Austrian doctor) will be able to use hypnosis to finally awaken it. The hypnosis is successful, but the Creature immediately kills Khotan (and the Creature itself is also killed in the struggle). Khotan awakens but finds his mind has been transferred into the body of the Creature, and Frankenstein strongly implies that this had been his plan all along. Khotan hypnotises Frankenstein and attempts to put his own mind into a less monstrous body, but fails. In his last act he hypnotises his daughter into killing him, making her instantly forget the moment she does it.

This synopsis is notable as, like Rawlinson's, it has a number of key similarities with an eventually produced Frankenstein film, in this case, *The Evil of Frankenstein* (Francis, 1964). The film is again written by Tony Hinds (under the pseudonym John Elder), and sees the Baron seek the services of the hypnotist Zoltan in waking his Creature. Zoltan plays a more antagonistic role than Khotan, hypnotising the Creature for his own malevolent purposes. Despite this small alteration, the similarities are startling, particularly as it was Tony Hinds who initially commented on Bryan's synopsis, noting 'I like this. There may be too much plot, but this can be remedied in the screenplay' (Hinds to Bryan: 8 May 1958). Although neither Rawlinson nor Bryan was credited in later productions (although not stated in the document, it is likely Hammer owned the rights to the synopses once submitted), Bryan did go on to work for Hammer, writing the screenplays for *The Hound of the Baskervilles* (Fisher, 1959), *The Brides of Dracula* (Fisher, 1960) and *The Plague of the Zombies* (Gilling, 1966).

The name Zoltan also appears in these synopses before *The Evil of Frankenstein*. In Cyril Kersh's synopsis, Zoltan is not a mystic but an acquaintance of Frankenstein who is obsessed with life after death. When Frankenstein is visited at his castle by Ulrich, a doctor looking to fund a new hospital in the village, Frankenstein convinces Zoltan to help him kill Ulrich in his sleep and instantly revive him, to ask him if there is truly life after death. Zoltan agrees, and Ulrich stays at the castle and is killed and revived that night. Waking up complaining of horrible dreams, Frankenstein tries to convince Ulrich to tell him what they were, but Ulrich resists and escapes the castle. Ulrich arrives home but is uncaring, angry and cruel to everyone he sees, even killing the family cat. After killing a woman, Ulrich is pursued by the police. Frankenstein finds him and begs to know what Ulrich saw, but as Ulrich begins to tell him, the police burst in and shoot Ulrich dead, with Zoltan theorising that in death, Ulrich had lost his soul.

Kersh's synopsis is the only one listed that Hinds seems completely happy with, with Hinds simply writing, under 'Producers Notes', 'None, I like this'. All the other synopses receive notes from Hinds (some more extensive than others), with one of the most recurring critiques being the mischaracterisation of the Baron. As mentioned in the previous section on Subotsky's *Frankenstein*, one of the most notable changes made by Sangster was his positioning of Baron Frankenstein as the main antagonist. This focus within the narrative on Frankenstein and not the Creature is a key facet of what made Hammer's *The Curse of Frankenstein* stand out from the previous Universal iterations, and it is interesting to note the difficulties some of the writers of these synopses had aligning Frankenstein with Hammer's own expectations of what the character should be.

For example, in Hugh Woodhouse's synopsis dated 1 April 1958, Frankenstein creates a clone of himself in his own image (referred to as F-2), who is an exact copy physically but can only speak in reply. When Frankenstein is visited by his cousin Margaretha, she tells him she has arranged an interview for the Baron with a prominent journalist. First telling Margaretha how much he hates journalists, Frankenstein agrees but sends F-2 in his stead who, remembering his creators words, kills the journalist. F-2 goes on to kill again when he overhears Frankenstein having a row with a priest pleading with Frankenstein to stop his experiments. Margaretha informs Frankenstein he is wanted for the murder of the journalist and Frankenstein confronts his creature, leading to one of them being flung from the balcony to their death. While the police are satisfied on finding the body that the journalist's murderer has been brought to justice, the last shot of the proposed episode would have been the Baron standing in his lab, the viewer unsure whether it is Frankenstein or F-2 who had survived the fight. Hinds's note on the synopses are all related to what he perceives as the mischaracterisation of the title character:

> The character of Frankenstein is not right as suggested here. He should have more dignity, be more adult. I suggest that the journalist should not be murdered by Frankenstein but just beaten up. Frankenstein must not be so careless as to let his creation wander about as he likes. The introduction of the priest is dangerous and unnecessary; change it. (Hinds to Woodhouse: 1 April 1958)

With the exception of the 'dangerous' murder of the priest (which he no doubt realises would be impossible to get on American television at the time), Hinds's key concern is with the lack of 'dignity' the character of Frankenstein has here. While some are justifiable issues (the point as to why the Baron would let this new creature identical to him wander around unsupervised is a good one), others are slightly more difficult to pin down, such as what Hinds means by 'more adult'.

The synopsis does centre on Frankenstein's general exasperation with people (he is irritated by Margaretha's arrival, dislikes journalists and has a heated argument with the priest), but at the same time it is clear in the synopsis that Frankenstein has not deliberately sent F-2 to kill the journalist or the priest, but that the acts had been committed essentially through a tragic misunderstanding. While only speculation, perhaps this is Hinds's issue. In *The Curse of Frankenstein* the Baron premeditates all of the murders he is involved with. When the maid Justine tells him she is pregnant with his child, he deliberately puts her in the path of the Creature, knowing it will lead to her death. Perhaps the Baron in Woodhouse's synopsis, essentially entirely unaware of the death and destruction happening around him until the very end, is not active enough in the story for Hinds's liking.

On the other end of this spectrum, Hinds's key complaint with another synopsis, written by Edward Dryhurst and dated 10 April 1958, is that 'Frankenstein has been indicated rather as the 'mad scientist' which is wrong; he should be made to behave more reasonably, more intelligently' (Hinds to Dryhurst: 10 April 1958). The synopsis sees a man, Hans, arrive at Frankenstein's castle frostbitten and near death, telling the Baron that his friend Carl was still out in the cold wilderness. Frankenstein goes to retrieve Carl, but returns with Carl's body, telling Hans that his friend is dead. However, Frankenstein suggests to his assistant Johann (his only appearance in any of these synopses) that this might not be the case. Johann traps Hans in the castle, and it quickly dawns on Hans exactly where he has sought shelter. Carl awakens in Frankenstein's laboratory, where Frankenstein explains he is going to freeze Carl to death and then revive him, in order to discover the restorative and preservative properties of ice and snow. Hans escapes his room and confronts Frankenstein, and with the help of some priests who were out looking for the missing pair, escapes the castle and saves Carl.

This synopsis undoubtedly leans further into Cushing's version of the Baron, having no qualms with taking a life in the pursuit of scientific advancement. With Hans panicking when realising exactly whose castle he has stumbled upon, there also a suggestion that tales of the Baron's experiments have become widespread, and the Baron is an infamous figure. Hinds here is again clearly not satisfied with the Baron's characterisation within the synopsis, but for very different reasons, with Dryhurst's depiction of the Baron proving too unhinged for Hinds and Hammer's tastes.

This points to a broader problem with the series as a whole, which is a lack of creative consistency in the creation of the show as well as episode by episode. Before these synopses, there had already been multiple possible versions of the show as noted previously, with one potentially featuring Karloff as a host and another utilising the ideas set out by Sangster in his correspondence with Michael Carreras. Even after settling on the episode format laid out in the 'General Information for Writers' document, there is no clear or cohesive creative direction given. The only creative brief is a short character description of Frankenstein. Noting that Diffring had already been cast, the document states:

> Baron Victor Frankenstein is at all times 'correct', although he is sometimes so abrupt in his manner as to seem rude. He is completely unemotional except in relation to his work – the scientific research into the nature of man; the mystery of the life-force – to which work he has dedicated his life.

With the exception of this note, the document primarily gives the writers logistical information on the sets that can be used, the maximum number of characters each episode could have (no more than ten speaking parts including Frankenstein), and the instruction that 'visual horror should be kept to the absolute minimum. The stories should be fascinating rather than frightening or revolting'. Tracking *Tales of Frankenstein*'s genesis through these multiple iterations makes it clear the show was developing rapidly with no real fixed creative vision in place.

Despite these issues, Hammer and Screen Gems pushed ahead with the pilot episode. Initially, Tony Hinds was sent to oversee the production of the pilot, but soon returned to England frustrated with the project (Hearn and Barnes 2007: 36). Michael Carreras reportedly flew out to Hollywood in mid-November (Anon. 1957e: 16), and star Diffring followed in early December (Anon. 1957f: 52). According to the 'General Information for Writers' document, the production commenced in January 1958. Carreras would later note that the experience in America overseeing the pilot was 'one of the unhappiest experiences of my screen career' (Hearn and Barnes 2007: 36), and it is clear that there was a significant tension between Columbia/Screen Gems and Hammer over the portrayal of the Baron and his creation, and the tone of the Frankenstein television series.

Jimmy Sangster's early involvement indicated Hammer were looking to replicate the success of *The Curse of Frankenstein*. Sangster himself, in his brief plot synopses sent to Michael Carreras, suggested that this will be the same antagonistic and ruthless Baron he wrote in *The Curse of Frankenstein*. The pilot however is far from Hammer's depiction of the Baron, and the overall tone of the pilot (widely available since falling out of copyright) is more aligned with Universal's 1930s/40s horror cycle. Notably, the director of the pilot and executive producer on the project was Curt Siodmak, who had been a crucial figure in much of Universal's 1940s horror output. Siodmak had written the screenplay for *The Invisible Man Returns* (May, 1940), *The Wolf Man* (Waggner, 1941) and *Frankenstein Meets the Wolf Man* (Neill, 1943), as well as the story outline for *Son of Dracula* (Siodmak) in 1943. Compounding this notion, Screen Gems' acquisition of Universal's horror output for television also gave the company the right to utilise elements of Universal's *Frankenstein* on the small screen. This is clear in the design of Frankenstein's Monster in the pilot. Quite clearly a direct homage to Jack Pierce's make-up, this move away from Hammer and towards Universal's original design proved to be a point of contention for Michael Carreras. On 9 December 1957, Carreras sent producer Irving Birking a memo regarding the Creatures' appearance. Attaching Hammer's own planned designs, Carreras noted that the current design of the Creature does not go far enough, and that Columbia 'should seriously consider marking the face itself with further scar tissue and signs of burns' (Carreras to Birking: 9 December 1957). These suggestions clearly went unheeded, with Columbia preferring to utilise Pierce's original design. This obvious shift away from Hammer's own iteration of *Frankenstein* is also clear in their depiction of the titular character. While Diffring's Baron is scheming and emotionless, he is far from Sangster and Cushing's murderous antagonist in *The Curse of Frankenstein*.

The difference is perhaps most striking in a sequence in the pilot where husband and wife Paul and Christine seek out the Baron in order to save Paul's life. Paul is dying from an unspecified illness and the Baron, whose Monster needs a brain, refuses to help. When Paul succumbs to his illness shortly afterwards, the Baron digs up his body and transplants Paul's brain into the Monster. This is in marked contrast to the strategy laid out by Cushing's Frankenstein when he is searching for a brain for his Creature in *The Curse of Frankenstein*. Cushing's Baron invites the distinguished Professor Bernstein to his castle and after he arrives, asks him to examine a painting at the top of the stairs. The Baron then throws Bernstein from the top, killing the Professor and thus securing an intelligent brain for his Creature. In the television pilot, the Baron's crime (for which he is arrested at the end) is grave robbing. Whereas Hammer's Frankenstein leaves a multitude of bodies in his wake on the quest to create life, Diffring's more neutral Baron, Siodmak's direction and the clear homage to Pierce's make-up result in an episode which lacks any of Hammer's identity.

As seen in the examination of Subotsky's *Frankenstein*, this is clearly due to the fact that nearly every production decision made on *The Curse of Frankenstein* was in direct opposition to Universal's film cycle. *Tales of Frankenstein* offered Hammer what would have been at the time their greatest opportunity to penetrate the American market. This was not just a co-financing or distribution opportunity, but the chance to have creative control over what could have potentially been a long-running series on American television. However, the show was ultimately undone by Screen Gems relying more on the legacy of Universal than the recent Hammer iteration of *Frankenstein*. The recruitment of Sangster and Hinds, two of Hammer's key architects on *The Curse of Frankenstein*, demonstrates that Hammer was clearly hoping that *Tales of Frankenstein* would offer a means to bring their unique interpretation of the character to the small screen. However, Screen Gems had recently acquired Universal's library of horror films for distribution on television, and after having great success airing them, was seemingly reluctant to move away from a tried and tested formula. This left Hammer in an impossible position. Although it is highly unlikely that Screen Gems would have entered a co-production deal with Hammer without the previous success of *Shock*, trying to merge the traditions of Universal's gothics with Hammer's new approach proved untenable, and the television show was never picked up.

Conclusion

The importance of these two projects for Hammer, at a crucial period in the company's history, has been outlined throughout the chapter. However, in a broader context, these case studies demonstrate how unmade projects can disrupt and challenge pre-existing notions in established film histories. This is clear in the examination of the production process of Milton Subotsky's *Frankenstein*. Subotsky's script was a crucial stepping stone to *The Curse of Frankenstein*'s production, however, Subotsky's importance to *The Curse of Frankenstein* is often minimised in other studies of Hammer, with some instead looking to the company's previous filmography to explain their move to gothic horror. This is apparent in *A History of Horrors* (2009), where Meikle looks to draw a direct parallel between *The Quatermass Xperiment* and *The Curse of Frankenstein*. Meikle quotes an interview with Michael Carreras regarding a meeting at Hammer on the special effects used to create the final monster in *The Quatermass Xperiment*, and the decision to give the decidedly unhuman looking creature a human eye. Carreras recounts:

> [...] the idea of putting an eye into it came up ... and the semblance of the last human cry ... and the whole thing changed. And I remember at the meeting only a few sentences later, I heard somebody say: 'You mean like the monster in *Frankenstein* ... '? I'd never heard the name Frankenstein mentioned before then, but there was certainly a spark at that meeting (Carreras cited in Meikle 2009: 24).

Meikle goes on to note that 'it was a spark that would ignite into a flame' (Meikle 2009: 24), and he is not alone in encouraging this direct connection between *The Quatermass Xperiment* and *Frankenstein*. This is perhaps most blatantly demonstrated in Picart's *The Cinematic Rebirths of Frankenstein* (2002), where the author gives credit for the conception of Hammer's gothic horror cycle solely to chairman James Carreras, suggesting 'he conceived of the idea of remaking the "classic" horror films of the thirties and forties, but this time in vivid and graphic color' (Picart 2002: 99). This suggestion that it was James Carreras who envisaged *Frankenstein* as the next property for Hammer to adapt, or that it was through the production of *The Quatermass Xperiment*, discounts the fact that the eventual *Frankenstein* project did not even originate at the company but with the American producer Eliot Hyman, and can lead to erroneous conceptions of Hammer's own production methods. However the foregrounding of unmade projects can offer crucial and original insights into existing areas of enquiry.

For example, while only examining Hammer's produced slate of films within the period 1956–8, one could see a frictionless transition to a production and distribution model that relied heavily on American finance and distribution. However, the unmade *Tales of Frankenstein* television show demonstrates that this fledging relationship was tenuous and not without difficulties. The project saw Hammer struggling to adapt to Screen Gems' own methods of production, a fact made all the more difficult due to Screen Gems trying to incorporate elements of the Universal cycle as well. This project may not have made it to the screen, but I would argue it is crucial to any examination of Hammer's emergence in the horror genre as it shows another potential path the company could have taken, with a focus on television over theatrical production. These unmade projects therefore not only illuminate crucial details in Hammer's own development, but reflect the importance and necessity in contextualising unmade case studies into wider industrial and production studies within film histories.

2

The Night Creatures and the censor

While Subotsky's *Frankenstein* and the *Tales of Frankenstein* series foregrounded the transition of Hammer Films to a system which relied on transatlantic partnerships, this chapter will examine another one of Hammer's early obstacles, the British censor's opposition to the X-rated horror film's steady rise in Britain, a surge led by Hammer's success with *The Curse of Frankenstein*. To explore this relationship with the British censor, this chapter will examine one of the best-known unmade projects in Hammer's history, Richard Matheson's screenplay *The Night Creatures*, based on his novel *I Am Legend* (1954). Hammer flew Matheson to London to adapt his novel almost immediately after the release of *The Curse of Frankenstein*, and the screenplay that followed would have offered Hammer a strikingly different trajectory in comparison to the company's eventually released gothic horrors. *I Am Legend* is a contemporary set novel which sees the last man on earth, Robert Neville, looking to find a cure to a worldwide epidemic which has left the remnants of humanity as plague-ridden vampires. *The Night Creatures*, as one would expect from a self-adaptation, remained relatively faithful to its source, and Hammer were no doubt looking to capitalise on its new-found infamy as horror experts cultivated after *The Curse of Frankenstein*.

However, the project stalled due to the British Board of Film Censors (BBFC) refusal to pass the screenplay. Hammer had encountered some difficulty with the censor in the past with its X-rated *The Quatermass Xperiment* and *The Curse of Frankenstein*, but for Hammer, the Board's refusal to pass the screenplay entirely was unprecedented. This decision came at a crucial time for Hammer. *The Night Creatures* was submitted simultaneously with sequel *The Revenge of Frankenstein* (Fisher, 1958) and six weeks earlier Hammer had also submitted *Dracula* (Fisher, 1958) for consideration by the BBFC. *The Night Creatures* therefore came at the exact same time the company looked to cement their credentials in the field of gothic horror, and if it had been produced would have initiated a markedly different style of 'Hammer Horror'. Utilising the screenplay held at the Hammer Script Archive and documentation held at the BBFC Archive and the Margaret Herrick Library, this chapter will offer a detailed analysis of how one of Hammer's most ambitious projects was curtailed, and examine what effect the screenplay's rejection by the censor had on Hammer. However before doing so it is important to underline the history of horror in Britain up to this point, and the intrinsic connection the censor had in stifling it.

In *Hammer and Beyond*, Hutchings notes that, as the American horror cinema thrived in the 1930s, 'throughout this period British cinema was strikingly deficient in horror production' (Hutchings 1993: 24). This was in no small part due to the BBFC, and its distaste towards the formation of a British horror cinema. However, although the censors explicitly looked to dissuade the production of horror films, some of the methods that actually impeded British horror material over other national cinemas were far subtler. For example, as detailed in Guy Phelps's *Film Censorship* (1975), the emergence of sound in the 1920s gave the censor significant difficulties, as the Board did not have the relevant sound equipment to watch the films. This led to a lasting tradition of scripts being sent to the censor before a production. As noted by Phelps:

> This, of course, allowed the Board an even greater degree of control than it had previously enjoyed. It is easier to insist on alterations to a project that exists only on paper than demand cuts in a finished film representing huge financial investment. (1975: 35)

Naturally, it was far easier for the British censor to procure scripts from British productions than international ones, 'thus penalizing the home industry at the expense of foreign productions' (35). However, the primary reason horror production in the United Kingdom was curtailed was the censor's belief that the material would have a damaging impact on society. Discussing the 'H' certificate, put in place to designate films featuring horrific material in 1933, then President of the Board Edward Shortt wrote:

> Although a separate category has been established for these films, I am sorry to learn that they are on the increase, as I cannot believe that such films are wholesome, pandering as they do to the love of the morbid and horrible. (Cited in Phelps 1975: 36)

With this kind of rhetoric from the President of the British Board of Film Censors, it is clear that Phelps's assessment of the censors 'continuing belief in their role as protectors of public morality, as a buffer between the public and a rapacious industry' (Phelps 1975: 36) holds significant merit.

This is not to say that no British horror films were produced in this period. Two titans of the American Universal horror cycle, Béla Lugosi and Boris Karloff, came to the UK for horror productions. Lugosi came to England for *The Mystery of the Mary Celeste* (Clift, 1935), which is notable for the fact it was produced by the first iteration of Hammer Films in 1935. Karloff returned to England (for the first time in 24 years (Rigby 2002: 18)) for a more auspicious production – *The Ghoul* (Hayes Hunter, 1933). However, despite being a genuine British horror picture the film underperformed commercially and 'was considered a disappointment' (Rigby 2002: 20) on its release. Around the same period, actor Tod Slaughter starred in a number of British horror melodramas that are of note. David Pirie dismisses Slaughter's series of quota quickies as 'pretty unwatchable' (Pirie 2008: 14) and Slaughter's performance as 'even less filmic I think than Lugosi' (Pirie 2008: 13). However, Hutchings, although not examining Slaughter's films in detail, notes that they at least demonstrate that 'elements which would later be mobilised within a distinctive British horror genre were already in existence in British Cinema before the war' (Hutchings 1993: 25). Although Slaughter's work contains fragments of a British horror cinema, Hutchings claims that Ealing Studios' *Dead of Night* (Cavalcanti, Crichton, Hamer and Dearden, 1945) 'is the first important recognisably British horror film' (1993: 25). *Dead of Night* is an anthology film which sees architect Walter Craig (Mervyn Jones) arrive at a strangely familiar house party, leading several guests to confide their own strange (and supernatural) experiences. *Dead of Night* is perhaps primarily remembered for the section that sees ventriloquist Maxwell Frere (Michael Redgrave) growing increasingly paranoid and obsessed over his dummy, Hugo. Forshaw notes that the 'subversive nature of this deeply creepy episode should not be underestimated, and the murderous, independently minded dummy at war with its putative master has been much imitated since' (Forshaw 2013: 107). *Dead of Night* is unquestionably a British horror film but would prove to be an anomaly for Ealing and a 'false start for the horror genre in this country' (Hutchings 1993: 36). Hutchings himself attributes this to the inherent strangeness of *Dead of Night* as a film. Calling it 'one of the most formally aberrant films British cinema has ever produced', Hutching suggests that the film was so anomalous that Ealing 'retreated from what in many ways was a complete dead end' (1993: 36). In the decade that followed *Dead of Night*, British horror production slowed to an almost complete stop.

The 1950s saw changes not only for Hammer, but for British cinema generally. The decade saw a financial crisis in British cinema, with 'declining admissions and the closing down of a large number of cinemas' (Hutchings 1993: 37). Hammer also found themselves in a period of transition in the mid-1950s. As noted in the previous chapter, Hammer's deal with Lippert was coming to an end, and in 1954 the National Film Finance Corporation (NFFC) ceased funding second features (Harper and Porter 2003: 143). This necessitated a complete change in Hammer's production strategy, and Hammer found themselves with 'neither the markets nor capital' (Harper and Porter 2003: 143) to facilitate that change. The production of *The Quatermass Xperiment* proved not only a lifeline for Hammer, but an unqualified success and was enough for Hammer to change course and start them on a path towards their gothic horror output.

Contextualising *The Night Creatures*

Whereas the success of *The Curse of Frankenstein* had buoyed Hammer and rekindled audience enthusiasm for the gothic horror genre, the diminishing returns of Hammer's X-rated science fiction cycle and the then recent collapse of *Tales of Frankenstein* demonstrated that Hammer were by no means invulnerable. As such Hammer looked beyond *Frankenstein* and *Dracula* to other horror novels which could potentially lead to mainstream success. Perhaps the most pertinent example of this is Richard Matheson's 1954 novel *I Am Legend*, which has permeated popular culture since its initial publication nearly seventy years ago. This is in no small part due to the three film adaptations that have been produced – *The Last Man on Earth* (Salkow, 1964) starring Vincent Price, *The Omega Man* (Sagal, 1971) starring Charlton Heston and *I Am Legend* (Lawrence, 2007) starring Will Smith. Several renowned films, while not direct adaptations, have also bore a number of similarities to *I Am Legend*'s general concept, for example, George Romero's *Night of the Living Dead* (1968) and Danny Boyle's zombie thriller *28 Days Later* (2002), the latter of which was so similar to Matheson's novel that it nearly curtailed Lawrence and Smith's eventual adaptation (Hughes 2008: 143).

The Night Creatures is also one of the only unmade Hammer films to have received any academic attention. Stacey Abbott, in *Undead Apocalypse: Vampires and Zombies in the 21st Century* (2016), examines the many adaptations of the novel in the chapter 'The Legacy of Richard Matheson's *I Am Legend*' (2016: 9–39). In this chapter, Abbott contextualises *The Night Creatures* in relation to other adaptations of Matheson's novel, noting how the script's shocking imagery fell afoul of the British and American censors (23–9). Peter Hutchings's chapter 'American Vampires in Britain: Richard Matheson's *I Am Legend* and Hammer's *The Night Creatures*' (2008: 53–71) utilises a comparative account of Matheson's novel and script in order to interrogate 'the relation between British and American models of horror' (Hutchings 2008: 55). Examining the process of an American contemporary horror novel being adapted by the same author for a British production company, Hutchings compares thematic and narrative similarities between Matheson's novel and his unmade screenplay for Hammer, and suggests that these two types of horror 'might not be as distinct and separate from each other as has sometimes been supposed' (2008: 68).

However, in his chapter Hutchings also stresses that, despite *I Am Legend*'s standing as a classic horror novel and Hammer's own popularity in the horror genre at the time, *The Night Creatures* was not an indispensable project for either Hammer or Matheson. Hutchings suggests that 'before we rush to install *The Night Creatures* in the canon of "unfilmed greats", it is instructive to note the response to its abandonment of some of the key figures involved in its creation' (Hutchings 2008: 55). He then goes on to note that Matheson, producer Michael Carreras, and would-be director of the film Val Guest

> [show little] in the way of artistic lamentation ... but instead just expressions of annoyance at the time and money wasted on the project. It is precisely the attitude that one might expect of jobbing

directors, producers and writers, all of whom had busy careers and quickly moved onto other projects after *The Night Creatures* shut down. (Hutchings 2008: 55)

Hutchings here touches on one of the key recurring issues in work on unmade films – the tendency to position the project in question as somehow being an essential or valuable object, which through its failure to be produced has been lost forever. As a result, many works take on a reverence for the unmade project, looking to recreate or imagine the would-be film, as opposed to analysing its historical development or production context. Despite Hutchings's argument being both pertinent and rational, I would suggest that, by emphasising it so keenly with *The Night Creatures*, he arguably undersells the importance the film had in shaping Hammer's trajectory.

Despite Hutchings's insistence that *The Night Creatures* was essentially a short-lived annoyance for Hammer and Matheson, the project was remarkable in a number of ways. Firstly, it stands as a notable blemish on an impressive record of produced films in a period where Hammer was gaining international recognition. Secondly, the reasons for *The Night Creatures* not making it to the screen are markedly different from every other notable unmade Hammer film. Whereas later chapters will chronicle the financial and even cultural roadblocks Hammer faced, *The Night Creatures*'s key undoing was the BBFC. This section will utilise documentation held at the BBFC Archives and reports on *The Night Creatures* by the MPAA (Motion Picture Association of America) held at the Margaret Herrick Library in Los Angeles to examine the complex relationship *The Night Creatures* had with the censor. Whereas Hutchings proposes that Carreras's attitude to the project demonstrated that Hammer 'quickly moved on to other projects', examining the BBFC files alongside the MPAA documents shows that Michael Carreras was potentially still involved with the project in 1961, four years after Hammer first submitted the screenplay to the BBFC. This section will cross-reference the screenplay for *The Night Creatures*, held in the Hammer Script Archive, with this documentation to reposition the project's place in Hammer's filmography at a time when their identity as horror specialists was by no means assured.

Matheson's script was submitted to Hammer in November 1957 and as such can be considered as a response from Hammer to the success of *The Curse of Frankenstein*, which entered production in November 1956 (Anon. 1956: 21). *Dracula* followed a year later, beginning production on 11 November 1957. Just over a month after *Dracula* began, an article in *Variety* noted that Richard Matheson has arrived in London 'to write screenplay [*sic*] of his upcoming novel, "I Am Legend," for Hammer Film Productions' (Anon. 1957g: 74). Despite erroneously listing the novel as upcoming (it was first published in the United States in 1954 and in the United Kingdom in 1956), this announcement creates a symbiotic connection between *The Curse of Frankenstein*, *Dracula* and *The Night Creatures*. As discussed earlier, *The Curse of Frankenstein* demonstrated to Hammer that the horror genre offered the company new prospects in regard to American finance and distribution, and *Dracula* and *The Night Creatures* can be seen as the next potential step in their exploitation of this new market.

However, despite both dealing with vampirism, *The Night Creatures* and *Dracula* were markedly different properties for Hammer. Whereas the period setting, gothic iconography and Dracula's longstanding status in popular culture made a Hammer adaptation all but inevitable after the success of *The Curse of Frankenstein*, Matheson's novel is a different proposition entirely. *I Am Legend* is a contemporary set, post-apocalyptic science fiction horror novel in which vampirism is a plague as opposed to a supernatural affliction.

To go further, one could argue that one of the primary successes of Matheson's novel is that it works in direct opposition to Stoker's *Dracula*. This is apparent in Chapter 3 of *I Am Legend*, which begins with Neville reading a copy of *Dracula*:

> Thank *you*. Dr Van Helsing, he thought, putting down his copy of 'Dracula' . . . It was true. The book was a hodgepodge of superstitions and soap-opera clichés, but that line was true; no one had believed in them, and how could they fight something they didn't believe in? (Matheson 1954: 23)

By overtly referencing the 'superstitions' and 'clichés' of vampirism that had entered the public lexicon after Stoker's novel (and perhaps more pertinently after Browning's *Dracula* (1931)), Matheson not only pre-empted any comparisons between Stoker's novel and his own but also, by acknowledging that the story is happening in a contemporary setting in which the novel *Dracula* exists, Matheson aligned the world of *I Am Legend* more closely with our own. Late 1957 therefore proved to be an interesting time at Hammer. Weeks after beginning production on

Dracula, the company flew in the author responsible for a horror novel that redefined and challenged every assumption audiences had about *Dracula* and vampire mythology.

As a result of the fact that these productions were being developed simultaneously, I would argue that Hammer did not have a long-term strategy in place to capitalise on the success of *The Curse of Frankenstein*. As well as these remarkably different but high-profile horror projects, Hammer released *The Abominable Snowman* (Guest) in August 1957. Produced almost directly after *The Curse of Frankenstein* (which finished filming on 3 January 1957, while shooting on *The Abominable Snowman* commenced on 28 January 1957 (Hearn and Barnes 2007: 22–6)) the film utilises *The Curse of Frankenstein* star Peter Cushing, but in a markedly different film. Shot in black and white and forsaking visceral or overt horror sequences for a foreboding, tense atmosphere, the film is a far cry from the colour gothic opulence of *The Curse of Frankenstein*. Even the film's primary monster, the mythical Yeti, is never fully seen. The film received an A certificate, and despite featuring facets of the horror genre (for example, members of the Himalayan expedition are picked off one by one), the film felt more like a 'throwback' (Meikle 2009: 45) to an older school of horror cinema, before *The Curse of Frankenstein* had signalled a new way forward for Hammer.

With *The Abominable Snowman* seemingly a relic from Hammer's pre-*Curse* days, and *Dracula* following steadfast in the tracks left by *The Curse of Frankenstein*, *The Night Creatures* is arguably the one true outlier in Hammer's horror production slate immediately following *The Curse of Frankenstein*. An adaptation of a book only three years old which redefined the landscape of vampire fiction, it is almost impossible to configure how this film would have impacted Hammer on release. Ultimately, however, *The Night Creatures* stands as one of Hammer's earliest and most notable unmade projects, not due to Hammer's own reluctance to produce *The Night Creatures*, but the refusal of the censor to approve Matheson's script.

The Night Creatures was put into development at the beginning of Hammer's most prolific period. As suggested previously, the company had first seen success with X-certificate films with *The Quatermass Xperiment*. Although the cycle of films that followed it soon diminished, Hammer still utilised the X-certificate as it turned to gothic horror. This not only gave Hammer a unique selling point for its new horror product, but predictably put the company firmly in the sights of the British film censor.

This period was the beginning of a complex history between the company and the BBFC. In his memoir, former Secretary of the Board of the BBFC John Trevelyan briefly discusses the relationship the censor and Hammer had, suggesting an amicable agreement:

> Horror films were rarely a problem since most of them came to us from Hammer Films, the most successful company in this field, from who we always had full co-operation . . . I remember a talk I had with Sir James (Jimmy) Carreras many years ago in which we agreed that his company's horror films would avoid mixing sex with horror and would avoid scenes some people could regard as disgusting and revolting. (1977: 165–6)

Yet a cursory examination of Hammer's dealings with the BBFC, particularly in the period of 1956–61, shows that it was far from amicable. Sangster's script for *The Curse of Frankenstein* was almost rejected, with the report from examiner Audrey Fields, dated 10 October 1956, noting that the script had 'a lip-smacking relish for mutilated corpses, repulsive dismembered hands and eyeballs removed from the head' and that while they could not reject the story outline outright, 'a great many details will have to be modified or eliminated' (Fields 1956). Examiner Frank Croft went further, noting that Hammer 'should have the script re-written and send it in again' (Croft 1956).

The status of *The Curse of Frankenstein* as the first British colour gothic made it a risky prospect in regard to assessing the censor's reaction. With no precedent to compare it to, Hammer had no real idea how the BBFC would react. However, this arguably worked in Hammer's favour. Treated almost as an anomalous one-off, *The Curse of Frankenstein* actually came out of its battle with the censor 'relatively unscathed' (Kinsey 2002: 80). However, as Hammer began to capitalise on the success of *The Curse of Frankenstein*, a proliferation of horror output from the company and the industry more broadly led to a stronger stance by the censor.

This came to a head in 1960 with the release of *Peeping Tom* (Powell, 1960). The subsequent release and moral panic surrounding the film (Pirie 2008: 128; Rigby 2002: 73) saw the BBFC trying to salvage its reputation (badly damaged after passing *Peeping Tom*) by taking a much firmer stance against the new influx of British horror films. Meikle suggests that this new firmer stance by the BBFC nearly altered Hammer's path entirely (Meikle 2009: 107–8).

An example of this is Hammer's ultimately unproduced *The Rape of Sabena*, which provides an interesting case study of Hammer in this period, though it is not the focus of this chapter due to a lack of archival material held on the project. While the Hammer Script Archive does hold a screenplay for the proposed film (listed as the 'Master Scene Script – Final Draft'), other ephemera such as financial documentation or correspondence are not held within the project file. As such secondary accounts of such material which feature in work by Hearn and Barnes (2007), Hearn (2011), Kinsey (2002) and Meikle (2009) can be used to garner more insights into the project's development and eventual failure.

The script focuses on the Spanish Inquisition's occupation of the town of Sabena in 1560 and was written by Peter R. Newman. Newman had worked with Hammer before, having adapted his own teleplay *Yesterday's Enemy* for the Val Guest film of the same name in 1959. *The Rape of Sabena* screenplay starts by noting that 'at the beginning, in order to plant firmly in the minds of the audience the utter brutality of The Inquisition, we open on a scene of extreme cruelty' and this is exactly how the screenplay opens, with three men executed for the crime of heresy against the Church. Despite this brutal beginning, the project itself was not envisioned as a horror film, a point of contention for the distributor Columbia which will be examined later. Kinsey notes that the film moved through production quickly, with a director attached in John Gilling and the script to *The Rape of Sabena* and *The Curse of The Werewolf* submitted to the BBFC on 12 August 1960 (2002: 197). John Trevelyan responded in five days, and his thoughts on the two scripts are illuminating:

> Each of these is liable to run into serious censorship trouble; this may not surprise you. I am, however, more worried about the effect of these two pictures on your company's growing reputation. I know this kind of thing makes money, and I do not for the moment blame you for wanting to do so, but I do feel that the reputation of your company is important both here and abroad. (Cited in Kinsey 2002: 197)

What is fascinating here is how Trevelyan focuses on Hammer's 'growing reputation' as a company, suggesting, as I will discuss later in regard to *The Night Creatures*, that it is not the scripts in isolation being assessed in relation to their suitability for release, but also several contextual factors outside of these individual productions being considered by the BBFC. James Carreras replied the same day:

> I must say I agree with your comments entirely and had a meeting with Michael [Carreras] and Tony [Hinds] when we decided to be very careful as to the type of subjects which we will be making during the end of 1960/61, and I think you will find that subjects, as per the two above, will have been deleted from our programme. (Cited in Kinsey 2002: 197)

In an interview with Denis Meikle, Michael Carreras seems to recall this meeting:

> I suddenly got a call from my father, and he said, 'I'm stopping the picture.' It was the rarest occasion of all – the only time that Hammer ever stopped a film that was in production. I think a flash of light went before his Catholic conscience. (Cited in Meikle 2009: 108)

However, as Meikle goes on to note, this flash of light was 'more secular in origin'. Although James Carreras, in his response to Trevelyan, seems to frame the decision to meet with Carreras and Hinds and pull *The Rape of Sabena* as a response to Trevelyan's advice, it seems the key issue for James Carreras was the hesitancy of its potential distributor Columbia. Kinsey notes that Hammer's relationship with Columbia was flagging, as Columbia 'knew what Hammer were good at – horror pictures – and began to get cold feet about any ventures outside the genre' (2002: 196). However, Hearn and Barnes suggest the subject matter could have played a part in Columbia's decision to pull the film, with the distributor 'apparently fearing condemnation by the Catholic Church' (2007: 56). Producer Tony Hinds seemed to confirm this was a factor, noting that 'we got a tip that the Catholic Church would ban the picture so he [James Carreras] pulled out and I was left with these sets'. While this of course may have been a reason, Kinsey suggests that, in the case of *The Rape of Sabena*, 'Columbia were never going to swallow the project ... Too much money had already been poured into its pre-production, and now major rewrites were needed close to its proposed starting date' (2002: 197). A litany of factors from the subject matter, the BBFC's warnings and the wariness of the distributor ultimately led to *The Rape of Sabena* being pulled from

Hammer's schedule, though the film does have traces of its production on screen. Hearn and Barnes note that before the project's cancellation the 'construction of, among others, a church, a main street, the church interior and a wine cellar' had all been completed for the would-be film (2007: 56). To try and minimise their losses, *The Curse of the Werewolf*'s production was brought forward and utilised these pre-existing sets (Hearn 2011: 47). *The Rape of Sabena* provides a fascinating case study not only as the only Hammer film abandoned during its actual production, but as a clear example of the difficult situation Hammer found themselves in the advent of the 1960s, with the censor attempting to pull the company away from horror material, while distributors such as Columbia were only seemingly interested in horror features from Hammer.

While Trevelyan had cautioned Hammer about both *The Rape of Sabena* and *The Curse of the Werewolf*, Hammer had only heeded his warnings with the former, and as such put themselves on another collision course with the BBFC. *The Curse of the Werewolf* not only featured Hammer's now standardised practice of horror and blood, but also a rape scene at the beginning of the film, to which the censors strongly objected. After a lengthy battle, the film did eventually garner an X-certificate, but at some cost. The film had been substantially edited, with the BBFC 'imposing painfully visible cuts enhanced by tell-tale jumps in the soundtrack' (Kinsey 2002: 216). It was in between these tumultuous periods that *The Night Creatures* was developed, after *The Curse of Frankenstein* had ushered in a new phase of colour gothic horror, but just before the BBFC's hardened stance on projects such as *The Rape of Sabena*, *The Curse of the Werewolf* and a new wave of British horror films.

Censoring *The Night Creatures*

The screenplay for *The Night Creatures* takes place in Canada, in the town of Hudson, an alteration from the novel's American setting. This is particularly relevant to Hutchings's study of the American Matheson working with the British production company Hammer, as Canada signalled 'a neutral space where Americanness and Britishness might profitably co-exist and engage with each other' (2008: 62). The narrative begins with the protagonist Robert Neville doing his daily preparations in a post-plague world, such as checking his generator and food supplies and ensuring that his electric fence is working. At night he listens to the calls of his former neighbours (now vampires) as they try to persuade him to join them. The script flashes back to before the plague, with Neville and his wife and daughter. We see how the plague resulted in the death of his daughter and, eventually, his wife too. At night, Neville stays indoors and is tormented by the vampires surrounding his house. By day, he experiments on the vampires, and drives around the town killing them while they sleep, by either staking them or exposing them to direct sunlight. Towards the end of the screenplay he finds another apparent survivor, Ruth, who he takes to his house and eventually becomes romantically involved with. After Neville tests her blood and finds her infected by the plague, Ruth reveals she is part of a new group of the infected who seem to retain their higher brain functions and can walk in the day, and that she had been sent to spy on Neville. As the more rabid vampires break through Neville's defences and attack the house, Ruth's group of new

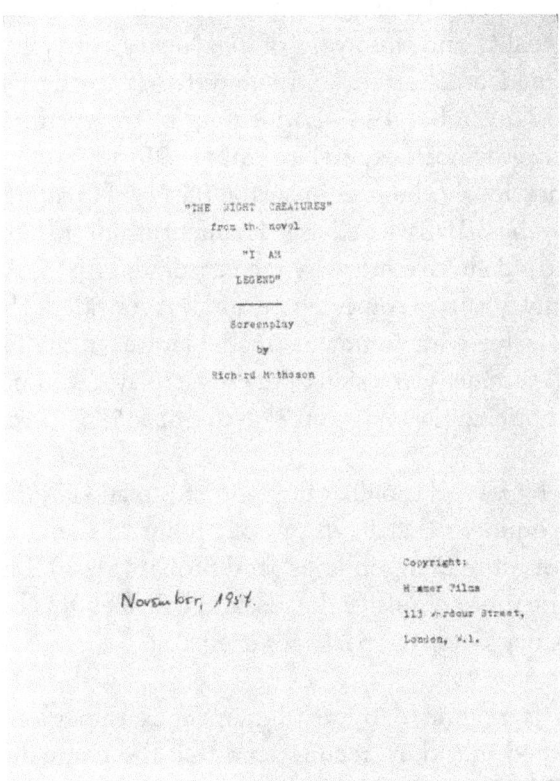

Figure 2.1 The cover page to Matheson's self-adaptation *The Night Creatures*

vampires also make their move, killing the rabid vampires and taking Neville away, to investigate his immunity to the plague.

Even by modern standards, the script's horror imagery remains potent, particularly in the film's first act flashback scenes. With Neville's daughter having succumbed to the plague and the government enforcing a law that all bodies should be burned, Neville is forced to take his daughter's body, in a sack, to a huge fire pit outside the town limits. As he arrives, two officials grab his daughter's body from his hands and take her away towards the pit, preventing Neville from having any chance of closure. It is a nihilistic and harrowing sequence, and the screenplay remains tonally bleak throughout. The film's contemporary setting may have also caused more issues than Hammer's gothic horror films. With most of Hammer's gothics located in a non-specific eastern European village decades ago, a degree of separation occurs which lends itself to some of the more fantastical elements of the films' narratives. *The Night Creatures* does not have this separation and, as is apparent in Chapter 3 of *I Am Legend* (where Neville finds a copy of Stoker's *Dracula*), even attempts to bridge the gap between reality and the world of *The Night Creatures*. Nevertheless, Hammer seemed undeterred, and submitted it to the BBFC and the MPAA on 20 November 1957 (Anderson to Trevelyan: 20 November 1957; Anderson to Shurlock: 20 November 1957).

As noted previously, the screenplay for *The Night Creatures* was strongly condemned by the BBFC who advised Hammer against making it. Although this seems like a definitive move by the censor, the BBFC Archive reveals that the screenplay caused some debate, and was considered by some examiners to be passable with some cuts made. However, the initial response from the first examiner was a sign of the screenplay's eventual fate. Audrey Fields, in their brief initial report on 25 November 1957, wrote:

> In a word, NO. I feel too ill at the moment to add anything to this, but I am confident that I can put our point to the company in a letter of not more than ten lines (and probably less). I have rough notes on the more repulsive details, and will keep this by me, but I think the story synopsis speaks for itself.

This opinion is reiterated by an unnamed examiner on 1 December 1957, who noted that they 'recommend that the company be told that we don't think a film based on this script would receive our certificate' before ending the report noting that 'it does not seem worthwhile to list the offending scenes, since the whole idea behind the story seems so unsavoury' (Anon. 1957h).

Although these early reports demonstrate the strong initial response to Matheson's script, it is notable that neither report actually referenced any specific scenes they find offensive, with both instead just referring to the general synopsis and story, as opposed to the way anything is portrayed or depicted. This is notable, as BBFC reports often listed specific instances within scripts which would prevent them from passing it, citing page numbers and suggesting alterations or deletions. The above reports did not go into these specifics, thereby suggesting a far more emotive reading of the screenplay. This is not to say that the BBFC's response was particularly reactionary. The script has many sequences throughout which would have been considered too gruesome or horrific to pass unchanged. However, these initial readings seem to refuse to engage with the specifics of the script, making it impossible for Hammer to know how to make the screenplay more agreeable.

Across the Atlantic, however, Hammer received more positive news. Not only did the MPAA, under the directorship of Geoffrey Shurlock, produce a detailed report on the alterations that Hammer would have to make, but the suggestions were far removed from the emotive outcry of the BBFC. The general conceit of the story, which seemed to offend the BBFC in principle, was not a problem for the MPAA, with Shurlock noting explicitly that 'the basic story seems to meet the requirements of the Production Code' (Shurlock to Hinds: 4 December 1957). Shurlock outlines seventeen alterations which would have to be made for the MPAA to consider passing the screenplay. Peculiarly, over half of these do not touch on the horror imagery throughout, but are primarily concerned with blasphemous language, such as 'Dam' [*sic*] and 'my God'.

Around the same time, the BBFC examiners also found themselves in an internal debate. Whereas the first examiners had rejected the script outright, a third found some positives, noting that 'the story ... is not a bad one with an interesting twist at the end' (Anon. 1957i). They noted that the script has 'a large number of incidents we would have to cut out'; however, they concluded by saying that the BBFC 'should get in Anthony Hinds and tell him our requirements' (Anon. 1957i). Audrey Fields, the initial examiner, wrote to the Secretary, John Nicholls, noting the divisiveness of the script: 'You will see that there is some difference of opinion here. I myself would not wish to try and draft a letter implying acceptance even of the underlying idea, unless the President decides this should be done' (Fields to Nicholls: 3 December 1957). Ultimately, the Secretary sided with Fields's initial assessment, writing to Tony Hinds to reject the script on 12 December 1957:

> I am afraid we can hold out no hope of being able to give a certificate to a film based on this script, which, in gruesomeness, horror and violence, goes well beyond what we should feel justified in accepting for screen entertainment, even in the X category. (Nicholls to Hinds)

Despite this initial setback, Hammer clearly sensed that *The Night Creatures* was not yet a lost cause. Although they were unaware of the BBFC's own internal discussions regarding the viability of *The Night Creatures*, Hammer had received the MPAA's verdict, and could see a notable difference in the BBFC and MPAA's assessment of Matheson's screenplay. This therefore allowed Hammer to again contact the BBFC, using the MPAA's verdict as their primary counterpoint to the British censor's decision.

Hammer took over two months to initially contest the decision made by the BBFC. James Carreras himself wrote to Nichols noting that Hammer had also submitted the script to the MPAA and thought that the BBFC 'would be interested in the letter which they [the MPAA] wrote to Tony Hinds dated January 28 1958' (Carreras to Nicholls: 26 February 1958). Carreras hoped that the MPAA's letter would make the BBFC reconsider the original decision, with Carreras wanting the opportunity to discuss the script with Nicholls in person. Nicholls passed the script back to the examiners, but the results were the same. One anonymised examiner refused to read the script, having read it when it was initially submitted. Noting that they will not read it just 'because of a letter from the MPAA to Hammer Films indicating general approval of it' (Anon. 1958b), the examiner only decided to pass it on to another reviewer rather than denying it again immediately due to the fact that one reviewer previously 'was less against it than the President, FNC (Croft) and myself' (Anon. 1958b).

This back and forth between Hammer, the MPAA and the BBFC demonstrates that the BBFC was far from united. The script not only caused an internal debate between the censors themselves, but also highlighted how different the MPAA and BBFC's own notions of censorable material really were. This is compounded in the official report made after

Carreras's letter (and after the examiner had refused to read it again and passed it on). If anything, the report was even more damming of *The Night Creatures* than Field's initial assessment in 1957. Observing that they had 'noted as many as 44 points which I disliked', the reviewer goes as far as to call the script 'the product of a diseased mind' (Anon. 1958c). The reviewer also openly attacked the assessment of the MPAA: 'I am astonished at Shurlock's letter. He is apparently prepared to accept all the real nastiness provided phrases like 'my god' and 'dammit' are deleted' (Anon. 1958c).

However, perhaps of most interest here is the reporter's seemingly preconceived notion of Hammer as a company. The report notes that if it was merely a 'straight horror film' it would 'probably be acceptable', but 'with the elements of sex and the gruesomeness, which the promoters will doubtless be most reluctant to abandon, it becomes quite prohibitive' (Anon. 1958c). This is the first overt reference to how Hammer's newfound reputation as horror specialists had perhaps hindered their chances of the film getting made. Whereas *The Curse of Frankenstein* got through the censors as an atypical one-off, the submission of the *Dracula* screenplay on 8 October 1957 to the BBFC, followed by the screenplays for *The Revenge of Frankenstein* and *The Night Creatures* on 21 November, made it clear that Hammer was planning on exploiting the horror genre long-term. Therefore, I would suggest that this perhaps led to the BBFC's presumption that Hammer was specifically looking to make shocking horror material, and as a result would simply refuse to contemplate toning down aspects of *The Night Creatures*. The reaction to the script can therefore be seen as a precursor to the BBFC's response to the influx of horror product two years later. Clearly aware that the release and subsequent success of *The Curse of Frankenstein* in May 1957 was the start of a new advent of horror product, the censor's reaction to *The Night Creatures* could arguably be seen as an attempt to demonstrate to Hammer that the censor had the power to stop a film in its tracks, and would utilise it when necessary.

The BBFC Archive holds correspondence from Nicholls to Carreras once again rejecting the screenplay for *The Night Creatures*. Nicholls noted that although he 'read with interest your copy of Mr Shurlock's letter', the film still passed 'the bounds of legitimate horror' (Nicholls to Carreras: 11 March 1958). What constitutes as 'legitimate' within the horror genre is never expanded on by Nicholls, and this vagueness as to why specifically *The Night Creatures* was impossible to pass with any changes was never elaborated on. In fact, even on its second submission to the censor no changes or specific scenes were discussed or noted. Despite the lack of concrete reasoning, this rejection would prove to be the final time Hammer officially submitted the script to the BBFC.

However, Hammer were still seemingly involved in the screenplay in the early 1960s. Nearly three years after Hammer's final submission of the script to the BBFC, John Trevelyan, now director of the BBFC, received a letter from R. Paul Elwood, writing in regard to *The Night Creatures* screenplay. Elwood is identified in an inter-office memo at the MPAA between Gordon White and Geoffrey Shurlock as

> having telephoned [the MPAA] from Atlantic City a few days ago and said that he had acquired rights to the script for THE NIGHT CREATURES. He said he had approached a big company about distribution of a film based on this script, and had been told that he would have to deal with Code objections first. (White to Shurlock: 30 March 1961)

Elwood wrote to Trevelyan regarding James Carreras. Elwood suggested that he had corresponded with Carreras, who had told Elwood he had recently 'obtained an unofficial reaction from the British Censor [regarding *The Night Creatures*], which is still by no means favourable' (Elwood to Trevelyan: 24 August 1961). Suggesting that this 'leaves him rather puzzled', Elwood went on to note that the script had undergone substantial changes, and now 'has the potential to become one of the screen's most popular thrillers' (Elwood to Trevelyan: 24 August 1961). Elwood's lengthy letter seemed to be aimed at trying to reverse the decision of the BBFC, using a tactic James Carreras had tried three years earlier – pitting the opinion of the BBFC against the MPAA. Elwood did so by noting that the substantial changes made to *The Night Creatures* had resulted in Geoffrey Shurlock at the MPAA finding the material acceptable under the production code.

Cross-referencing this correspondence at the BBFC Archive with the MPAA files at the Margaret Herrick Library, it is clear that Elwood did indeed engage in lengthy discussions with the MPAA through to March 1962. On 22 May 1961, after nearly eight weeks of correspondence, Elwood submitted a revised script of *The Night Creatures* to the MPAA, and Shurlock replied noting that 'with the extensive changes in this new version of your story, we wish to note that this material now seems acceptable under the requirements of the Production Code'

(Shurlock to Elwood: 24 May 1961). Clearly enthused by this, Elwood (still apparently coordinating with James Carreras) wrote the above-mentioned letter to Trevelyan. However, Trevelyan's own response to Elwood, held in the BBFC Archive, is illuminating. Noting that he would have to see the script again as it had been 'more than four years since [we] considered the original script' (Trevelyan to Elwood: 28 August 1961), Trevelyan also warned Elwood that even though time had passed, the script potentially would be more difficult to pass in 1961 than it was in 1957. Trevelyan wrote:

> In recent years we have found it necessary to be cautious about horror films, probably more cautious than we were a few years ago . . . [horror] films are now infrequent. As a result, when they are shown to the public they tend to invite a much greater degree of public criticism that the film would have invited even a few years ago. Criticism of what is shown on the cinema screens has increased substantially during the last two years and we think it might be inadvisable to issue certificates to films which we think will intensify this criticism. (Trevelyan to Elwood: 28 August 1961)

It was around this time that the BBFC encountered considerable criticism for their handling of *Peeping Tom*, and were keen to keep a closer eye on horror material shown to the public. Despite Trevelyan promising that any resubmitted script would 'receive fair and objective consideration', this excerpt from Trevelyan explicitly states that the BBFC was not giving certificates to these films based merely on the film itself, but were also considering their own relationship to the public, and the damage passing a horror film such as *The Night Creatures* might do for the censor's own reputation.

After noting that Michael Carreras 'is having Anthony Hinds take care of matters concerning script revisions' (Elwood to Trevelyan: 3 September 1961), Elwood assures Trevelyan that Hammer would resubmit the script again imminently. However, the correspondence took a bizarre turn with a handwritten note by Trevelyan on a copy of a letter from Elwood dated 16 September 1961. Trevelyan's note read:

> Spoke to Col. [James] Carreras on telephone. He said that he knows nothing of any proposal for Mike [Carreras] to be associated with making this picture. He himself would have nothing to do with it, and would stop Michael doing it. (Trevelyan 1961)

This note offers up a number of questions regarding this revival of *The Night Creatures* script, and the nature of Hammer's involvement. Perhaps most pressing is the nature of Elwood's relationship with Hammer. Throughout the correspondence, Elwood regularly referred to Hammer's involvement in the project's revival, and specifically mentioned Tony Hinds, James Carreras and Michael Carreras throughout his correspondence. However, the note by Trevelyan explicitly stated that James Carreras has no idea about the arrangement, while also casting significant doubt about Elwood's business relationship with Michael Carreras. Elwood clearly had a copy of the script (he gives detailed references to scenes throughout his correspondence with the MPAA and BBFC), but there is a potential scenario where Elwood perhaps exaggerated Hammer's involvement with *The Night Creatures* revival. However, it is pertinent to note that it would be wise of James Carreras to distance himself from what had already proved a controversial screenplay for Hammer. This is around the same time that the BBFC had not only played a part in the cancelling of *The Rape of Sabena*, but had exacted significant cuts to *The Curse of the Werewolf* and even strongly encouraged James Carreras to move away from horror films altogether. Frustratingly, neither potential scenario is confirmed in the correspondence between Trevelyan and Elwood due to this being one of the last pieces of correspondence held in the BBFC Archive between Trevelyan and Elwood, and Elwood's involvement with the project seems to cease entirely by early 1962.

The final chapter in Hammer's *The Night Creatures* saga came when 'an economical Hammer sold the screenplay to American producer Robert Lippert' (Hutchings 2008: 54). As noted, Hammer had a longstanding relationship with Lippert dating back to the late 1940s and therefore Hammer selling *The Night Creatures* on to Lippert in the early 1960s, after their great success within the gothic horror genre in the United Kingdom and United States, offers a neat, cyclical aspect to *The Night Creatures* turbulent development process. *The Night Creatures* underwent significant changes (so much so that Matheson took his name off the eventually used script), and the film was retitled *The Last Man on Earth* and finally shot in Italy. Despite these changes, one thing remained constant, and that was the difficulty the film had with the BBFC. Despite the film no longer having anything to do with Hammer, it was James Carreras who came to its aid when talks had seemingly stalled between Lippert and the BBFC. The BBFC Archive holds correspondence from Carreras to Trevelyan regarding *The Last Man on Earth*, noting that Lippert 'has had a lot of trouble' with the film (Carreras to Trevelyan: 23 November 1964). Not only did Carreras write to Trevelyan on Lippert's behalf, but he actually submitted the film to the censor. Trevelyan wrote back to Carreras three days later, noting that the film was submitted in July 1963, and that the BBFC 'gave Fox some cuts, but they decided not to proceed and the picture has therefore never been cleared by us' (Trevelyan to Carreras: 26 November 1964). Trevelyan ended the letter by saying that 'if your company, or any other company, will make these cuts we are prepared to clear the picture'. The film would eventually see the light of day, but 'had no noticeable impact at all when it opened in the mid-1960s' (Hutchings 2008: 67).

The Night Creatures looked to capitalise on *The Curse of Frankenstein*'s reception, but looked outside of the gothic horror genre to a more contemporary and darker story, which was seen by the British Board of Film Censors as unacceptable. *The Night Creatures* was undone not by Hammer, but by the BBFC, though Hammer was by no means blameless. Matheson's script features some harrowing scenes by today's standards, and clearly would not pass the censor unscathed in 1958. However, although Hammer was no doubt prepared to alter the script to the censor's satisfaction, the censor instead refused to engage with any specific issues in the script itself, deeming the story of the screenplay unsuitable in any fashion. Correspondence between Hammer and the BBFC and Hammer and the MPAA, show that the American and British censors differed in their opinions on the script, a fact Hammer tried to use to its advantage. However, the BBFC stood firm on its decision, and despite a brief and bizarre attempt to revive the script in the early 1960s, Hammer's *The Night Creatures* never made it to the screen. What effect it may have had on Hammer's production slate can only be speculated. At the time, its failure meant that Hammer's horror product was restricted almost entirely to the gothic horror genre. One can venture that if it had been released and proven internationally successful, it could have led Hammer down a different path entirely.

The collapse of American finance

While *The Night Creatures*, *The Rape of Sabena* and Chapter 1's case study of *Tales of Frankenstein* stand as key failures for Hammer, it is worth underlining that, within this period and throughout the 1960s, failures such as this would be rare, and the company would quickly find its footing as it moved into the 1960s. Anglo-American industrial relations grew even more robust throughout the 1960s and, by 1967, 'ninety per cent of funding for 'British films' came from the USA, with investment peaking in 1968 at 31.3 million dollars' (Magor and Schlesinger 2009: 302). James Carreras exploited this industry trend, proving adept at fostering a number of lucrative financial and distribution arrangements with major US production companies, primarily on the strength of their gothic horror product. Hearn notes that 'it is a measure of Hammer's reputation and success that almost every subject they pitched to distributors from the mid-1950s to the late 1960s found finance' (2011: 160). While this and the previous chapter covered a number of notable exceptions as Hammer began to adapt to its new position as horror specialists, for the most part this statement is correct. Through the majority of the 1960s, Hammer capitalised on its success in the horror genre, producing a slew of sequels to some of its late-1950s gothic horror films, and consolidating this success by diversifying into other genres.

However, while Hammer's output seemed to move from strength to strength, the 1960s were not bereft of behind the scenes incidents. In 1961, after escalating tensions between him and his father, Michael Carreras left Hammer and formed his own production company Capricorn Productions. This was in part due to the ongoing issues with Columbia and *The Rape of Sabena* project. Frustrated that this passion project had been cancelled and that he 'found himself playing second fiddle again as executive producer to nine out of the next thirteen of Hammer's pictures in "60–61"' (Kinsey 2010: 65), Carreras left shortly before production began on *Captain Clegg* (Scott, 1962). Despite his official departure Carreras still worked frequently with Hammer throughout the 1960s as an independent director, writer and producer, directing films such as *Maniac* (1963), *The Curse of the Mummy's Tomb* (1964) and *Slave Girls* (1967).

A more permanent change came when Hammer moved from Bray Studios to Elstree. Hammer had made their home at Bray Studios in 1951, where a home studio proved a shrewd financial move. The reused and redressed sets that recur throughout Hammer's Bray films undoubtedly contribute to the notion of a distinct Hammer style and aesthetic. Moreover, Hammer's time at Bray (1951–66) is intrinsically linked to Hammer's peak as a company, echoed in Laurie N. Ede's assertion that 'the best Hammer horrors were made when the company had a stable studio base at Bray, and a stable group of technicians' (2012: 54).

However, Hammer's change in fortune was not merely down to location, but due to a myriad of industrial factors which caused Hammer to have to rethink its entire finance and distribution strategy. Due to the Eady Levy and the cheaper cost of production in the United Kingdom (outlined in the previous chapter), 'by the 1960s American capital was flowing into the industry on an unprecedented scale' (Dickinson and Street 1985). However, this overreliance on American finance in Britain would prove to be costly for Hammer and the industry more broadly. In a remarkably prescient article in *Sight and Sound* entitled 'England their England' (1966), Penelope Houston discusses film funding in the United Kingdom and the dependency on American support. Noting how a great deal of American production money 'is now concentrated in London ... partly no doubt because it's easier, closer and offers the attractions of being abroad without the snags of having to work in a foreign language' (Houston 1966: 55), Houston outlines the positives of this influx of American finance in Britain:

> The Americans are not driving the British out of work: they are creating employment. They are not setting out to Americanise British films: they are using a good deal of British talent to develop an international cinema. (Houston 1966: 55)

Yet Houston also outlines the tenuous nature of this relationship, noting that 'everything is fine, in fact, unless and until the Americans move out. Then it has been suggested ... "the British film industry could collapse in a month"' (Houston 1966: 56). The lack of a more reliable or long-term financial plan is noted by Houston who emphasises that:

> there is of course, no guarantee of permanence, no tying investment in plant or fixed assets. This is mostly picture-by-picture finance, depending on such chancy things as the tastes of producers and directors, or the type of story in vogue at the moment. (Houston 1966: 56)

Houston's deliberations would soon come to pass. In the late 1960s/early 1970s, the American economy and film industry went into recession (Baillieu and Goodchild 2002: 95; Casper 2012: 48). Between 1969 and 1971 alone 'only one in ten films cleared a profit. About 40 percent of labor was unemployed' (Casper 2012: 48). This resulted in the withdrawal of 'the extensive American financial support for British production which had been such as key feature of the industry's optimism in the 1960s' (Higson 1993: 217). Outside of American finance, social factors also contributed to this decline in the industry, with cinema attendance dropping dramatically as television and other leisure activities became increasingly popular (Street 2009: 105; Higson 1993: 217; Hutchings 1993: 159).

The large-scale withdrawal of American finance alone would have been critical for Hammer, but it was not the company's only blight. Hammer's success within the horror genre led to a proliferation of horror product within the British market in the 1960s and 1970s, notably Amicus Productions, Tigon, Anglo-Amalgamated and Tyburn (Hutchings 2004: 29; Conrich 2008: 26). Amicus was perhaps the most notable, particularly as it was founded by Milton Subotsky and Max Rosenberg, who had so nearly worked for Hammer on the unmade *Frankenstein* project in 1957 detailed in Chapter 1. Amicus Productions was officially formed on November 1961 (Nutman 2008: 32), and produced fourteen horror films between 1964 and 1974. Hutchings notes that the frequency of which British stars such as Peter Cushing and Christopher Lee appeared within Amicus's films 'suggest that Amicus should be seen as an integral part of the British horror movement of the 1960s and 1970s' (Hutchings 2002: 131). Amicus's use of actors and directors notable for their work in Hammer 'cannily attempted to utilise the same creative approach' as Hammer (Forshaw 2013: 80). This use of recurring creative talent associated with Hammer meant that 'Hammer Horror' 'became a generic description' (Forshaw 2013: 80), as opposed to solely being associated with Hammer Films. As such, as the financial and distribution networks Hammer had relied so heavily on fell apart, competition within the genre actually increased in the first part of the 1970s (Conrich 2008: 26; Street 2009: 106), putting further strain on the company. How Hammer reacted to this pressure, and the internal fissures it caused, will be a key focus of the next four chapters.

3

The curse of *Dracula*

Despite the large-scale withdrawal of American finance and the proliferation of rival horror product detailed in Chapter 2, arguably the most seismic change at Hammer happened in 1973. James Carreras, who had led the company since his own father's death on 15 October 1950, sold his stake in Hammer to his son Michael on 31 January 1973. James Carreras had been looking to leave Hammer for some time. In 1969 he attempted to broker a deal with EMI head Bernard Delfont which would have seen EMI take a 75 per cent stake in Hammer Films. When this failed, he turned to Tony Tenser at Tigon in 1971. This deal came close to fruition, with contracts being drawn and a meeting held. However, disappointed in the terms offered (due to the fact it was on a performance basis, James Carreras was to be far less rewarded than he initially thought) this deal was also shelved (Hearn and Barnes 2007: 133–4). Michael Carreras had returned to Hammer as managing director in January 1971, and despite his prominent position at Hammer, he had not been aware that his father was looking to sell the company. As such he had to move quickly and took out a £400,000 loan with the Pension Fund Securities (PFS), making an official offer to his father for the company in 1973. James Carreras accepted the deal, making Michael Carreras the official head of Hammer.

Michael Carreras's tenure at the head of the company for what would prove to be its final seven years could lead some to consider a correlation between Carreras's appointment and the company's eventual failure. In his chapter 'The End of Hammer' in *Seventies British Cinema* (Shail 2008) Wheeler Winston Dixon notes that Hammer, 'still a significant force in British cinema in 1969, saw the 1970s as a period of decay and terminal collapse' (2008: 14). Personnel changes, the move to Elstree from Bray, and the change from James Carreras to Michael Carreras all arguably confirm the notion that Hammer was losing many of the facets that had once made it such a successful studio.

Despite the huge economic changes in the late 1960s and 1970s which fundamentally altered Hammer's entire production strategy, some studies on the decline of the company have placed a particular emphasis on the apparent stagnation of Hammer's films, citing this as a key factor in its decline and eventual closure. In his 1992 article 'Twilight of the Monsters: The English Horror Film 1968–1975', David Sanjek identifies George Romero's *Night of the Living Dead* (1968) as a crucial moment in horror cinema. Sanjek positions *Night of the Living Dead* as the film that broke the rules set firmly in place by British horror films such as Hammer's, with its impact setting in motion 'the decline of the British horror film and the myth it embodied' (Sanjek 1992: 112):

> Violence that once was implied ... now was shown in all its visceral details. The film's victims in several cases became themselves monsters, thereby muddying the distinction between the monstrous and the normal as well as locating terror in the everyday world. (Sanjek 1992: 111)

Sanjek specifically cites Hammer's output in stark contrast with Romero's film, noting how by 1968 Hammer's films had become 'increasingly safe and formulaic' (Sanjek 1992: 112). Sanjek notes that *Night of the Living Dead*'s moral ambiguity and bleakness put the 'tidy universe of the English horror film ... in jeopardy' (Sanjek 1992: 112). This is also echoed in Laurie N. Ede's chapter 'British Film Design in the 1970s', where they note that, by the 1970s, 'the Hammers were burdened by a lack of imagination' (2012: 54).

While it is difficult to look past the critical failure of Hammer's distribution and financial networks as the primary reason for the company's eventual downfall, this notion that Hammer itself struggled to innovate within the confines of a genre with which they were synonymous is a common one. Between 1957 and 1970, Hammer had produced twenty-seven films that could be categorised as gothic horror, with seven Frankenstein films and seven Dracula films amongst them (Hammer would go on to produce one more Frankenstein film and three more Dracula pictures). As such, this argument of a lack of innovation or creative stagnation is one worth considering. Yet this chapter will argue that an analysis of Hammer's unmade projects within this period makes it clear that Michael Carreras's tenure is not one that lacked innovation. This will be done primarily through an examination of arguably Hammer's most notable franchise, *Dracula*.

Reviving Dracula: the reinvention of Hammer's *Dracula* series

Hammer's 1958 *Dracula* cemented the company as the new standard-bearer for British gothic cinema. The first film to feature Hammer's most iconic character, *Dracula*'s reputation has only grown in stature, with the British Film Institute restoring and re-releasing the film in 2007, and then again in 2013, with additional footage recovered in Japan restored and integrated into the film. At the time of its release, the international success of the film saw Hammer put in the enviable position of devising a sequel for a character who had only ever originally appeared in a single stand-alone novel. Hammer had dealt with this before with the *Frankenstein* series (1957–74), continuing ably after the original adaptation (which took far more liberties with its original source material than *Dracula* did) had proven successful.

The issue was temporarily circumvented with the omission of Lee from the produced sequel. Instead, new vampire Baron Meinster (David Peel) faced off against a returning Peter Cushing as Dr Van Helsing. Yet despite featuring an original screenplay and a new villain, *The Brides of Dracula* (Fisher, 1960) can still be seen to 'reproduce the structures' (Hutchings 1993: 120) of the original *Dracula*, with the gothic iconography and recurring theme of the 'battle between vampire and savant-professional over the women within a weakened patriarchy' (Hutchings 1993: 120).

Christopher Lee eventually returned to the role in *Dracula Prince of Darkness* (Fisher, 1966). Set ten years after the original, the film is still anchored in the gothic archetypes and iconography which, even on Lee's second appearance as the Count, contained 'little that audiences hadn't seen before' (Hearn and Barnes 2007: 97). With *Dracula Prince of Darkness* putting an end to eight years of hibernation, Lee's Dracula began to stalk screens with increasing frequency. *Dracula Has Risen From the Grave* (Francis, 1968) saw the departure of Terence Fisher from the series, but the film proved a success at the box office, with the 39 November issue of *Kinematograph Weekly* noting that 'all records were broken by *Dracula Has Risen From the Grave* on the first day of its ABC release' (cited in Kinsey 2007: 97). Despite director Freddie Francis bringing a distinctive visual style to the franchise, the film's narrative remains similar to its predecessors, with Lee's Dracula terrorising a nineteenth-century 'cod mittel-Europe' (Hearn and Barnes 2007: 30). The franchise continued to be bound by these spatial and temporal limitations in the follow-up, *Taste the Blood of Dracula* (Sasdy, 1970).

By the time *Scars of Dracula* (Ward Baker, 1970) was released, it was the sixth entry in a series which was now over a decade old. Although the established formula was present in *Scars of Dracula*, it was the final instalment of it on screen and, behind the scenes, the beginning of a new finance and distribution deal for Hammer. With waning interest from American majors, James Carreras turned to Associated British Picture Corporation (ABPC), who had been under the ownership of EMI since 1969, to distribute the film (Kinsey 2007: 206). Under this deal Hammer effectively had 100 per cent British finance, but for the first time since the 1950s, Hammer had no American distribution guarantee. As well as this, the funding offered by the British independent ABPC was far below what had been given by American majors such as Warner Bros., meaning no film could cost over $200,000. ABPC were also not able to secure significant American distribution for *Scars of Dracula* and its double bill feature *The Horror of Frankenstein* (Sangster, 1970), meaning the films had a relatively limited theatrical run in the United States.

This is significant for several reasons. First, it underlines the point that although the correlation between Michael Carreras's instalment as head of Hammer and the company's decline is often cited, the seeds of Hammer's eventual failure were planted three years before James Carreras left the company. Not only had Tony Hinds and other Hammer regulars departed by this stage, but Hammer's most viable (and crucially, marketable) franchise had been turned down for distribution by the Hollywood majors. This left Hammer with limited budgets to make the films, and very few options regarding transatlantic distribution, the latter of which had been fundamental to Hammer's longstanding success. Second, this deal shows a lack of interest in the current Hammer *Dracula* product. With *Scars of Dracula* only being produced through a tight budget and limited United States distribution, it was clear that this formula was in drastic need of reinvention.

This reinvention came in the form of two contemporary set *Dracula* films – *Dracula AD 1972* (Gibson, 1972) and its sequel *The Satanic Rites* of *Dracula* (Gibson, 1973). Both projects got the backing of Warner Bros., which ensured American distribution, but failed to live up their enticing premise. In *Dracula AD 1972*, Dracula does not even venture outside the gothic church in which he is resurrected. This was seemingly at Michael Carreras's behest, who, in an interview with Alan Frank, said he 'was very strong in dragging in a deserted and empty churchyard as much as possible, to give it a midnight flavour' (cited in Hallenbeck 2010: 162). While there is clearly a tension between Hammer's traditional gothic iconography and the need for a new approach in these contemporary set *Dracula* films, it was an unmade project developed within the same period that arguably proved to be Hammer's most radical attempt to revitalise the character.

Developed by Don Houghton in 1972, *Victim of His Imagination* is a biopic of *Dracula* author Bram Stoker. The narrative begins with Stoker on his deathbed in 1912, tormented by visions of monsters from his previous works. Its status as a part of the Hammer *Dracula* series, however, is more difficult to define than other entries. By 1972, Hammer had been developing *Dracula* projects for fourteen years, yet a biopic focusing on the author of the novel is undoubtedly dissimilar to anything Hammer had produced at that time. The twenty-nine-page treatment features Stoker suffering from night terrors, and it is within these sequences that the character of Dracula features, appearing as a nightmarish vision that haunts Stoker. The narrative then flashes back to key moments in his life, focusing on his initial meeting with Henry Irving, the famous actor whom he managed for years, and Stoker's relationship with his wife Florence. Meanwhile, in 1912, his doctor looks for clues in Stoker's work which might help ease his suffering. Even at treatment stage, it is difficult to see how the ambitious narrative structure would have translated on to screen. Not only is there a flashback structure at its centre, but it also introduces dream sequences which incorporate scenes from Stoker's works. For example, as Stoker struggles to put a face to the character of Dracula, he sits watching Irving perform in the Lyceum theatre, before having a realisation: 'BRAM's brain reels as the figure of IRVING becomes transformed into the awesome spectre of – Count Dracula ... Is Irving the monster he has created?'

This three-pronged structure would have inevitably been convoluted on screen, though the treatment does contain several interesting metatextual elements. One of these is in regard to casting. The role of Stoker was offered to Shane Briant (who was under a two-year contract at Hammer), with Christopher Lee to play Henry Irving (Briant in Skal 2011: 15). The casting of Lee in particular seems like Hammer attempting to placate an actor who had grown tired of his most iconic role. Aware that Lee was growing increasingly frustrated at reprising his role of Dracula, but also keen not to overexploit their star attraction in other films, Hammer potentially saw that the role of Irving gave Lee the chance to develop a new role which drew heavily on Lee's association with the Dracula character (with Lee even playing Dracula in the nightmare sequences). This link between Irving and the vampire Dracula is also interestingly explored in Houghton's treatment. This connection has been made numerous times throughout biographical works on Stoker, yet Skal suggests that 'Houghton may be, in fact, the first biographical writer of any kind to have considered a direct Irving/Dracula connection' (16). With only one Stoker biography widely available at the time of his treatment (*A Biography of Dracula: The Life Story of Bram Stoker* by Harry Ludlam (1962)), Houghton's script focuses less on historical accuracy and more on the quasi-psychological reasons behind Stoker's horror works, drawing parallels between 'real life' events and his novels. As well as being structurally complex, the narrative is also somewhat muddled, with Houghton seemingly unsure whether to focus on the historical details of Stoker's life or the horror expected from a Hammer film that features Dracula. The nightmare sequences and biographical elements are so generically disparate it is difficult to see how it would have made it to screen as a cohesive whole.

Having never produced a traditional biopic and struggling to find international finance for anything but *Dracula* films at this stage (at the time Hammer were under contract with Warner Bros. for its two contemporary *Dracula* films), Houghton could have conceivably seen *Victim of His Imagination* as an easier sell by including genre set pieces such as the nightmare sequences. This would have allowed the film (and its marketing) to focus heavily on the character of Dracula through both the origins of the literary character and his appearance within the nightmare sequences. Michael Carreras was enthusiastic about the project, and in a pull-out celebrating Hammer's twenty-fifth anniversary in December 1972, the project is listed with other films as 'tuning up' at Hammer. However, Hammer chairman James Carreras and Warner Bros. were clearly less enthusiastic, and the project would never see the light of day.

Although *Victim of His Imagination* stands as a truly innovative attempt to utilise the Dracula character, perhaps the most well-known unmade Dracula film of the 1970s period is *The Unquenchable Thirst of Dracula* written by Tony Hinds (under his pseudonym John Elder). Perhaps due to its enticing premise, which offers a high concept approach to one of Hammer's most famous horror icons, the project has been Hammer's most tantalising 'what-if' scenario since its conception over fifty years ago. In 2015, the project was adapted as a dramatized script reading at the Nottingham Mayhem Festival in October, in association with De Montfort University's Cinema and Television History Institute (which provided the screenplay and ephemera for the event). In 2017, the project was adapted for BBC Radio 4, directed by Mark Gatiss and narrated by Michael Sheen. Both versions utilise John Elder's *The Unquenchable Thirst of Dracula* script, which is held in the Hammer Script Archive and dated February 1977.

The Unquenchable Thirst of Dracula began development seven years prior as a draft entitled *Dracula High Priest of Vampires*, and was Hammer's first attempt at mounting a Dracula in India project. Having resigned from Hammer on 19 May 1970, Tony Hinds delivered the *Dracula High Priest of Vampires* script only three months later, with board member Brian Lawrence informing Hammer's board of directors that they had received the script from Hinds, and that it had already been sent to Norman Katz, president of Warner International (Hearn, interviewed by Foster, 20 December 2016).

This script features the protagonist Penny travelling to India to find her missing sister, who is ultimately discovered to have been taken by Dracula. Dracula has fled to India after being driven out of his castle in Transylvania by the 'searching light of civilisation', and has aligned himself with the Rani, a high priestess with her own deadly cult, the Temple of Blood. In comparison to *Kali Devil Bride of Dracula* (which is discussed later in this chapter), Dracula himself features prominently within the script. Not only does Dracula act as the primary antagonist for Penny, but he also engages in something of a civil war against the Rani and her blood cult. Early in the screenplay, Dracula is furious that one of his most recently turned victims was taken by the cult and sacrificed by the Rani. This confrontation comes to a head on page 79 of *Dracula High Priest of Vampires*, where Dracula refuses to give them a sacrifice: 'What do you know of blood? To you and your foolish followers it is something to spill . . . to waste . . . to drench your unclean bodies in. You know nothing. Nothing of its life-giving spirit. Life without end.' This dialogue exchange also suggests that Dracula has somehow corrupted the local Indian authorities to turn a blind eye to the Rani's crimes: 'who is it that controls the authorities . . . that makes it safe for you to continue your childish games'. This inversion of the *Dracula* novel, which saw the Eastern aristocrat corrupting the West, is explored partially in *Legend of the 7 Golden Vampires* (Ward Baker, 1974), which will be discussed in the next section. However, in *Legend of the 7 Golden Vampires*, it is arguably undermined by the decision to have Dracula represented for the majority of the film as a Chinese nobleman. Here, however, four years before *Legend of the 7 Golden Vampires* had even been considered for production, Hinds presents a similar thematic inversion but to even greater effect. Not only does Dracula remain as the Western aristocrat of Hammer's series throughout, but he also features much more prominently in *Dracula High Priest of Vampires* than *Legend of the 7 Golden Vampires*.

The script also predicts future franchise offerings by utilising a contemporary setting. Far from *Dracula AD 1972*'s overt foregrounding of its new modern setting, *Dracula High Priest of Vampires* does not actually feature an explicit date in which it is set. However, the action certainly takes place significantly later than any Hammer *Dracula* story had before. The third act set piece features a car chase through a parade celebrating the Hindu god Krishna and his bride. More specifically, when Penny is bitten by a snake on page 59 of *Dracula High Priest of Vampires*, she is rescued by her friend Prem, who rips off her trousers, and with a knife, cuts open the wound before sucking the poison out. As Penny recovers, she 'feels the bandage under the cloth of her jeans'. Although far from definitive, the reference to cars, contemporary clothing, and no explicit date given in the script referencing a period setting suggests a contemporary time period. This is one of the key differences in *Dracula High Priest of Vampires* and the eventual rewrite *The Unquenchable Thirst of Dracula*, which features the same plot and characters, but is explicitly set in the 1930s.

Another crucial difference between *Dracula High Priest of Vampires* and *The Unquenchable Thirst of Dracula* is the former's nude scenes, which are all removed from the latter. *Dracula High Priest of Vampires*'s nude sequences could perhaps be connected to the time the screenplay was written. In an interview I conducted with Hammer historian Marcus Hearn, he suggests that Hinds likely wrote the project after leaving Hammer in May 1970. As previously mentioned, the board meeting in which *Dracula High Priest of Vampires* is first discussed was in September of the same year, meaning that it is likely that Hinds wrote the screenplay between May and September 1970. As noted by Hearn, 'one of the crucial things that happens during that time . . . is the nature of the X-certificate changes' (Hearn, interviewed by Foster, 2016). On 1 July 1970, the AA category was introduced, intending to 'reduce the wide gap between the "A" and the "X"' (Phelps 1975: 120). The new AA certificate was designated to films suitable 'to persons of fourteen years and over' (Trevelyan 1977: 63). With this new certificate introduced between the A and the X, the X-certificate age restriction was raised from sixteen to eighteen. As a result, films could begin to feature more explicit material. Post-1970, Hammer would use this new certificate to dramatic effect in their films, with *The Vampire Lovers* (Ward Baker, 1970), *Lust for a Vampire* (Sangster, 1971) and *Twins of Evil* (Hough, 1971) all examples of films released after the new X-certificate was introduced which feature far more nudity and overt violence than former gothic horror offerings. Trevelyan himself notes this in *What the Censor Saw*, suggesting in relation to Hammer, 'nudity became quite common in these films, and by 1970 we even had lesbian vampires' (1977: 166).

Therefore Hinds, either due to pressure by Hammer or his instincts as a former producer at the company, could have added more nudity into the script as a response to the more lenient certificate. This not only includes the sequence where Prem rips off Penny's jeans and sucks the poison from her leg, but even more explicitly, a scene where Dracula forces one of his victims (Prem's sister Lakshmi) to dance naked. Hinds's later draft of the script, *The Unquenchable Thirst of Dracula*, notably removed these sequences, with Prem instead cutting through Penny's jeans to draw out the poison. The scene with Lakshmi and Dracula is also altered, as it ends with Lakshmi only beginning to remove her sari. With this redraft occurring in 1977, the reasons for toning down these sequences is not definitively stated. However, one could argue that with the more lenient X-certificate model now in its seventh year, audiences no longer found these exploitative pictures new or exciting, and subsequently they were no longer necessary. Hinds himself was no fan of the more exploitative model Hammer had begun to adopt in 1970, noting that he 'hated the tits-and-bums films that Jim [Carreras] was keen to make' (Murphy 1998: 11).

In hindsight, *Dracula High Priest of Vampires* contained many of the facets that would be featured in later Hammer *Dracula* Films, namely the contemporary setting, a new location and a heavier emphasis on more exploitive components. Yet the project was ultimately turned down by Warner Bros., with Hearn suggesting it was a meeting between Michael Carreras and Norman Katz in January 1971 that decided the fate of *Dracula High Priest of Vampires*. Hearn also notes that since the project's initial inception in September 1970, Hammer were keen to stress to Warner Bros. that the film would be more expensive than previous Dracula entries: 'Lawrence tells the board that Warner must be informed of the fact that this script cannot be produced in India for anything less than £225,000' (Hearn, interview with Foster, 2016). However, as noted earlier, Hammer's previous Dracula film *Scars of Dracula* had been made for under $200,000 and had a limited release in the United States. Consequently, one could see why Warner Bros. would be reluctant to not only increase the budget significantly for the next film, but also allow Hammer to shoot on location in India. Instead, buoyed by the success of contemporary vampire films such as *Count Yorga, Vampire* (Kelljan, 1970), shooting for what would become *Dracula AD 1972* commenced in September 1971.

Yet this was not the last time Hammer attempted to develop *Dracula High Priest of Vampires*. After a failed attempt in 1974 to again sell the project to Warner Bros. (which will be discussed in the following section of this chapter), Michael Carreras turned once more to Hinds's script in 1977. The script, entitled *The Unquenchable Thirst of Dracula*, is dated February 1977 and is a redrafted version of Hind's *Dracula High Priest of Vampires*. Correspondence suggests that it was Carreras who first asked Hinds to revisit this concept. On the 31 January 1977 Hinds wrote, in what is clearly a response to Carreras regarding *Dracula High Priest of Vampires*, 'I'll certainly have a look through this, and see if it needs updating or anything'. On the 3 February, only four days later, Hinds sent the script back, writing to Carreras:

> I've gone through the script page by page and have done some tightening and eased some of the dialogue. I like this story, always have. But I must be the first to admit it has dated in the seven years since I wrote it, and in the event that you're able to set it up, I would strongly suggest a fairly substantial rewrite using all the incident but giving it much more punch. But I do not suppose you would want to become involved in anything that would cost money, until you are sure of a deal. (Hinds to Carreras: 3 February 1977)

Why at this stage Hammer were looking once more to pursue Hinds's script is unknown. Hinds's suggestion that Hammer would not want to spend any money until 'sure of a deal' suggests that Carreras was yet to secure a financier or distributor for the project. Perhaps *The Unquenchable Thirst of Dracula* was Hammer, financially strapped in 1977, attempting to use a pre-existing and pre-bought script featuring one of their most marketable characters. If this was the case, it is a clear example of how dire circumstances had become at Hammer by the late 1970s.

Kali Devil Bride of Dracula

After *Dracula High Priest of Vampires* was initially declined by Warner Bros. in 1971, that specific project would lie dormant for six years. However, Hammer would revisit the concept of Dracula in India only three years later in 1974. Due to the general concept similarities, *Kali Devil Bride of Dracula*'s production history is often conflated with that of *The Unquenchable Thirst of Dracula*, and it is regularly described as a redrafted version of the latter. For example, Kinsey's *Hammer Films: The Elstree Years* (2007) suggests that 'Don Houghton revised Hinds script, submitting a nineteen-page treatment under the striking new title *Kali- Devil Bride of Dracula* [sic] in June [1974]' (394). Meikle's *History of Horror* states that 'Hind's script was later dusted off, retitled (as *Kali Devil Bride of Dracula*) and handed over to the resourceful Chris Wicking' (Meikle 2009: 213), and Hearn, in *The Hammer Vault* (2011), says that that '[Hind's story] was overhauled and various drafts of *Kali . . . Devil Bride of Dracula* were written by Don Houghton and Chris Wicking' (162). Yet from the materials in the archive it is clear that they are distinct projects, which were developed at different times by different creative talent. In fact, in relation to both production and narrative *Kali Devil Bride of Dracula* had far more in common with the produced *Legend of the 7 Golden Vampires* than it did Hinds's *Unquenchable Thirst*.

Legend of the 7 Golden Vampires was released in 1974, after the contemporary *Dracula* films had proven a financial disappointment for Warner Bros. and Hammer. As a result, Hammer's next *Dracula* film not only had to re-energise the character on screen, but also keep Warner Bros. on board as distributors. In order to do so, Hammer found themselves having to dramatically alter the way they produced and financed their films. Utilising writer Don Houghton's family connections (his wife's father was a personal friend of Run Run Shaw (Kinsey 2007: 380)), Hammer entered into a co-production with Hong Kong studio Shaw Brothers.

Famed for their kung fu films, the studio were also struggling in 1970s. As Bettinson suggests, this deal with Hammer seemingly 'betrayed the instability of two studios in decline' (2011: 123), with both looking for new ways to refresh their diminishing genre cycles.

After two entries in the series had seemingly exhausted a contemporary time period, Hammer took the character to the advent of the twentieth century and looked to innovate the ailing franchise with a change of location, with the film being primarily set in China. Set in 1904 and starring Peter Cushing as Van Helsing, the temporal shift back to a more familiarly gothic time period, and Cushing's reprisal of his original character, suggest that Hammer may have been looking to minimise some of the more subversive aspects of the previous two entries. This is compounded in the film's prologue, which opens in 1804 in Transylvania, and features John Forbes-Robertson's Dracula (replacing Lee, who played the character for the final time in *The Satanic Rites of Dracula*) emerging from his coffin in the customary fashion of Hammer's former gothics. Yet the traditional gothic norms are altered by the end of the prologue, which sees Dracula possess the body of Chinese acolyte Kah, who, for most of the film, is the visual representation of Count Dracula.

As noted briefly earlier in the chapter, the notion of the Western figure of Dracula invading the East offers an interesting inversion of Stoker's original *Dracula* (1897) novel, which sees an Eastern European menace invade the Western bourgeoisie. Stoker's novel had played on fears of Dracula as the foreign other, yet this had never been a primary factor in Hammer and Lee's interpretation of the character (primarily due to Sangster and Fisher never having Dracula travel to England). This offered Hammer a fascinating opportunity with *Legend of the 7 Golden Vampires* to present a new facet to a character they had been portraying for sixteen years. However, I would argue that by having Dracula possess the Chinese noblemen Kah at the beginning of the film, the notion of the Western aristocrat invading Eastern culture is squandered. This, like *Dracula AD 1972* limiting Dracula to the gothic trappings of an abandoned church, once more suggests Hammer was not fully comfortable with the dramatic changes they were making with the character. Nevertheless, Warner Bros. were seemingly pleased enough with the film as in December 1973, shortly after *Legend of the 7 Golden Vampires* had completed filming, Warner Bros. invited Hammer to prepare a similar *Dracula* film, this time set in India. Carreras outlined one key difference in the approach between *Kali Devil*

Bride of Dracula and *Legend of the 7 Golden Vampires* in a board meeting at Hammer – instead of a co-production, the project was to be funded wholly by Warner Bros., who were looking to utilise frozen rupees held in India to finance the film. These rupees were profits from Warner Bros. films they could not, due to the laws at the time, repatriate. As a result, Warner Bros. had a significant sum of money it could only invest in India (see Ivory, cited in Long 2006: 1).

A piece of correspondence from Brian Lawrence to Michael Carreras dated 12 March 1974 (when Carreras is in Los Angeles to meet Warner Bros.) suggested Hammer's original idea was to dust off Hinds's *High Priest of Vampires* script, and four years later, offer it to Warner Bros. again. Lawrence wrote:

> [. . .] trust you have received Hinds Dracula High Priest of Vampires script, and that you may be able to get the Indian situation sorted with Warner. While India I assume will present as many problems as Hong Kong, we would at least be spending all of Warner [sic] money and not ours. (Lawrence to Carreras: 12 March 1974)

However, the Hammer Script Archive indicates that only two months later, *Dracula High Priest of Vampires* had once again been rejected, and Hammer had already begun work on the first draft synopsis of what would become *Kali Devil Bride of Dracula*. The archive holds a twenty-page synopsis entitled *Dracula and the Curse of Kali*, dated May 1974 and written by Don Houghton. In total, the archive holds three *Kali* outlines written by Houghton, and one brief four-page synopsis, all dated between May and November 1974.

Dracula and the Curse of Kali focuses on the impending wedding of two entities, Dracula and the Hindu goddess Kali. This was not the first time Kali had been utilised in a Hammer horror film, with the goddess being the focus of *The Stranglers of Bombay* (Fisher, 1959). *The Stranglers of Bombay* told the story of the thuggee cult of Kali, an organized crime group who worshipped Kali and were responsible, according to the film's end title card, for 'over a million' deaths, before eventually being wiped out by the British forces in India. Attempting to replicate its fledging gothic horror cycle by presenting a clear dichotomy of good and evil, the story's focus on a group of white, Western saviours against an Eastern menace is extremely problematic.

Houghton's treatment, at first glance, also seems to be attempting to depict Kali as an omnipotent force of evil. It begins with two 'historical notes' (Houghton 1974: 2), the first of which outlines the significance of Kali in Hindu culture. Houghton's treatment relies on Kali being presented as the film's primary antagonist, and therefore he focuses specifically on the facets of Kali that would lend themselves to a Hammer horror film. Kali, the goddess of time, doomsday and death, is often artistically depicted with a 'necklace of skulls, her skirt made of severed arms, and above all her lolling tongue which is shown oversize, red and dripping with the blood of sacrificial victims' (Blurton 1993: 173). This gruesome imagery, coupled with Kali's association with death, allowed Houghton and Hammer to realise Kali as an antagonistic, demonic entity, enabling them to foreground the spectacle of Eastern tortures used in *Legend of the 7 Golden Vampires*. Describing her as a 'vision of violence and debauchery ... [who] represented the lust for life terminating in tormented death', Houghton essentially attempts to equate Kali as a female equivalent of the Judeo-Christian Devil. However, Kali's standing within Hindu culture is more complex. Heather Elgood in *Hinduism and the Religious Arts* notes that, 'despite her gruesome appearance Kali holds ... a key position in Hindu religious devotion' (2000: 73). In fact, it is often the case that Kali's frightening image is only there to act as a 'barrier placed before the devotee, who must have the courage to seek the inner depths of her compassion ... or universal power she represents' (Jones and Ryan 2006: 221). Worshipped as a mother figure, Kali has also become adopted by feminist movements. This is in part due to one of the most iconic images of Kali depicting her stood over the god Shiva, who is lying prone, suggesting that the 'transcendent power of Shiva can only be made immanent through interaction with the dominant goddess' (Blurton 1993: 173).

Houghton's foregrounding of Kali as the treatment's antagonist does, however, allow him to minimize the role of Dracula within the story. Whereas *Dracula High Priest of Vampires* would have most likely been reliant on Christopher Lee reprising his role as Dracula once again (due to the prominence of the character within the script), *Dracula and the Curse of Kali*, similarly to *Legend of the 7 Golden Vampires*, would only feature the Count in a handful of scenes. Although one could assume this was due to Lee no longer wanting to reprise his role, Carreras himself suggested this was a deliberate story decision. In an unpublished interview with Steve Swires at the Famous Monster Convention in 1975, Carreras

Figure 3.1 Houghton's 'historical notes', which precede his synopsis

discussed the depiction of Dracula in *Dracula and the Curse of Kali* and the possibility of Lee playing the role:

> I will not, to be perfectly honest, offer the part to Christopher Lee. We will be treating this Dracula as a young and virile sensual character, because he will have to have a romantic involvement with Kali, the goddess of the thuggees. With all due respect to Christopher and his talents, he would not suit this particular interpretation. (Carreras in Swires 1975)

In Houghton's treatment Dracula appears twice. First, eleven pages into the twenty-page treatment he is introduced on his way to India, killing a merchant and his family in Afghanistan, before he 'gallops away from Jalalabad, eastward to the Khyber Pass'. Secondly, he appears in the third act to marry Kali, only to find he has been tricked and 'Kali' is not the goddess herself but a fake, an unwilling woman sacrificed and reincarnated by an evil high priest named Shinwar Khan.

By having the physical manifestation of Kali be an imposter and positioning the fictional Shinwar Khan as the true villain of the film, Houghton displays some awareness of the necessary sensitivity needed to utilise a Hindu deity within the context of an exploitation film, showing a clear distinction between *Kali* and *The Stranglers of Bombay*. Houghton also goes one further than just distancing Kali from the horrific acts of the antagonist, by suggesting that the actual goddess Kali is responsible for the destruction of the villains within the film. As Dracula attacks Khan for deceiving him, the temple begins to collapse:

> The giant stone effigy of Kali cracks. The statue pitches forward. The granite swords in her six arms sweep down . . . Kali had answered her High Priest. As the statue crashes – the stone swords impale them, striking through their chests – and into their evil hearts.

This suggestion that the real incarnation of Kali is in fact acting as a force for good is arguably Houghton attempting to circumvent any potential issues or controversy that could arise from having Kali herself featured within the film.

The protagonist of the film is Dr Louis Van Helsing, the father of Laurence (who is eventually 'destined to become the renowned Vampire-Hunter immortalised by Bram Stoker'). Houghton's storyline necessitates that *Dracula and the Curse of Kali* would have to be set fifty years before Stoker's original novel. Meaning that while Hammer's 'original' Van Helsing appears in the treatment, it is only briefly as a child.

This shift in protagonist is required due to the treatment's temporal and spatial setting being crucial to the overall narrative. Many of Hammer's *Dracula* films feature an inconsistent chronology throughout the series, but in *Dracula and the Curse of Kali*, the setting of the film is of crucial importance. In the previously mentioned 'historical notes', Houghton first details Kali's place in Hinduism, before then providing historical context to the time the film is set – 1856, months before the Indian Rebellion of 1857. The Rebellion saw several sepoy soldiers in the East India Trading Company's army revolt, which quickly escalated into widespread army and civilian rebellions. Houghton describes it in his historical note as 'a savage war of massacre and reprisal', and notes that in the lead up to the rebellion, 'there was a sense of unrest and impending disaster'. This feeling of unrest and tension in the months preceding the rebellion is accurate, with Saul David in his historical account *The Indian Mutiny* (2002) noting that the Governor General Dalhousie, as early as 1855, had reflected on 'the danger of withdrawing for any purpose too many troops from a country which, though tranquil and unwarlike in itself, is yet liable to such volcanic outbursts of popular violence as this now before us' (cited in David 2002: 10). As noted by Houghton, this feeling of dread leading up to the rebellion is referred to as 'the devil winds', and one of Houghton's most effective choices within the treatment is to make this a literal presence within the narrative, stirring forebodingly to foreshadow the impending arrival of Dracula in India.

The specificity of the setting creates an effective atmosphere of tension, and is referenced directly in the narrative, not only through the 'devil winds', but by a plot point that sees two British officers found mutilated and killed, and the Indian soldiers nowhere to be found. The British Captain Purnell 'is certain that the Sepoys have mutinied, killed their Officers and are now roaming the countryside hell-bent on destroying every Englishman in the Northwest Frontier'. It is later revealed that the sepoys have been kidnapped for ritual sacrifice by the same killers of the British soldiers, but this tension between the Indian and British soldiers forms a crucial crux within the narrative.

Yet by setting the film in such a contentious and bloodied period of colonial Indian history, Houghton arguably creates some serious production issues for the prospective film. Hammer had primarily received funding for its *Dracula* films through majors such as Warner Bros., smaller companies such as ABPC, or co-production deals. However, *Dracula and the Curse of Kali* would have necessitated a funding strategy which, at least in part, played a key role in the film remaining unproduced. While the film was to be backed by Warner Bros., they had insisted on setting it in India due to accruing a significant number of rupees which could only be utilised by filming on location in India. This is referenced in correspondence from Michael Carreras to Don Houghton, who notes that the eventual screenplay 'must be submitted to the Indian authorities by Warner and no-one else, if they are to obtain use of their "frozen" rupees' (Carreras to Houghton: 14 October 1974). As a result of this situation, Warner Bros. and Hammer were therefore reliant on the Indian government approving the film for production.

Houghton's script would likely have been extremely difficult to get approved by the Indian government. Its use of Hindu gods in an exploitation/horror context (and the antagonistic denotations they have until the very end), coupled with it being set at one of the most turbulent and bloodied times in India's colonial past creates a prospective film that could have attracted a considerable amount of controversy if released. This is not to say that Houghton was necessarily ignorant of the potential pitfalls of the story. As noted, he subverted this view of Kali as an antagonistic figure at the end of the film, and showed the cult's victims to be the Indian soldiers and villagers as well as British soldiers. Houghton also has several Indian protagonists within the film such as Lal Gomal, an Indian professor and contemporary of Van Helsing, Hugh Fennell, an Anglo-Indian politician who is the first to believe Van Helsing and Gomal about Dracula's impending arrival, and Ranji Hissar described as a 'prince of the mountain tribes' and eventual ally of Van Helsing. There is also an important sequence featuring the character Bahrud Singh, a sepoy sergeant who is part of British soldier Lieutenant Ashwood's regiment. After Ashwood and his men are ambushed by Khan's cult, Ashwood tells Singh to ride and get help. Utilising the seeds of discord sown through the treatment's setting, Houghton attempts to make the reader doubt Singh's loyalty as he retreats:

> [. . .] he stumbles to his horse, mounts it with difficulty and gallops out of the Valley. It is impossible to know whether the Sepoy Sergeant intends to actually return to the Fort for help – or make good his escape and get as far away from the Temple as he can.

Yet at the climax of the film, as the protagonists are overwhelmed by Khan's forces, Singh returns with reinforcements, 'the Sepoy Sergeant has remained faithful to Ashwood – and returned with Captain Purnell and the Lancers'.

One could argue that despite Houghton's attempt at a more diverse cast of characters and the heroic moments he gives them, these are merely conciliatory gestures. The main characters of the story are undoubtedly the British Van Helsing and Ashwood, and even Singh's heroic moment is problematic, seemingly suggesting that on the brink of the Indian Rebellion, it is remaining faithful to the British colonisers that is an attribute worthy of admiration. However, when compared to *The Stranglers of*

Bombay, it is undoubtedly a more nuanced depiction of nineteenth-century India, featuring an attempt to complicate the antagonistic associations of Kali within the treatment, and feature a more diverse cast of protagonists.

Houghton submitted a new draft of the treatment in June, with minor changes and a new title – *Kali Devil Bride of Dracula*. Seemingly in response to this treatment, Carreras wrote to Houghton in October that 'Warners (A. Kananack) have indicated to me that we should develop this project into Screenplay form as quickly as possible' (Carreras to Houghton: 14 October 1974). This strongly suggests that both Carreras and Warner Bros. seemed relatively content with Houghton's efforts, with Warner Bros. only having one key issue with the script. Carreras notes that Warner 'feel[s] the Treatment needs more horror to arrive at a final balance of 50% Hammer ingredient and 50% Bengal Lancers' (Carreras to Houghton: 14 October 1974). Carreras also suggested a prologue for the film almost identical to that of *Legend of the 7 Golden Vampires*, with 'emissaries from Kali calling on Drac in Transylvania and signing the wedding pact'. Yet Carreras's main note for Houghton was to have the literal incarnation of Kali as the film's villain, a proposal that clearly caused tension between Houghton and Carreras.

Carreras suggested that the film should, during the main story, 'cut to either Drac and his "Bats" causing havoc as they travel south, or Kali and her thugees causing havoc as they travel North'. This suggestion would have given Dracula a larger role than in Houghton's original treatment and would also fulfil Warner's desire for more horror material. Carreras envisages the literal embodiment of Kali as a 'sort of motivated mummy' and perhaps even more troublingly, sees the opportunity to utilise the British Film Censors' more lenient X-certificate for a sex scene involving Kali, as she 'has young village lads brought to her for sex (with six hands – wow!) and then she emasculates them' (Carreras to Houghton: 14 October 1974).

Carreras's notes seem to suggest that his own issues with the treatment came from Houghton's attempts to complicate the simple good and evil dichotomy of Hammer's traditional gothics. Whereas *The Stranglers of Bombay* presented the moral certainty of the protagonists against the evil otherness of the cult of Kali, Houghton attempts to subvert this dichotomy, suggesting that while Shinwar Khan had used the image of Kali to indoctrinate his murderous cult, Kali herself was a fair and just deity entirely removed from the villain's evil schemes. By suggesting that

Houghton should increase the horror elements of the film and have Kali as its primary antagonist, Carreras was essentially asking him to strip away this subversive element.

Don Houghton's response to Carreras's proposal, sent two days later on the 16 October, clearly shows that it is Houghton, and not the managing director Michael Carreras, who was aware of the huge production issues that would arise from utilising Kali in this way. Houghton writes that 'with one very important and vital exception, I agree, in the main, with the suggestions outlined in your memo of 14/10/74' (Houghton to Carreras: 16 October 1974). Houghton's vital exception was Carreras's suggested use of Kali, with him noting that narratively

> [...] this new conception gives me a lot of plotting troubles and makes my job more difficult – without I believe adding anything significant to the property ... Kali is a Goddess and therefore cannot be destroyed – how, then, do I bring the picture to a climax? We can hardly have Kali and Dracula walking off, hand in hand, into the sunset. (Houghton to Carreras: 16 October 1974)

However, Houghton's primary concern was that using Kali in this way would almost certainly curtail any hopes Hammer and Warner Bros. had in getting the film made. Noting that in Hinduism 'Kali is very much venerated', Houghton underlined that any presumption that Kali would 'marry Dracula, a western figment of imagination, would be totally unacceptable to the majority of Indians'. To cement his point, Houghton draws parallels between Kali and the Virgin Mary, noting how it would be 'unpleasantly blasphemous for us to visibly reincarnate, say, the Virgin Mary in fiction – and then linking her with Dracula'. Houghton emphasised that he has already pre-empted this potentially controversial aspect of the script by presenting Shinwar Khan as an antagonist who 'uses the Kali Cult for his own base purposes' with Kali destroying Khan in the film's climax an act of 'retribution for the blasphemy that has been perpetrated in her name' (Houghton to Carreras: 16 October 1974).

Houghton also demonstrated that he is knowledgeable about the process of gaining approval from the Indian authorities. His fax to Carreras named both Nandini Satpathy, who was chief minister of Odisha at the time, and the deputy minister Dharam Vir Singh as key figures in the process. Houghton emphasised how both were 'prominent (and somewhat strict) leaders of the Hindi and Sikh communities' who would not tolerate Carreras's vision of a real Kali. Houghton was also clearly aware of how difficult the process would be regardless of this change:

> It is going to be extremely difficult for Warners to negotiate with the Indian Authorities anyway, but I maintain it will be an impossible task to present a Script to Delhi for production anywhere in India which features Kali in the form suggested. (Houghton to Carreras: 16 October 1974)

If the production of *Kali Devil Bride of Dracula* really did hang so precariously on the reaction of the Indian authorities, why would Carreras risk potential catastrophe by including the literal embodiment of Kali? Although general cultural ignorance could be to blame, it could also come down to Carreras merely attempting to replicate his last successful horror film as closely as possible. As noted earlier in this chapter, *Kali Devil Bride of Dracula* only became a viable proposition for Warner Bros. after the relative success of *Legend of the 7 Golden Vampires* (Kinsey 2007: 394). With *Legend of the 7 Golden Vampires* therefore the key reason for the interest from Warner Bros., Carreras would understandably want to reproduce the film's structure and style as much as possible. For the most part Houghton's script does correspond to this. For one, *Legend of the 7 Golden Vampires* emphasises action as well as horror through David Chiang's character Hsi Ching. Hsi Ching, along with his five martial arts-trained brothers, engage in several kung fu action set pieces against the seven Golden Vampires. In *Kali Devil Bride of Dracula*, a similar balance is struck through the use of the British army and sepoy soldiers in India going up against Khan's cult.

As well as sharing action set-pieces throughout, the two projects also share a number of similarities in their narratives as well. In *Legend of the 7 Golden Vampires*, Hsi Ching's love interest Vanessa is bitten by a vampire, and when Ching attempts to save her, Vanessa seduces him and bites him. Realising his fate, Ching sacrifices himself and Vanessa, throwing them both onto a wooden stake. In *Kali Devil Bride of Dracula*, Prince Hissar joins Van Helsing's party to find his partner Lalamir. However, at the film's climax it is revealed that Lalamir has been turned into the 'fake' Kali, and after a failed rescue attempt, Hissar throws both himself and the undead Lalamir into a fire pit. The doomed romance subplot in both films, as well as the action set pieces, clearly demonstrate that Houghton was aware that although *Kali Devil Bride of Dracula* did not chronologically follow on from *Legend*, it was for all intents and purposes a spiritual sequel to the Hammer and Shaw Brothers' co-production.

With this in mind, one can see why Carreras would see no problem exploiting the films setting to include a physical manifestation of Kali. *Legend of the 7 Golden Vampires* itself had also attempted to utilise Eastern religious practices to expand upon its vampire mythology, with Van Helsing noting that the Golden Vampires will recoil from images of Buddha as well as a crucifix. However, although the treatment for *Kali Devil Bride of Dracula* and the film *Legend of the 7 Golden Vampires* are remarkably similar, their production contexts were not, and this, as Houghton identifies, is the crucial issue. Whereas *Legend of the 7 Golden Vampires* had required the backing of a Chinese production company to ensure its completion, it did not require the express permission of the Chinese government to go ahead. In the case of *Kali Devil Bride of Dracula*, Warner Bros.' rupees are a legal issue and therefore, in order for them to be cleared to use in film production, the Indian authorities must have the final say. Warner Bros. and Hammer were essentially at the behest of the Indian government, which meant their usual use of exploitation tactics became a direct pitfall for the film's potential production.

This disagreement between Carreras and Houghton about the story of *Kali Devil Bride of Dracula* was not their first. As noted earlier in the chapter, Houghton's family connections had been instrumental for ensuring the co-production deal between Hammer and the Shaw Brothers went ahead. Due to his importance both as the screenwriter of *Legend of the 7 Golden Vampires* and as Hammer's key contact point with Hong Kong, Carreras promoted Houghton to the role of associate producer for both films (Hearn and Barnes 2007: 164). However, Carreras flew from California to Hong Kong to find the production of *Legend of the 7 Golden Vampires* in complete disarray – 'he was supposed to be doing schedules and so on, but I don't know what he was doing' (Carreras cited in Kinsey 2007: 389). As a consequence, Carreras dismissed Houghton from the set of *Legend of the 7 Golden Vampires*, and off the upcoming production of the second film in Hammer and Shaw Brothers two picture deal, *Shatter* (Meikle 2009: 212–13). Principal production for *Legend of the 7 Golden Vampires* ran between 22 October and 11 December 1973, meaning there was only five months between Houghton's firing and him turning in the treatment for *Dracula and the Curse of Kali*. Whether these issues affected the production of *Kali Devil Bride of Dracula* is only speculation, but the disagreements on the project could have only exacerbated any tension between the pair.

Houghton's strong rebuttal of Carreras's alternate story did initially seem to have been taken on board. In November 1974, only weeks after Carreras and Houghton's correspondence, Houghton wrote a four-page synopsis entitled *A Devil Bride for Dracula* which was expanded into a twelve-page treatment titled *Devil Bride of Dracula*, a rewrite of the *Kali and the Devil Bride of Dracula* treatment. Notably one of Carreras's requests, for a prologue featuring Dracula being summoned from his castle, was granted. However, the most fundamental changes are twofold. Houghton moved the story away from the Indian Rebellion, with the script now set primarily in 1899 and as such putting the film five years before *Legend of the 7 Golden Vampires*, effectively making it a prequel. Unlike previous drafts, this treatment also makes direct allusions to the fact it is only one instalment in an ongoing series. The treatment begins with Dracula destroyed, with his casket having a 'plain wooden stake' driven through it, before Dracula is eventually resurrected by the end of the prologue. Dracula and Van Helsing's paths are clearly supposed to have crossed in previous adventures, with Dracula seeing Van Helsing at the film's climax and 'remembering the stake that pierced his evil heart and turned him into dust ... promises that Van Helsing will know Eternal Torment'.

The shift away from the historical context of the Indian Rebellion from a narrative standpoint arguably diffuses some of the more interesting character interactions and the foreboding atmosphere found in Houghton's previous draft, as well as throwing up a number of confusing questions about the series chronology. However, from a production perspective, this move makes a good deal of sense. Having the film set on the precipice of one of the most bloodied and violent moments in the country's colonial history could have caused several difficulties in getting the film passed by the Indian authorities, meaning that ultimately this temporal shift seems a safer direction for the project's production.

To this extent, the second major change to the script also sees Houghton trying to circumvent any potential controversy with the Indian authorities. Instead of utilising the thuggee cult of Kali, Houghton entirely fictionalises the antagonistic cult within the treatment. The primary villain is now 'the Snake Goddess', whose evil followers, 'the Cult of the Cobra', cut swathes of destruction across India in anticipation of the Snake Goddess's marriage to the vampire Dracula. Although Houghton had been careful in his first draft to not have Kali as the actual antagonist, he has clearly concluded that even invoking Kali in relation to the film's primary antagonists would be too much of a risk. Instead, Houghton not only changes the name of the villain, but has one of the treatment's new protagonists, a mystic called Maya Devi, be a 'disciple of the Mother-God, Kali'. As a result, the treatment's only reference to Kali is to associate her with the forces of good, demonstrating again Houghton's attempts to pre-empt any issues the Indian authorities may have with his treatment. Yet despite these alterations made by Houghton, this was not seemingly enough for Hammer. Although the Hammer Script Archive holds no evidence as to why this change came about, this was to be Houghton's last draft of the *Kali Devil Bride of Dracula* project.

Kali Devil Bride of Dracula, as a project, simply ran out of time. In their correspondence on 14 October, Carreras emphasises to Houghton that 'speed was of the essence', due to the precarious situation Warner Bros. was in with regards to their rupees in India. Ultimately, Carreras's failure to settle on a treatment or proposal for *Kali Devil Bride of Dracula* proved fatal to the project. A change of government policy in India meant that Warner Bros. no longer had to use its assets solely in India (Kinsey 2007: 394). *Kali Devil Bride of Dracula* was quickly discarded by Warner Bros., and *Legend of the 7 Golden Vampires* remained Hammer's last Dracula film.

Conclusion

Whereas the brief summary of the produced Dracula films in the first section of this chapter arguably lends credence to the suggestion that Hammer's gothic cycle was stagnating and lacked innovation, it is clear to see why Hammer would have persevered with this formula for so long. The 1970s saw the slow withdrawal of nearly every major American investor in Hammer, and one of the company's only consistent internationally funded film series was *Dracula*. While this funding was still available, it would have been unwise for Hammer to dramatically alter this formula. It was only when ABPC struggled to find large scale American distribution for *Scars of Dracula* that Hammer was forced to react to a changing international market.

This, I would argue, counters any accusation that Hammer were sluggish to respond to cultural or industrial changes. Between 1970 and 1973, Hammer considered Hinds's *Dracula High Priest of Vampires* and Houghton's *Victim of His Imagination*. These unmade projects, coupled with the two produced contemporary *Dracula* films, clearly show that Hammer was aware that the current state of the film industry necessitated a dramatic change to its premier franchise. This attempted innovation of the *Dracula* series is apparent in Hammer's final Dracula film, *Legend of the 7 Golden Vampires*, yet the production of the film itself exposed some of the internal pressures within Hammer at the time. A tumultuous and ultimately costly co-production between Hammer and Shaw Brothers, the project would not only prove complex financially, but also created tensions between Houghton and Carreras which eventually carried over into the pre-production of *Kali Devil Bride of Dracula*.

Kali Devil Bride of Dracula proved a project that, at the time of inception, had too many pressures, external and internal, thrust upon it. Warner Bros.' complex financial situation with the Indian government led to enormous time pressures for Hammer, and Warner Bros. necessitating that Hammer's eventual script had to be approved by the Indian government was creatively restricting for Houghton and Carreras. It is apparent when reading the treatment that the horror material which features in *Kali Devil Bride of Dracula* is no more gruesome or shocking than other Hammer horror films of the 1970s. Even the use of the goddess Kali would probably not have caused Houghton or Carreras much consternation if not for having to be approved by the Indian government. Hammer's own film for example, *The Stranglers of Bombay*, had utilised the spectre of Kali effectively. Even outside of Hammer, Kali has been utilised throughout Western film and television for decades. In 1973, the year before *Kali Devil Bride of Dracula* was developed at Hammer, *The Golden Voyage of Sinbad* (Hessler) saw Sinbad and his allies engage an enchanted statue of Kali in a sword fight (with Kali holding a sword in each of her six arms).

Perhaps the best-known example of Kali and her cult in cinema is *Indiana Jones and the Temple of Doom* (Spielberg, 1984), which shares many similarities with Houghton's first draft of *Kali Devil Bride of Dracula*. The film sees archaeologist and adventurer Indiana Jones uncover a Kali worshipping cult led by Mola Ram, whose blood rituals and sacrifices at the altar of Kali call to mind the character of Shinwar Khan in Houghton's draft. *Indiana Jones and the Temple of Doom*, made a decade after *Kali Devil Bride of Dracula*, is arguably more egregious than anything Houghton wrote. Not only is there never a distinction made between the horrific acts of Mola Ram and the actual goddess Kali, but Kali is portrayed in effect as a Hindu devil figure, with Indiana Jones at the film's denouement shouting to Mola Ram: 'Prepare to meet Kali, in Hell'! *Indiana Jones and the Temple of Doom* was temporarily banned in India, but this proved little hindrance to the film's financial success. Its buoyant box office in the

United States ensured the film had the highest grossing weekend of 1984, and the third highest overall gross that year.

This is the crucial difference for Hammer. Whereas *Indiana Jones and the Temple of Doom* was not reliant on the backing of foreign investment or box office, Hammer in 1974 was almost completely dependent on it. The departure of James Carreras in 1973 and the subsequent loss of American backing left Hammer and new owner Michael Carreras in a desperate position, and despite Warner Bros. backing, *Kali Devil Bride of Dracula*'s subject matter meant the project was always going to struggle to meet the Indian government's approval. Carreras, however, clearly aware that horror remained Hammer's most marketable international export, remained steadfast in retaining the exploitation element, arguably to the project's detriment. Despite this reliance on the horror genre, Houghton's *Kali Devil Bride of Dracula* showed at least some promise. Its diverse cast of characters and setting on the precipice of the Indian Rebellion (at least in *Dracula and the Curse of Kali*) creates a more nuanced approach to a *Dracula* story than many before it. Ultimately it was the restrictive production process and not the treatment itself that proved the primary hindrance.

Perhaps *Kali Devil Bride of Dracula*'s most significant lasting legacy is the death knell it sounded for the *Dracula* franchise. Although Hammer would not know it at the time, *Legend of the 7 Golden Vampires* was to be their final Dracula film. *Kali the Devil Bride of Dracula* was commissioned by Warner Bros. on the back of *Legend of the 7 Golden Vampires*, therefore making it the last Dracula project for which Hammer had upfront financial support. One could perhaps see *Kali Devil Bride of Dracula* as merely a victim of circumstance, with the Indian government's decision to change their monetary policy and thus free Warner Bros.' rupees entirely out of their hands. However, the strained relationship between Houghton and Carreras, as well as Carreras's ignorance (wilful or not) of what kind of exploitation material would get past the Indian authorities, created a laborious production process. Even after months of development, *Kali Devil Bride of Dracula* never seemingly made it to screenplay stage. Ultimately Carreras came to realise that Hammer not only had to change its entire financial and distribution structure to survive, but, even with radical reinventions, the company could also no longer rely on the gothic icon that had helped build Hammer's house of horror. Instead, as I will go on to explore in Chapter 4, Carreras opted for a bold new strategy that would see Hammer risk everything in an attempt to gain back the support of the American majors.

4
Grave encounters: *Vampirella* and *Vlad the Impaler*

If this book was split into sections, the previous three chapters could have been grouped together as a chronicle of the origin, consolidation and eventual demise of Hammer's gothic horror cycle. Once the lynchpin of Hammer's entire international distribution strategy, by the mid-1970s wider industrial factors had left Hammer radically in need of new direction. In response Hammer began developing several productions that, despite being significantly more expensive than former Hammer pictures, had in Carreras's eyes the potential to garner big returns for the company and its potential investors through their global appeal. This new production plan, described by Hearn as a 'shit or bust' strategy (2011: 162), took up a great deal of financial and creative resources in the latter half of the 1970s and accounts for the lack of actual productions released by the company in this period.

Chapters 4–6 will focus specifically on the final years of the company under Michael Carreras and his bold new attempts to radically alter Hammer's fortunes. This chapter in particular will focus on a key tension I will argue undermined Hammer's attempt to forge ahead with a new innovative strategy, namely a self-reflexive harkening back to past successes. If the failure of *The Unquenchable Thirst of Dracula* and *Kali Devil Bride of Dracula* had underlined for Carreras the need to move away from former franchises, there was still a clear reluctance on the part of the company to do so fully. *Vlad the Impaler* and *Vampirella* are two unmade projects developed in the mid-1970s that foreground this tension at Hammer. Both are developed on a larger scale than any other Hammer project before, while still being over reliant on past genres, tropes and characters.

Vlad the Impaler was a Dracula origin film which looked to refresh Hammer's associations with the character by producing a large historical epic which would have had the biggest budget of any Hammer film to date. The comic-book adaptation *Vampirella* is an ambitious science fiction adventure with a sizeable potential budget, and was a project Carreras saw as key to helping Hammer once again breakthrough in the US market. Both unmade projects share many surface similarities, they are adaptations developed within the same period which both rely in part on associations with the horror genre, specifically vampire lore. Moreover these films, while they were genuinely innovative attempts at making a new kind of Hammer film, also heavily relied on existing gothic horror tropes. As such they perfectly highlight the tension at Hammer which sees the old way of doing business directly conflicting with the new.

Carreras's *Vlad the Impaler*: 1974–9

On the 27 April 1974, BBC Radio 4 produced a one-off drama from Brian Hayles entitled *Lord Dracula*. The ninety-minute drama tells the story of Vlad Tepes, the tyrannical ruler of Transylvania who is arrested for his brutal war crimes at the beginning of the play. After years in prison, he pledges himself to God under the stewardship of a monk called Benedek and is released, returning to his castle in Transylvania. Vlad has a wife, Ilonya, with the two having fallen in love as she cared for him in prison. He is greeted by his oldest son, Istvan, and reveals that he and Ilonya are expecting a child. Ilonya and Vlad's unborn son dies in childbirth, and Vlad renounces God. With Benedek as his captive 'witness' (Hayles, 1974), he begins another reign of terror and is soon seduced by the witch Militsa, who introduces Vlad to the dark arts. In the play's third act, Vlad is reborn as the undead Dracula and is confronted by Benedek and Istvan. In the ensuing struggle, Militsa is killed and Dracula is supposedly beheaded. However, it is revealed that they had not killed Dracula but, through Dracula's sorcery, a monk called Jacob. Benedek and Istvan are both arrested and eventually executed for the crime.

While the Hammer Script Archive holds screenplays on the project, another key source utilised in this examination of *Vlad the Impaler* will be an interview with Carreras printed in the February 1978 issue of *House of Hammer* magazine (Skinn and Brosnan, 1978). The interview took place four years into the development of the project, but provides details on how *Vlad the Impaler* initially came to Hammer in 1974. Even at the time of the interview, the project seemed to still be on Hammer's slate: 'we're going to do a film about Vlad the Impaler, the original Dracula. It will be based on a radio play by Brian Hayles' (Carreras in Skinn and Brosnan: 21). Discussing how the project originated in 1974, Carreras remarked that Hammer immediately bought the rights to the project after its original airing in April of that year, noting that although he missed the original broadcast he 'finally played it the following Friday night . . . it was one of the most marvellous broadcasts I'd ever heard. It was tremendous! So I quickly rang Brian, we met and did a deal' (21).

The archive holds a screenplay by Brian Hayles entitled *Dracula The Beginning* which is a clear self-adaptation of *Lord Dracula*, and as one might expect from a self-adapted work, it is extremely faithful to the original radio play. No date is given on the screenplay itself, but the passing of Brian Hayles in 1978 and the title change in all other drafts to *Vlad the Impaler* suggest this is likely to be the first draft of the project for Hammer. The screenplay features only superficial differences to the radio play, with even entire dialogue sections reproduced verbatim. The largest change is in the third act, where Dracula frames Istvan and Benedek for the death of Ilonya and his unborn child, not that of the monk Jacob, who is jettisoned from the script entirely. Istvan is also spared execution in the screenplay, instead being sentenced to life imprisonment. Benedek however, suffers the same fate.

At this point in Carreras's tenure, *Vlad the Impaler* seemed to be a natural fit on Hammer's production slate. It was to be an ambitious and expensive production, in line with Carreras's 'shit or bust' strategy, yet there were many inherent familiarities with the project that tied it closely to the company's past. *Vlad the Impaler* effectively acted as an origin story for Hammer's most famous franchise, and as a result the project was both inherently familiar as a Hammer product while diversifying enough from the *Dracula* formula discussed in the previous chapter to demonstrate Carreras's new ambitions for Hammer in the mid-to-late 1970s. Hayles's script moved quickly through pre-production, being sent to potential directors only six months after the radio play had aired. In October 1974, Carreras offered directorial duties on the project to Ken Russell.

Hammer's attempt to bring Russell into the fold chimes with Carreras's overhaul of Hammer's production strategy at this time, and could be seen as a response to the resurgence of the horror film in America and an attempt to gain critical legitimacy. This critical support of the new wave of American horror film can be traced back to the late 1960s, when Hollywood began to harness the talents of several European directors who 'were associated, to varying degrees, with self-consciously artistic movements and "new waves" in European cinema' (Krämer 2005: 86). Films such as *Rosemary's Baby* (1968) and *Night of the Living Dead* (Romero, 1968) signalled a new wave of American horror films that spoke 'to the rapidly changing social and sexual values of the era' (Shiel 2006: 30). This fusing of horror cinema with that of the independent art film added critical credibility to the genre, and provided a new and distinctive blueprint for horror cinema. Perhaps the most prominent example of this is William Friedkin's *The Exorcist* (1973). Following Friedkin's previous critical and commercial success *The French Connection* (1971), *The Exorcist* is combatively visceral and explicit and 'bore as little resemblance to the gothic chillers of the 60s as Nixon did to JFK' (Kermode 1997: 9). Its subsequent box office success suggested a significant shift in what audiences wanted from horror films, with Hammer's own gothic formula (which, despite the proposed strategy shift was still in effect as late as 1974 with *Frankenstein and the Monster from Hell*) in clear need of an overhaul.

To Carreras's credit, his letter to Russell seems like a significant step in this direction. Russell's reputation as an audacious and provocative director had been truly cemented by the release of *The Devils* in 1971. Critically reviled on its release ('*The Devils* is so totally and manically hated by nearly every critic I have read that it seems an excess to select the parts which are hated more than the entire film' (Atkins 1976: 59)), the film is undoubtedly the work of a filmmaker with a singular distinctive vision. Matthew Melia goes even further, noting that *The Devils* (along with Stanley Kubrick's *A Clockwork Orange* (1971)) embodies:

> The nihilistic and transgressive milieux of (cult) British cinema at the end of the 1960s and the start of the 1970s where the cliched and naïve aspirations to free love and liberalism had given way to a Sadeian cinematic impulse towards violence, libertinage, and cruelty. (2022: 9)

However, in correspondence with Carreras, Russell was extremely critical of the script itself, particularly the third act: 'the bloodbath at the end is as unnecessary as it is obnoxious. Blood, particularly movie blood, is not synonymous with horror' (Russell to Carreras: October 1974). Russell ended his letter just as bluntly, signing off by writing 'please don't misunderstand me, I would like to make a horror film with you – a real one' (Russell to Carreras: October 1974). In Carreras's reply to Russell, he noted that he 'heartily agree[s]' (Carreras to Russell: October 1974) with Russell's comments about the script. Yet it is clear, at least publicly, that Carreras really believed in the *Vlad the Impaler* project. In 1978, he stated that 'I think it will be a hell of a movie' (Skinn and Brosnan 1978: 21) and nine years later, in an interview with *Fangoria* in May 1987 long after leaving Hammer, Carreras stated that 'the script is still my prize possession and I will never give up the idea of doing it. If we were allowed to make one more film, *Vlad the Impaler* would be it' (Swires 1987: 64). These comments from Carreras suggest he was in fact pleased with the script, and denote a significant divide between the projects Carreras felt Hammer should be producing, and the tastes of a more radical director such as Russell.

Despite Carreras's apparent affection for the project, progress on *Vlad the Impaler* notably slowed after 1974. Hammer saw the systematic collapse of its international finance and distribution networks in the mid-1970s, and like other projects in his bold new strategy for Hammer, Carreras clearly realised he had to think outside of the United Kingdom and the United States if he were to find funding for *Vlad the Impaler*. While examining funding options for *Nessie* (discussed in the next chapter), Carreras sent a fax to Doctor Helmut Gierse of Constantin Films in West Germany on 26 August 1976 laying out an ambitious co-production plan:

> I would like you to consider the possibility of Hammer Films setting up a Production Organization in Germany using the availability of the current Tax Shelter situation and a direct relationship with your Company in terms of investment, to secure the distribution rights of the German, Swiss and Austrian Territories. (Carreras to Gierse: 26 August 1976)

Along with this proposal, Carreras listed several mooted television and film projects, with the common denominator being to 'base the productions in Germany' (Carreras to Gierse: 26 August 1976). One of these potential projects was entitled *The Blasphemer*, with the synopsis noting it would be 'based on the historical character of Vlad Tepes' (Carreras to Gierse: 26 August 1976). Unfortunately for Hammer, the deal with Gierse never developed. An article in the 21 November 1977 issue of *Der Spiegel*, detailing Gierse being summoned to the Dusseldorf Chamber of Commerce and Industry by investors after the recent failure of 'the Constantin film loan' (Anon. 1977c), perhaps indicates why. Yet despite this, Carreras was still clearly considering filming in Germany even after the collapse of this deal, demonstrating the dire financial situation Hammer had found itself in at the time. Carreras noted: 'it is more economically viable – there's more film finance available in Germany today than in America at the moment, and certainly much more than is available in this country' (Carreras in Skinn and Brosnan 1978: 21).

Whereas *The House of Hammer* interview in 1978 saw Carreras looking back at the initial production of *Vlad the Impaler*, Carreras also discussed ambitious plans for the project's future as well. Carreras suggested that the project will seek an A-list star, noting that Hammer had 'sent the script to people like Richard Burton and Richard Harris' (Skinn and Brosnan 1978: 21) even though Hammer 'hadn't selected a director yet' (ibid.). However, these details offered by Carreras were notably vague. Carreras's iteration of *Vlad the Impaler* seemed to have suffered the same fate as projects such as *The Unquenchable Thirst of Dracula*. Carreras, whether due to his admiration for Hayles's script or as part of his strategy to try and produce more ambitious films, had touted that *Vlad the Impaler* 'will be four, if not five, times as expensive as any single Hammer film' (ibid.). This would ultimately be the project's undoing, as Carreras notes in 1987 that the project failed because he 'was never able to find one company willing to finance the entire project' (Swires 1987: 64).

Hammer's *Star Wars?* Michael Carreras and *Vampirella*

While *Vlad the Impaler*'s links to the earlier years of Hammer's gothic horrors are more overt, another project developed round this period, *Vampirella*, also shares tensions between the old Hammer and Carreras's new attempts at innovating the company. The first notable similarity to the old Hammer method is the focus on adapting existing work within the horror genre. *Vampirella* was initially developed as a comic-book character by Forrest J. Akerman, and published by James Warren's Warren Publishing in 1969. The first issue of *Vampirella* was published in September that year, envisioned as a supplement to Warren's two flagship horror comics *Creepy* and *Eerie*. The character of Vampirella not only starred in the comic but 'hosted' it as well, breaking the fourth wall to introduce and narrate the events that would unfold in each issue. The character's origins also lay bare the comic's tonal balance between horror and comedy, with Vampirella an inhabitant of the dying planet 'Drakulon', a planet where the rivers literally run red with blood. With the planet running out of blood, Vampirella travels to earth in the hopes of saving her planet, and it is here most of the comics take place.

In the August 1975 issue of the magazine *Famous Monsters of Filmland*, Hammer asked readers 'what will Hammer do next' (75)? The full-page advertisement came with a small form where readers of the magazine could send in suggestions for Hammer's next project. The advertisement is notable for its direct appeal to Hammer fans to help guide the company's production slate, with the text promising that all suggestions will be sent 'direct to Hammer Films in London', and as such offered audiences who sent in their potential project ideas the 'unique chance to make film history' (75). The advertisement also makes overt reference to the resurgent American horror market, noting that Hammer 'has the know-how to take you beyond *Rosemary's Baby*, beyond *The Exorcist*'.

The magazine in which the advertisement is placed, *Famous Monsters in Filmland*, is also notable as it was owned by Warren Publishing, the same company which produced the *Vampirella* comics. This is by no means coincidental, with the Hammer Script Archive holding evidence that Hammer were already exploring the possibilities of adapting *Vampirella*. The earliest documentation held on the project is dated 8 August 1975, and is entitled 'Merchanising [sic] Promotional Concepts for the Trade Launch of "Vampirella"' (Anon. 1975a), and lists a potential strategy for how to approach the promotion of the project. Even this early document shows evidence that Hammer were unsure how to approach *Vampirella* tonally. This is particularly apparent in a specific sentence in the document which has been altered in pen but still readable. The original sentence read 'the major appeal of the film is to children and teenagers, although some adult appeal along 'Barbarella' lines should be considered' (Anon. 1975a). However, the altered text reads 'the major appeal of the film is to adults along "Barbarella" lines' (Anon. 1975a). This alteration is certainly more in line with Hammer's previous horror films, which despite not always being played straight (and entries such as *The Horror of Frankenstein* (Sangster, 1970) being explicitly comedic) always catered to an adult market. An attempt to market the film to children as well as adults would have been a significant departure for Hammer, but the decision to alter this and state that the project would look to appeal to adults exclusively seems to suggest that Hammer were still reluctant to dramatically alter their pre-existing strategies.

Despite clear issues with the tone of the project in August 1975, only ten weeks later the project had a completed screenplay by Christopher Wicking, dated 27 October 1975. Wicking was a screenwriter who, as the 1970s progressed, became a crucial part of Hammer's production outfit, with Kinsey noting that by the end of Hammer in 1979, the company 'basically consisted of Carreras, [Hammer board member] Tom Sachs and Wicking' (2010: 115). Originally working for Hammer on *Blood from the Mummy's Tomb* (Holt, 1971) and *Demons of the Mind* (Sykes, 1971), Wicking's only other credited Hammer film was *To the Devil a Daughter*. Yet despite only having these three credits for Hammer, Wicking was an integral part of many unmade Hammer projects such as *Nessie*, which will be discussed in Chapter 5 and Chapter 6. *Vampirella* is perhaps Wicking's most significant creative contribution to Hammer, particularly as it was through Wicking that the idea to look to comic-books for inspiration began.

In an interview with Meikle, Wicking notes that in the mid/late 1970s, 'I had all sorts of ideas – including comic books. I talked to Stan Lee about doing a Marvel-Hammer connection. But it all came to nothing because we had no money to afford to pay anybody to develop it' (2009: 215). Wicking's notion in the 1970s to use Marvel Comics' roster of superheroes for inspiration predates Warner Bros. adaptation of the iconic Detective Comics (DC) character Superman in 1978, as well as the seminal CBS show *The Incredible Hulk* (1978–82). The box office performance of *Superman* (Donner, 1978) and the success of *The Incredible Hulk* (which ran for five seasons and five television films), ably demonstrates a clear appetite for comic book adaptations in the late 1970s. While the adaptations of DC and Marvel's superheroes would have been a significant departure for Hammer, *Vampirella*, despite also being a comic-book, played knowingly with horror tropes and vampire lore, and as such gave Hammer a tether to their previous gothic horror films while still ostensibly presenting the project as a new chapter in Hammer's story.

The script is generically disparate, invoking the horror genre, science fiction films and spy films in particular (the press synopsis for Hammer's *Vampirella* held at the BFI explicitly labels the character as an 'Inter-Stellar 007'), and it relies on a comedic tone throughout. The plot of the screenplay sees Vampirella and her 'father-figure' Pendragon touring the theatres and clubs as a magic act, with Vampirella relying on her alien powers to charm audiences. When earth is attacked by the very same aliens who invaded and destroyed Vampirella's home planet, Vampirella and Pendragon are recruited by the 'Space Operatives For Defence and Security' (SODS), to help stop the invaders before they achieve global domination. Wicking's script leans heavily on its comic-book associations, and in many places actually directly features artwork from the comic itself, with comic-book panels replicated on the script page. Its experimentation with genre, ambitious set pieces (which would have seen a notable increase in budget in comparison with earlier Hammer films) and contemporary setting all give the indication that Carreras's Hammer was aware that the company must change to survive. Yet the script also shows a company unwilling to let go of its own legacy.

For example, Wicking's script features a number of overt allusions to Hammer's history. Some are merely knowing winks which wouldn't have made it to the screen, such as when, after a masked woman reveals herself as a demon, Wicking notes that the woman 'now unmasked, is no Raquel Welch' (1975: 65). Wicking's invoking of one of Hammer's most famous actors (Welch starred in Hammer's most internationally successful film *One Million Years B.C.* (Chaffey, 1966)) would have stayed on the page, but Wicking also makes narrative choices which directly reference Hammer's most famous gothic franchise – Dracula. For example, the screenplay features Conrad and Adam Van Helsing, the father and son vampire-hunting duo who are direct descendants of the original Van Helsing. Although both of these characters do appear in the original comic series, their minor presence in Wicking's script evokes Peter Cushing's vampire hunter, with Van Helsing (or a descendent of Van Helsing) featuring in Hammer's *Dracula, The Brides of Dracula* (Fisher, 1960), *Dracula AD 1972* (Gibson, 1972), *The Satanic Rites of Dracula* (Gibson, 1973) and *The Legend of the 7 Golden Vampires*. More explicitly, Wicking's screenplay ends by teasing a future film pitting Vampirella against Dracula. After being approached by an employee of 'the Count', Pendragon and Vampirella are invited to 'perform for him at his private mansion' (1975: 116). After Pendragon and Vampirella ask to meet him, the employee of the Count escorts them to a clearing, and the last page of the script reads:

> Awaiting them are Six Black Horses – A long hearse and a coffin. The coffin lid moves fractionally, a hand protrudes momentarily. Bearing a lustrous ring decorated with the big initial 'D'. But that, as they say, is another story for – Vampirella. (Wicking 1975: 117)

These instances are notable examples of Hammer deliberately harking back to its former gothic horrors, and one could see why Carreras and Wicking would consider Hammer's legacy a positive facet worth emphasising. Their gothic horror films had legitimised the company as an international production force, and created a franchise of innovative films which had garnered the company a loyal following. Yet if *Vampirella* was supposed to shift perceptions away from Hammer being solely reliable for low/mid-budget gothic horror films and instead demonstrate that the company was capable of more ambitious fare, the *Vampirella* project offers a confusing message. *Vampirella* may have been trying to break new creative ground for the company, but the screenplay frequently references the company's former success with horror films despite the increasing lack of interest in the gothics from American financiers and distributors.

This tension is exacerbated in Hammer's choice of director, with a document, dated 7 October 1975 (Anon. 1975b) revealing that John Hough

Figure 4.1 An example of a page of Wicking's *Vampirella* screenplay, which features comic-accurate artwork

had been signed on to direct the film. Hough had a close relationship with Hammer before the *Vampirella* project, directing the Hammer horror film *Twins of Evil* in 1971 and Hammer picking up a previous Hough film, *Wolfshead: The Legend of Robin Hood*, for distribution in 1973. After Carreras was forced to give up the company in 1979, Hough would continue to have a strong connection with Hammer, directing three episodes of the television show *Hammer House of Mystery and Suspense* (1983), and even trying to buy the company outright on two separate occasions (Kinsey 2010: 165).

Hough's former gothic horror experience again tied *Vampirella* to the company's past successes, a fact compounded by the casting of Peter Cushing as Vampirella's paternal sidekick Pendragon. Peter Cushing had starred in Hammer's very first gothic horror *The Curse of Frankenstein* in 1957, and became, along with Christopher Lee, one of the company's most prolific stars. Cushing had worked with Hough before on *Twins of Evil*, and his involvement with *Vampirella*, perhaps more than anything else, created a clear link between this new phase of the company and the former Hammer gothics.

Cushing was joined by Barbara Leigh in the titular role of Vampirella. Described on the 30 October 'Proposed Cast List' as 'Hammer's New Discovery' (Anon. 1975c), Leigh had in fact made several appearances in film and television before, most notably in *Junior Bonner* (Peckinpah, 1972) alongside Steve McQueen. Leigh's casting and Hammer's promotion of Leigh as 'the sex sensation of the seventies' (ibid.), also called back to Hammer's previous promotional techniques, which utilised their exploitation credentials to foreground their female stars' physical appearance (with female nudity also becoming commonplace in Hammer films in the 1970s), a tactic that saw the coining of the term 'Hammer Glamour'.

With the two key roles cast and a completed script, Carreras took the *Vampirella* project to the Famous Monsters convention in November 1975, a fan event that took place in New York. A clever bit of synergy on the part of Hammer and Warren Publishing (who ran the convention), Carreras looked to garner awareness of the project for fans and financiers alike. Cushing and Carreras in particular were received as 'guests of honour' at the convention, with both featuring in extensive interviews in the convention's programme. The Margaret Herrick Library holds two transcripts of separate unpublished interviews with Carreras and Cushing at the convention, both of which are particularly illuminating about the *Vampirella* project and Hammer's position in the industry more broadly. Notably Carreras addresses his current frustrations with Hammer's former American financiers:

> Warner Bros, with whom we have had a number of very successful world-wide releases, feels that the expensive American marketing of a Hammer horror film isn't justified by the returns they will get. They maintain, contrary to what our hard-care [sic] fans believe, that the American horror market is 'soft', and has been so for the past two years. (Carreras in Swires 1975)

The above quote acts as a direct acknowledgment by Carreras of how Hammer had become synonymous with a specific brand of horror, which had now fallen out of favour with the Hollywood majors. As a direct response to this, Carreras spent a good deal of the interview discussing future plans, offering updates on *Vlad the Impaler*, *Kali Devil Bride of Dracula* and *Vampirella*, noting on the latter that they 'have a full screenplay written by Christopher Wicking. We have already cast Barbara Leigh in the title role, with Peter Cushing as her side-kick Pendragon, and we are hoping for a summer 1976 release date' (Carreras in Swires 1975).

Cushing's career-spanning interview also touches on the upcoming *Vampirella*, with Cushing clearly aware of the project's novelty in relation to his other Hammer roles:

> Hammer Films have just cast me in 'Vampirella', in what will be an entirely different part for me. I play a rather seedy, not very successful impresario named Pendragon, who tries to do conjuring tricks which never come off. He has taken to drink and is always a little besotted... the role contains great humour, as well as a great deal of pathos. It could lead me into all sorts of new things. (Cushing in Kelley and Kelley 1975: 15)

The optimism regarding the opportunities a project like *Vampirella* could offer is apparent in both interviews, and it is worth noting how real a proposition *Vampirella* seemed to be for the company at this time. Not only did the project have a script, director and two lead roles cast, but the Hammer Script Archive holds documentation that shows how extensively developed *Vampirella* had been by this stage. A revised budged dated 10 September 1975 (Anon. 1975d) shows that Hammer had worked out a deal with Warren Publishing in regard to adapting the comic (with a copyright cost of $35,714 listed and a fee to Warren Publications also listed at $4,762), and had negotiated a deal with American International Pictures (AIP) to co-produce the film. AIP, like Hammer, had seen a decline in their once successful horror pictures, but clearly both saw an opportunity with *Vampirella*. In the short-term this deal, which Carreras noted was negotiated with head of AIP Sam Arkoff (Frank 1978: 30; Swires 1987: 61), would have been an essential piece of *Vampirella*'s development. However as will be discussed later in the chapter, the AIP deal would have long-term ramifications which ultimately impeded the project from ever making it the screen.

As well as the budget, Hammer were also actively scouting locations, with a shooting schedule dated 15 September (Anon. 1975e) and a detailed breakdown of the necessary sets and settings dated 23 September (Anon. 1975f). October would prove just as fruitful for the project, with a proposed cast listed dated 3 October (Anon. 1975c) (including notable additions such as Donald Pleasance, Orson Welles and Ringo Starr), a preliminary crew list dated 7 October (Anon. 1975g), and a location report dated 15 October (Anon. 1975h). This burst of activity culminated less than a week before the convention with Wicking's completed script, dated 27 October 1975. Carreras therefore attended the convention with the project in an advanced stage of development, with an extraordinary amount of creative and economic labour already put in it.

Yet while Carreras hoped that attending the convention in New York would result in increased interest from American financiers and distributors, his decision to leave London had tangible consequences on active Hammer productions. Specifically, it overtly effected the production of *To the Devil a Daughter*, which was in post-production at the time of the convention. *To the Devil a Daughter*, which would turn out to be Hammer's final released horror film under Carreras, was, like *Vampirella*, a gamble for Hammer, albeit much less ambitious. Forsaking the temporal and spatial settings of the gothic horror, the contemporary setting and narrative of *To the Devil a Daughter* had more in common with the American horror films of the time than Hammer's previous gothics, with a plot derivative of *Rosemary's Baby* and *The Exorcist*. The film had a tortured production which delayed it getting to the screen, an issue exacerbated by the absence of Michael Carreras. Described by Meikle as 'a catalog [sic] of misfortune and mismanagement' (2009: 218), Carreras's absence was keenly felt, particularly as one of the key issues the film had was that it was being extensively rewritten on set by director Peter Sykes. Even in a promotional behind the scenes interview during the films production, the journalist on set notes that:

> When we were visiting, the film was in the seventh week on an eight-week shooting schedule, and Peter [Sykes – the director] showed us the latest version of the script: about eighty per cent of which was made up of pink revised pages. 'We're known as Pink Page Productions!' he said, grinning. (Moore 1976: 27)

Skeggs and Sykes had hired writer Gerald Vaughan-Hughes without Carreras or Wicking's knowledge, to provide rewrites while filming continued. Carreras's absence promoting *Vampirella* in New York meant that he found himself isolated and unable to get the production back on track even after Wicking reported issues, with Carreras remembering:

> What could I do? I told him, sort the bloody things out! What do you think I'm doing over here? I'm living in a cheap hotel, I've got no money and I have to take the bus to meetings. (Koetting 1994: 52)

Carreras's own situation broadly highlights Hammer's dire position. The company was clearly aware that they need to radically innovate to stay active in the industry, and the *Vampirella* promotion in New York gives the impression that Hammer are in a position to do so. Yet Hammer's failure as the 1970s progressed to maintain or develop any relationships with international financiers and distributors had put the company in a weakened and vulnerable position. Now running on a threadbare staff, Carreras's gamble to leave during the production of *To the Devil a Daughter* to promote *Vampirella* ultimately failed. In November 1975, *Vampirella* was the closest it would ever get to production. It had a cast and director, locations scouted, detailed budget breakdowns and a deal with AIP to co-finance the picture. Yet despite Carreras's overseas efforts, the crucial backing of an American distributor never transpired. The progress of *Vampirella* seems to slow dramatically after this point, with a budget summary dated 26 March 1976 (Anon.) held in the archive being the only item related to *Vampirella* for the entirety of 1976.

Although it is difficult to chart the development of the project at this time, a completely new draft of the script, written by John Starr and dated 22 February 1977, indicates that further work had been done on the screenplay since Wicking's 1975 draft. Wicking's draft has in black marker down the spine the number '2A' written on it. Starr's draft has the number '5' written on its spine, suggesting that extensive work had taken place on the project's story. Starr's draft supports this, with the script being a complete rewrite and bearing little resemblance to Wicking's draft. Starr's script makes a number of key changes to the core story, as well as Vampirella herself. Her planet no longer extinct (and renamed Triangulon), Vampirella has been sent by Triangulon's high council, 'The Three' (Starr 1977: 53), to find the planet's war criminal Starlock, a female supervillain who after being banished from Triangulon comes to earth to create a race of subservient monsters. Oddly, one of Vampirella's key characteristics, her need to drink blood, is completely excised from this draft, with Vampirella instead drawing her power from a pendant originating from her home planet. There is also no reference to the Van Helsing family or Dracula, making Starr's draft far less self-referential than Wicking's. Peter Cushing, another tether to Hammer's former glory, also seems to be missing from the project, with the script listing John Gielgud, Robert Morley and Ralph Richardson as potentially casting choices for Pendragon (Starr 1977: B). Barbara Leigh also seems to be out as Vampirella, with the script noting 'we will arrange for a widely publicised talent search for the finest young unknown actress we can find' (Starr 1977: B). Director John Hough is also gone, with Gordon Hessler, director of the 1970s horror *Scream and Scream Again*, an AIP/Amicus co-production written by Christopher Wicking and starring Peter Cushing, now in his place. Despite a new director, writer, plot and cast, this phase of Hammer's *Vampirella* project never garnered the traction of its original 1975 iteration, and by April 1978, just over a year later, Carreras declared the project effectively dead at Hammer.

Examining interviews with Carreras (primarily one with *Little Shoppe of Horrors* in April 1978 and another with *Fangoria* in 1987), the two primary reasons for the project's failure become apparent. First, to quote Carreras, 'there were too many cooks' (in Frank 1978: 30). Carreras elaborates, noting that he 'never had the rights to *Vampirella* directly, because I had not familiarised myself with *Vampirella* at all' (30). As a result, the project did not come cleanly to Carreras, but through 'an American company' (the archive holds no record of who this company was, but Carreras explicitly notes AIP's involvement came later in the process, ruling them out). This complex situation was exacerbated by the necessary involvement of AIP, which led to the second key issue in the production. In the 1987 *Fangoria* interview, Carreras notes that when AIP came aboard the project 'the budget was approved. We had everything ready to go', but 'unfortunately, AIP had a production executive who couldn't cast the picture to Sam's [Arkoff – head of AIP] satisfaction' (in Swires 1987: 61). John Hough elaborates on the AIP contract in an interview with Wayne Kinsey:

> It wasn't till later, when we read the contract that they'd signed, the deal provided that we get a host of other big name American artists in support. We couldn't get anyone and that's why at the eleventh hour AIP pulled out and it never happened. (2010: 164)

Hough's assertion that it 'wasn't till later' that Hammer even realised the contractual stipulations placed on *Vampirella* by AIP perhaps reveal the extent of Hammer's desperation to get the project into production, though it should be noted the discrepancy in Carreras and Hough's accounts, with Carreras placing the blame on AIP themselves. Despite this, it is clear that the casting of the picture proved an insurmountable hurdle, and perhaps more broadly illustrates Hammer's vulnerable position in the international market at the time. While at the height of the company's power their name alone was enough to close multi-picture deals with American majors (an example being a three-picture deal with Columbia in September 1957 for *The Snorkel* (Green, 1958), *The Camp on Blood Island* (Guest, 1958) and *The Revenge of Frankenstein* (Fisher, 1958) (Myers 1957: 7, 12)), Hammer were now operating on a project by project basis, with Hammer's reputation no longer enough to close the deal, leading to strict conditions which complicated the production process.

It was the protracted development of *Vampirella* which would force Carreras to conclude in 1978 that the project was dead. In the *Little Shoppe of Horrors* interview, Carreras alludes to an acrimonious split with the project's once mooted director Gordon Hessler, noting that 'somebody else, not us, is doing a ripoff [*sic*], or there is an intention' (in Frank 1978: 30). An author's note specifies that Carreras is referring to a project titled *Devilina*, which is to be directed by Gordon Hessler and produced by Henry White. White is also listed on the Starr *Vampirella* script as a producer, but why Hessler and White left *Vampirella* to attempt to make *Devilina* (a comic produced by the short-lived Atlas comics in 1975 which only ran for two issues) is unclear, though ultimately that project also failed to make it into production.

While *Devilina* is the first thing Carreras mentions when the interviewer asks about *Vampirella*, another recent science fiction film also looms large. Carreras suggests that Hammer's instincts to pursue an adaptation of *Vampirella* have been vindicated:

> I think our desires and intentions have been proven right, because had we made that picture when we wanted to make it, and it was going to be made as a full comic book/space adventure, we would have been parallel if not slightly ahead of *Star Wars*. (In Frank 1978: 30)

While, as the script summaries in this chapter attest, *Vampirella* shared little in similarity to George Lucas's *Star Wars* (1977), Carreras clearly saw parallels with the production and (correctly) predicts that with the unprecedented success of Lucas's film, the science fiction market would soon be hugely oversaturated: 'you've only got to pick up *Variety* today to see 18 others that are being ripped off and coming out' (in Frank 1978: 30). For Carreras, this is a critical issue in relation to the feasibility of *Vampirella*: 'If we started to think about "we" doing it now, getting it into production next year, it is nowhere near as viable a project as starting it a year ago' (30).

While Hammer's *Vampirella* was dead by 1978, the project would go on to have a tangible effect on those involved for numerous decades afterwards. For Hammer, the consequences of the project's failure were almost immediate. Carreras's strategy to reinvent Hammer as a big-budget genre studio with international appeal never resulted in a produced film, and would prove extremely costly for the studio itself. However no project would prove as costly to the company as *Vampirella* with Carreras himself noting:

> I managed to find people to pick up all the bills for *Nessie* . . . The one that really cost me was *Vampirella*. I spent a lot of time on that, had 25 different versions made and everyone spent a lot of money on that. That was a major set back [sic] for me, because the others were mostly picked up by somebody or the other. (Carreras in Kinsey 2007: 414)

In April 1979, only a year after the interview in which Michael Carreras declared *Vampirella* dead, he was removed as managing director. Hammer would not produce another film for three decades.

Barbara Leigh would go on to be intrinsically linked with the character for years after the project's failure. In 1995 she appeared in full *Vampirella* costume on the front of the magazine *Femme Fatales*, a move that resulted in a cease and desist letter being sent to both Barbara Leigh and *Femme Fatales* from the then owners of the *Vampirella* property Harris Publications. The letter, which is held in the Margaret Herrick Library and dated 13 September 1995 (Coleman), notes that the magazine's 'extensive bannering of the name *Vampirella* on the cover of this issue could very well be construed as a violation of our client's rights under trademark/unfair competition laws'. The firm also keenly stresses that 'Ms. Leigh's performances have occurred without any authorization by our client, and in our opinion, constitute a serious infringement of its rights' (Coleman 1995). This strict policing of the rights to use the *Vampirella* name coincides with the release of a film adaptation of *Vampirella* in 1996. Directed by Jim Wynorski and produced by AIP stalwart Roger Corman, the film starred Talisa Soto as Vampirella and The Who frontman Roger Daltrey as the antagonist Vlad. The film was a critical and commercial failure, with Wynorski distancing himself from the production: 'What went wrong??? Wrong choice for the star, massive union problems in Vegas, studio interference, theft, accidents, 112 degree heat, you name it, we had it happen' (Wynorski 2013). The film bears no resemblance to Hammer's failed adaptation, but perhaps suggest that, even if Carreras's *Vampirella* would have made it into production, it was far from guaranteed that the film would have had a positive impact on Hammer, and could have just created further problems for the already ailing company.

Conclusion

Developed within a year of each other, Hammer's *Vlad the Impaler* and *Vampirella* both speak to Hammer's wider ambitions in the mid to late 1970s, and the issues they had extricating themselves from their own history. *Vlad the Impaler*'s production under Carreras demonstrates that, despite Hammer only producing two films in the last five years of his tenure, he was keenly aware that Hammer's existing gothic horror films were in need of radical alteration to appeal to American studios. Hammer's pursuit of Ken Russell suggests an acknowledgment of the director driven ethos emerging in American horror cinema, as does their search for A-list stars such as Harris and Burton to lead the film. Yet while the horror of

American cinema took place in apartment blocks and children's bedrooms, Hammer still seemed fixated on the gothic iconography that had served it so well in the past. Carreras also seemed reliant on Hammer's previous propensity for adapting popular works. His clear enthusiasm for Hayles's radio-play and the subsequent hiring of Hayles to self-adapt his own work arguably leads to a project that, with its gothic iconography and period setting, undermines any attempt to reshape Hammer in the wake of the new American horror cinema. This focus on adaptation would also fatally undermine the *Vampirella* project, with the would-be film marred in legal issues relating to who had the rights to adapt the comic book. However, like all good vampire stories, *Vlad the Impaler* would live much longer after its 'death' in 1979. Despite Hammer not producing any films for thirty years, *Vlad the Impaler* continues to appear on Hammer's production slate until the late 1990s. As such, this project is an extremely useful vehicle to examine the Roy Skeggs's era of Hammer, which lasted from 1979 to 2000, and will be used to do so in Chapter 7.

Like *Vlad the Impaler*, *Vampirella* also stands as one of Hammer's most infamous unmade projects, and while the file held on the production at the Hammer Script Archive is one of its most extensive, there are still clear limitations with work that heavily utilises primary archival materials. As noted by A. T. McKenna 'what the researcher wants from an archive and what the researcher gets are often two very different things' (McKenna 2012: 112), and despite offering a comprehensive overview of the project, there are still gaps in the story of Hammer's *Vampirella* project. Perhaps most significantly the numbering on the spines of both Wicking's (2A) and Starr's (5) drafts suggest that there were multiple rewrites on the script that the Hammer Script Archive does not have access too.

However, these limitations do not prevent a number of key findings becoming evident in the study of the project. Primarily, it is clear in an examination of Hammer's *Vampirella* how the company, despite being clearly aware of a need to change its production processes, still relied heavily on its former reputation as experts in the gothic horror genre. While Hammer had certainly lost its footing in an industry that had rapidly changed, the company struggled to present itself as a studio with new ideas and ambitions.

Michael Carreras's own legacy at the company could be in part attributed to this. His grandfather Enrique Carreras had been the co-founder of Hammer and after his death in 1950, James Carreras took overall control of the company for over two decades, before selling it to

Michael in 1973. As such, Hammer had been with Michael Carreras for nearly his entire professional life, with Carreras having an active role (as a producer), in the development and release of *The Curse of Frankenstein*, which would change everything for Hammer. By the early 1960s, with multiple sequels to *The Curse of Frankenstein* and *Dracula*, and new gothics such as *The Curse of the Werewolf* (Fisher, 1961) and *The Gorgon* (Fisher, 1964), Hammer themselves had cultivated a reputation as a franchise in itself. Michael Carreras played a significant part in this development as a producer and director, and as such, Carreras's vision of a new Hammer in the 1970s is inevitably compromised by his own nostalgia and instincts as a producer.

Vampirella is the perfect microcosm of this issue. The film is in many ways a bold project for Hammer to take on. It presented a shift away from the classic gothic formula and towards a more ambitious science fiction narrative, and with a projected budget of $1,750,000 (Anon. 1975c), would have been Hammer's most expensive film ever. Yet the strictures of Hammer's former successes are still present in *Vampirella*. Wicking's script in particular leans heavily into Hammer's legacy, invoking Hammer stars such as Raquel Welch and the company's most iconic character – Dracula. Outside of the screenplay, the cast and crew did little to dispel the notion that this was a Hammer film, with John Hough directing and Peter Cushing cast in a key role. Some of the primary elements that had once made the company so successful ultimately impeded the project, with AIP never satisfied with the casting. Ultimately, *Vampirella* shows a company desperately trying to evolve in a rapidly changing market, but failing to move past the preconceived notions that had served Hammer so well in the past. By the 1970s, their reputation ultimately impeded any chance the company had at reinvention, with *Vampirella* proving not to be the company's brand-new start, but the beginning of the end for Carreras's iteration of Hammer Films.

5

International waters: *Nessie* and overseas finance

The following two chapters will detail the pre-production of Hammer's most ambitious unmade project – *Nessie*. Developed between 1975 and 1978, *Nessie* was a multimillion-dollar co-production with major financing from Japan, Hollywood, Germany and South Africa, as well as other production outfits in Britain such as Paradine. The international scale of the production was reflected in the screenplay, which sees the Loch Ness Monster rampage across the world from Scotland to the Canary Islands and Hong Kong harbour.

This chapter will specifically focus on Hammer's attempt at garnering international finance for *Nessie* over its near four-year production. Hammer's ambitious attempts to put together a complex financial package to fund their films would not be apparent through a focus on their produced features, as within this period Hammer only released two films (*To the Devil a Daughter* (Sykes, 1976) and *The Lady Vanishes* (Page, 1979)). Vital production context for this period can often be missing from other studies of Hammer due to their focus on Hammer's produced films, and not their unmade projects. This chapter will therefore attempt to foreground *Nessie*'s development in this period to reveal the significant shift in production strategy for Hammer that would, within other studies, go unnoticed. In order to do so, these two chapters will primarily use materials held in the Hammer Script Archive. The archive holds two screenplays for *Nessie*. One labelled 'third draft', is 135 pages long and is dated August 1976 (Forbes). The other, dated 28 March 1978 (Forbes, Wicking and Starr), is only 120 pages long and has fewer and much less ambitious action and special effects sequences. The archive also holds the '*Nessie* File', a ring-binder containing extensive pre-production materials on the project dating from 1976 to 1978. These range from internal office memos and correspondence with potential financiers, to notes on the script and letters on the search for a director.

Nessie acts as a salient case study of how a British independent studio such as Hammer, who had relied so much on American finance and distribution streams since the late 1940s, attempted to operate as the major American studios became less inclined to finance and distribute British films. An examination specifically of Hammer's relationship with Toho studios in Japan, who were brought on in the early stages of the project to provide the special effects (as well as a third of the $7 million budget) will detail Hammer's strategy of co-production with a studio outside of America, and will draw some comparisons with Hammer's previous co-production deal with the Hong Kong studio Shaw Brothers. This chapter will also examine Hammer's relationship with Columbia Pictures in the United States. As discussed in Chapters 1 and 2, Columbia had distributed several Hammer films throughout the late 1950s and 1960s, partnering with them for *The Revenge of Frankenstein*, and continuing with films such as *The Gorgon, The Curse of the Mummy's Tomb* (Carreras, 1964) and *Fanatic* (Narizzano, 1965). Despite this earlier relationship with Columbia, since 1972 Hammer had no real support from Hollywood outside of Warner Bros. By examining the complex financial arrangements and utilising Hammer's relationship with Toho and Columbia as case studies, the chapter will highlight the insurmountable difficulties Hammer had in attempting to finance a $7 million genre picture as an independent studio, in a film industry which was rapidly changing.

Before examining the complex financial packaging of *Nessie* over the four years of its production, it is important to contextualise how Hammer had attempted to find international production and distribution deals elsewhere, after the initial collapse of American backing in the early 1970s. Previous chapters have detailed Hammer's original courting of American finance, which began in the mid-1940s with Robert Lippert Productions. James Carreras had then utilised his connections at the Variety Club to pursue a deal with Eliot Hyman and Warner Bros. for *The Curse of Frankenstein*, with the subsequent success of that film opening up a number of opportunities for finance from American majors. However, as this book has documented, these once reliable avenues of production finance and distribution eventually began to fade, with even Hammer's most reliable franchises struggling to gain attention.

With Hammer no longer being able to rely on the United States, Michael Carreras had to pursue distribution and finance from other territories, with perhaps the most significant international deal Hammer brokered within the mid-1970s being a co-production between Hammer and Shaw Brothers. As noted in Chapter 3, this venture with the Hong Kong production company saw the release of Hammer's final *Dracula* film *Legend of the 7 Golden Vampires* as well as the crime thriller *Shatter*. Both productions were fraught with difficulties. Shot entirely in China at the Shaws' Movietown complex, Hammer found itself struggling to adapt to the Shaw Brothers' production methods, with Hammer finding the studio inadequately soundproofed due to most Shaw Brothers films at the time relying on post-production dubbing as opposed to recording sound on set (Hearn and Barnes 2007: 165; Kinsey 2007: 383). Hammer were not the only ones frustrated by the co-production process, with Shaw Brothers unhappy with how the action set pieces were progressing and insisting on setting up a second unit for the action sequences, with Ward Baker 'forced to cede the staging of *Legend*'s martial arts scenes to Shaw's leading action choreographers' (Bettinson 2011: 125).

However, the issue which caused Hammer lasting damage was the films running over budget. Hammer had already taken out a 'significant loan' (Hearn and Barnes 2007: 165) to finance the two films, and the increased costs damaged both their long-term financial standing as well as their relationship with Shaw Brothers, with the Hammer Script Archive holding correspondence between Vee King Shaw (Shaw Brothers head of production and distribution) and Michael Carreras still settling accounts on *Shatter* in November 1977, nearly three years after the film had finished shooting.

Despite the arduous production process the films were completed, yet Carreras struggled to find American distribution, with Warner Bros. deciding not to distribute *Shatter* in the United States until 1976 and *Legend of the 7 Golden Vampires* eventually appearing in 1978, distributed by Dynamite Entertainment. Even after partnering with an international studio to produce two feature films, a venture Hammer found taxing from both a production and financial standpoint, American distribution remained elusive. Carreras was aware that Hammer's reliance on the horror market to secure international finance was no longer a viable strategy. While the previous chapter argued *Vlad the Impaler* and *Vampirella* were still in some ways tethered to the gothic horrors of Hammer's past, *Nessie* can be seen as Carreras shifting completely away from the gothic genre and characters such as Dracula and instead focusing on big-budget genre films with the potential for cross-market appeal. Yet the deliberate strategy to increase the budget of these potential projects, in a market where Hammer was struggling to distribute their mid-to-low budget films, is one with clear risks attached.

This move away from genres with which Hammer had previously found success was also echoed in the production of their final film under Carreras, *The Lady Vanishes*. A remake of Hitchcock's 1938 thriller, this project would not have been out of place on Hammer's production slate in the mid-1960s, where it produced a slew of black and white thrillers. However, by the mid-1970s and with Carreras fully aware of the general apathy towards the current Hammer product, Carreras deliberately distanced the project from this genre. The Margaret Herrick Library holds a piece of correspondence sent with a screenplay for *The Lady Vanishes* by George Axelrod and a separate treatment by *Vlad the Impaler* writer Brian Hayles (Anon. to Carreras: 14 November 1974). In this correspondence, Carreras was being asked to decide between the two approaches to *The Lady Vanishes*. The unnamed sender noted that despite being 'very ingenious' (Anon. to Carreras: 14 November 1974), Hayles's version 'rests on suspense, requires complete credibility and I don't believe that is possible with the basic material involved' (ibid.). Instead, the writer recommended going with Axelrod's script as it 'has a zany style which would be acceptable and, with some adjustment and addition, could supply an audience with lots of surprises and fun' (ibid.). Axelrod's screenplay was indeed chosen for the project, notably demonstrating Carreras's belief that the genres Hammer had previously relied upon were no longer viable.

The Lady Vanishes originally had funding both from American International Pictures (AIP) and Rank Film (Hearn and Barnes 2007: 170; Kinsey 2007: 416; Meikle 2009: 222), but after AIP dropped out due to disagreements over casting, Rank took over the financing of the film (Hearn and Barnes 2007: 170; Kinsey 2007: 416; Meikle 2009: 222), which was released in 1979. However, with the British film industry in decline throughout the late 1970s, the deal with Rank proved more an exception than any kind of recurrent strategy. Even this one instance of Hammer attempting to co-produce a film with another British company ended badly, with the budget ballooning to the point where Rank removed Hammer and Carreras from the film entirely (Hearn and Barnes 2007: 170; Kinsey 2007: 41). *Nessie* then, seems to be a synthesis of *The Lady Vanishes*'s production strategy and the deal with Shaw Brothers, reliant initially on the backing of UK distributors, before expanding to the point that international finance became a necessity for the project.

Toho, Columbia and the financial complexity of *Nessie*

Before its expansion necessitated international finance, Nessie was very much a British production. The idea germinated at Hammer with a treatment written by Clarke Reynolds (who wrote *The Viking Queen* (Chaffey, 1967) for Hammer), with Hammer's script editor Christopher Wicking also involved (Carreras to Lloyd: 6 January 1976). Euan Lloyd, despite being a member of Hammer's board of directors at the time, came aboard the project as a separate producer under his own company Euan Lloyd Productions, effectively making *Nessie* a co-production from the beginning. Yet only three weeks later, on 5 February 1976, the *Daily Mail* reported that the broadcaster David Frost was planning a rival Loch Ness film, *Carnivore* (Carreras to Frost: 5 February 1976). Carreras contacted Frost that same day to alert him to this (ibid.), with Frost suggesting they join forces on one Loch Ness Monster project and Frost's Paradine Films co-produce *Nessie* as well (Carreras to Lloyd: 10 February 1976).

Even in this very early stage of development, and with no international finance or distribution deals in place, *Nessie* was becoming a complex production, with three British companies – Hammer, Euan Lloyd Productions and Paradine – all having a financial stake in the film. However, even with three production companies in place the project still had vital hurdles to overcome. Firstly, there was the pressing need to find an international distributor for the film but secondly, for the film to work at all, Hammer and its partners had to find a way to bring Nessie herself to the big screen.

In the first correspondence held in the archive for *Nessie*, dated 6 January 1976 and written when the project was at treatment stage, Carreras identified that the special effects would be vital to the project's success: 'the key to the whole film still remains as who will be in control of the special effects and co-direct these sequences' (Carreras to Lloyd: 6 January 1976). Carreras suggested Jim Danforth for the role, noting that 'if Danforth is still uncommitted to King Kong, and could become involved, then this would be the answer' (ibid.). Danforth had created the impressive prehistoric monsters for Hammer's *When Dinosaurs Ruled the Earth* (Guest, 1970), which had earned him an Academy Award nomination. The suggestion of Danforth at this stage of the production indicates that Carreras originally perceived *Nessie* as being like other Hammer films that had relied heavily on creature effects, with a specialist taking over from the film's director to stage these sequences separately. This method had been used with Danforth on *When Dinosaurs Ruled the Earth* and Ray Harryhausen on *One Million Years B.C.* (Chaffey, 1966). However, Danforth proved unavailable to Hammer due to his work on *The Legend of King Kong*, a film that, like *Nessie*, would never be produced.

As a result of Danforth's unavailability, Hammer entered into a deal that had notable similarities to their previous venture with Shaw Brothers. On the 11 March 1976, an agreement was drafted between Hammer Productions, Euan Lloyd Productions and Toho Studios of Japan (with Paradine not yet an official partner on the project). *Nessie* was still at treatment stage at this point, but the contract stated that 'subject to Toho-Towa approving the screenplay ... the British Companies and Toho-Towa will enter into a joint-venture for the co-production of the film' (Toho Draft Agreement: 11 March 1976). *Nessie* was budgeted at $3 million in the contract and it was stated that: 'One third of the budget shall be advanced by Toho-Towa and spent directly or indirectly in Japan on the Special Effects sequences, including the services of Mr. Shokei Nakano together with the facilities under his supervision (ibid.).'

In many ways, the co-production deal was a shrewd decision by Hammer. Not only did they secure a considerable amount of the film's budget (as well as a distributor in Japan), they also enlisted a company which specialised in creating special effects for genre films. Toho had become internationally synonymous with the kaiju film after the success of Ishirō Honda's *Godzilla* in 1954. In 1956, a re-edited version of the film with newly shot footage was released in the United States as *Godzilla, King of the Monsters!* (Honda/Morse), 'a version made palatable both linguistically and politically for the American market' (Tsutski 2006: 2). The film grossed more than $2 million, an extremely respectable figure when considering the rights for the project were purchased from Toho for only $25,000 (Tsutski 2004: 41). By the time Hammer entered into a co-production arrangement with Toho, *Godzilla* had become an international success, with fifteen Godzilla films being produced by 1976.

However, despite the seemingly astute nature of the deal, there are clear parallels with the troubled co-production with Shaw Brothers. For example, the establishment of a second unit to shoot all the special effect sequences recalls Shaw Brothers bringing in their own choreographers to direct the kung fu set pieces in Legend of the 7 Golden Vampires. On Legend of the 7 Golden Vampires, the entire production was located in China, and although this in itself caused many issues for the production, it at least allowed Hammer and Shaw Brothers to respond in real time to any issues they had with the project itself. However, the co-production deal with Toho relied on long distance correspondence and sporadic visits from Hammer to Japan and Toho to England. The deal also led to time pressures being put on the development of the screenplay. Only one day after the contract was signed between Hammer, Lloyd and Toho, Lloyd faxed Carreras informing him that he had promised Toho a first draft of the script 'within four weeks' (Lloyd to Carreras: 12 March 1976). Toho would have been understandably anxious to see a script from Hammer, with the contract agreed at only the treatment stage. Carreras responded informing Lloyd that the 'first draft script is to be ready by April 12th' (Carreras to Lloyd: 15 March 1976), leaving less than a month for the script to be completed. This inevitably resulted in a rushed writing process (a factor I will consider later within the next chapter), but undoubtedly caused an initial strain on the relationship between Hammer and Toho. On the 2 April, as Lloyd was about to leave for Japan to visit Toho in person, Carreras sent two packages to Lloyd and a letter explaining that one of the packages contained 'a copy of Chris Wicking's second draft as far as he has got' and the second package contained 'a presentation and screenplay of Vampirella' (Carreras to Lloyd: 2 April 1976). What is notable about the letter initially is that Carreras is attempting to capitalise on the deal with Toho by expanding it to other projects. As discussed in the previous chapter, Carreras had been pursuing an adaptation of the science fiction comic Vampirella since 1975 and, less than a month after signing the Nessie deal with Toho, he looked to capitalise on this deal by offering Toho the 'Far East' distribution rights to Vampirella (Carreras to Lloyd: 2 April 1976). Although this may have suggested confidence in the arrangement between Toho and Hammer, this piece of correspondence also indicates that Hammer had not been able to fully complete a script to send to Toho with Lloyd. The phrasing of Carreras's fax, noting that the script is as far as 'he [Wicking] has got', implies that Hammer had failed to meet the first deadline agreed with Toho. Therefore, less than one month into the deal Hammer found themselves under increased pressure to complete a script, and despite having started to tout potential future collaborations with Toho, they already ran the risk of frustrating Toho by not producing a screenplay on the agreed date.

However, perhaps the biggest concern to the viability of the deal came at the Cannes Film Festival in May 1976, only two months after the deal between Toho, Lloyd and Hammer had been struck. The project was well-represented at Cannes, with a significant advertising campaign in trades such as *Variety*, who ran a full-page advertisement in the 19 May 1976 issue. What is immediately apparent in the advertisement itself is the budget for the film, with the project announced as the '$7,000,000 Production/Nessie the Loch Ness Monster' (Anon. 1976a: 40). Between the signing of the original deal and Cannes, the project's budget had more than doubled from its initial $3 million, with Toho's original $1 million contribution, once a third of the film's budget, now only a seventh. No information is held in the Hammer Script Archive that suggests why the budget increased so dramatically, but a document dated 8 July 1976 written by Carreras gives a detailed budget breakdown, and lists Toho's contribution as $1,900,000, nearly double the original figure.

Despite the project being in development for another eighteen months after this point, it is the move to increase the budget to $7 million that arguably hindered any real chance *Nessie* had of being put into active production. Not only did it require Hammer and its partners to look for other investors, but this new budget also put a strain on Hammer's relationship with existing partners. On 23 July, a new contract was drafted by Lloyd and sent to Toho films. The contract was between Richmond Film Production (West) Ltd and Toho, with Richmond being a production subsidiary set up by Lloyd (Toho Draft Agreement: 23 July 1976). This new contract signifies the beginning of a difficult period between Hammer and Toho. Hammer had still failed to send a final production script to Toho, with Hammer board member Tom Sachs sending script revisions on 30 July. This seemed to be a frequent occurrence, with Sachs calling the pages 'revisions to the pages which we sent you last week' (Sachs to Matsuoka: 30 July 1976). Less than a week later, Carreras and Lloyd cancelled a trip to visit Toho just five days before their intended departure due to 'casting and British production planning' (Carreras and Lloyd to Toho: 4 August 1976). These missed deadlines and the prioritising of other production needs over Toho's concerns undoubtedly put a strain on the partnership with the Japanese company.

In the next chapter, I will examine Hammer's own role in the failure of *Nessie*, largely as a result of its inexperience at mounting such a large production. However, at this juncture it is noteworthy that Hammer's relationship with Toho is further strained not only by a new contract and budget, but by Hammer's own failure to meet agreed arrangements, in regard to both the script and the meeting in Japan. These issues came to a head in a telex sent by Toho on 4 August 1976, which contested fifteen separate articles within the newly drawn up contract. The first, and most notable, was the budget for Toho's special effect sequences. The telex stated that 'the budget of one million nine hundred thousand dollars for special effects sequences is based on first draft of script and any further departure therefrom required by Richmond cannot be included in said budget' (Matsuoka to Lloyd and Carreras: 4 August 1976). Toho was clearly concerned that with the script still being developed key sequences may be altered. Their subsequent request that 'any sequences additionally required by Richmond should be photographed at Richmond's expense' (ibid.) clearly showed the company looking for assurances from Hammer, Lloyd and Frost that any dramatic changes in the screenplay would not result in Toho having to contribute further to the budget. Toho also looked for guarantees that the film's quality would match its budget: 'Richmond to provide director of international fame and top box-office drawing stars' (ibid.). Also of note in the telex is Toho asking for the partial ownership of the Nessie character: 'Toho to become co-propertier [sic] of copyrights to special effects sequences, including name and character of Nessie' (ibid.). This is a significant request as, for the most part, the deal with Toho had centred on the film's production and distribution in Japan and other territories in the Far East. Owning the rights to the character would potentially extend to the worldwide marketing and merchandising, as well as theoretically impacting any possible sequel to the film. Although the vagueness of the request makes it difficult to specify what Toho were explicitly looking for by becoming co-owner of the Nessie character, the telex sent by Matsuoka, and the points discussed within it, make it clear that Toho was looking for more from Hammer both in assurances about the project's production as well as financial recoupment now that their contribution to the project was close to $2 million.

Lloyd replied within five days of Matsuoka's telex, providing answers to each individual issue raised about the contract. There are two significant passages in Lloyd's response. First, his reaction to Toho's request to co-own the character:

> The entire copyright of this film and everything contained therein must rest with the Maker of the film, namely the London company. However, under the terms of our final distribution agreement

> Toho will share in the benefits of licence and elsewhere in the world through its equity position. To that extent therefore you are co-proprietors. (Lloyd to Matsuoka: 9 August 1976)

In this response, Lloyd effectively dismissed Toho's request to partially own the character of Nessie, suggesting that the already agreed terms make them, 'to that extent', co-proprietors. However, despite Lloyd attempting to suggest Toho already effectively co-owned the rights to the character, this point does show the potential complications of having another studio co-directing sequences of the film. Although Toho was only providing $1,900,000 of the $7 million budget, the company was responsible for all effects sequences featuring Nessie and the design and creation of the creature itself. Consequently, their request to co-own the rights to the character held some weight, and further complicated the relationship between Toho and Hammer. This was perhaps best expressed by Toho's Isao Matsuoka nearly a month after the contract was first sent: 'rights resulted from creative work by each party should rest with the party who did said creative work' (Matsuoka to Lloyd: 13 September 1976). As a result, the Toho and Hammer deal in effect became even more complex than their previous deal with Shaw Brothers, as Hammer were handing over almost complete creative control to Toho in the creation of Nessie, and, as a result, Toho were vital to the film's production. However, in relative financial terms Toho was a minor partner, with other companies such as Columbia and a German tax shelter group (both discussed later in the chapter), holding a larger financial stake in the project.

The nature of Toho's relationship with *Nessie* was further complicated by Lloyd in his initial response to Toho's 4 August telex regarding issues with the contract. In responding to Toho's concerns, Lloyd attempted to clarify the nature of the relationship between Hammer and Toho. However, his explanation contradicted the initial contract in one key area:

> To avoid any possible misunderstanding between us I feel it is necessary to reconfirm that our relationship should not be construed as a full coproduction. You are, of course, a minority partner in this enterprise and are providing facilities (and to that extent an investment) in return for distribution rights and equity in the film. (Lloyd to Matsuoka: 9 August 1976)

Although Lloyd stated that he is merely 'reconfirming' the nature of the deal, the insistence that the deal 'should not be construed as a full coproduction' was obviously a significant alteration from the initial contract (signed only five months before this exchange). The contract signed in March specifically stated that this was a co-production deal (Toho Draft Agreement: 11 March 1976), and therefore this shows a dramatic departure from the original deal with Toho. The thinking behind this was most likely that, due to the budget increase for the film, Toho's stake in the production had been significantly reduced, at least in financial terms. In regards to creative input on the project, however, the latter part of this chapter will foreground just how crucial Toho were to the production of *Nessie*.

These many setbacks in the Toho deal could be construed as a sign of incompetence at Hammer, yet it is important to reaffirm the mammoth task Hammer had given itself in trying to bring *Nessie* to the screen. In August 1976, the month in which these contract negotiations between Hammer and Toho took place, Hammer was concurrently attempting to garner finance and distribution from various outlets around the globe. Carreras himself was attempting to put together a complex financial package in Germany with Dr Helmut Gierse and Constantin Film, which would not only secure a large part of the finance for *Nessie*, but also potentially secure Hammer's long-term future. Carreras suggested utilising the 'current Tax Shelter situation' (Carreras to Gierse: 26 August 1976) to set up a production outfit for Hammer in Germany. The German tax shelter group went on to offer a significant share of the budget, '$2,450,000 (35%) on the basis of pari-passu recoupment and 17 ½ % of world profits' (Carreras to Begelman: 27 October 1976). This was a sizeable sum, but the fact that Carreras still had to find a significant amount of the budget, even with this deal in place, underlines the enormity of a project like *Nessie* for a British independent such as Hammer.

While Carreras brokered this deal, Lloyd not only dealt with the contract negotiations with Toho, but also entered negotiations with Martin Wragge of Martin Wragge Productions to provide 'certain financial facilities up to $500,000 for the purpose of filming certain sequences of this film in South Africa' (Lloyd to Wragge: 18 August 1976). Lloyd looked to take advantage of the fact that South Africa is one of the many key locations in the film script, with Lloyd noting in a letter to Wragge's associate that 'Nessie is coming to Cape Waters and in a way to make your mind boggle' (Lloyd to Pierotti: 18 August 1976). Even using just the month of August as an example, it is clear that Hammer, or more specifically Carreras and Lloyd, were attempting to juggle a number of complex financial arrangements. This once again led to Toho becoming frustrated with Hammer. Lloyd, in a letter to Carreras, acknowledged that it was essential to Hammer's relationship with Toho that they visit Japan in September, with Lloyd noting that 'any postponement will make them unduly nervous as we are already behind schedule' (Lloyd to Carreras: 30 August 1976). As such, it was not necessarily ineptitude or incompetence that led to a fractious relationship with Toho, but this was rather just a symptom of a comparatively small independent production outfit such as Hammer attempting to secure finance and distribution deals for a $7 million project.

Calling Columbia: *Nessie* and American finance

As Hammer continued to grapple with the enormity of a project such as *Nessie*, October 1976 saw Hammer turn its attention to another crucial component of *Nessie*'s production, American distribution and finance. Despite Hammer's attempts to garner American distribution for previous projects having proven increasingly difficult throughout the mid-to-late 1970s, it became inevitable that they would once more have to turn to the United States to salvage *Nessie*. Even with pieced-together financing from around the world, such as the previously mentioned deals in Japan, South Africa and Germany, a project of *Nessie*'s size necessitated the backing of an American studio. With the project first broached in January 1976, it seems surprising that Hammer didn't officially approach an American studio until October, nine months after the *Nessie* project began. However, by waiting until some of the other financing was secured, Hammer approached Columbia in October with $4,350,000 of the $7 million dollar budget already in place and, perhaps even more crucially, a director signed on to the project.

Assigning a director to the project had been no easy task. Bryan Forbes was signed on as a writer and potential director in June 1976 (Anon. 1976b), and his work on the project will be examined in detail in the next chapter. However, by July 1976 Forbes had declined Hammer's offer to direct *Nessie* (Forbes to Carreras and Lloyd: 22 July 1976), and by September 1976, Mark Robson (*Von Ryan's Express* (1965) and *Earthquake* (1974)) and Richard Fleischer (*20,000 Leagues Under the Sea* (1954) and *Soylent Green* (1973)) had also turned Hammer down (Carreras to Gersh: 22 September 1976). These setbacks aside, by November 1976 Hammer had finally secured a director in Michael Anderson. Anderson had directed *Logan's Run*, which was released in 1976 and, despite a near $9 million budget, proved to be a substantial box office hit for its studio MGM, saving them from potential bankruptcy (Brock 2014: 105). However, Hammer were perhaps more drawn to Anderson due to the film he had just completed, *Orca* (1977). *Orca* is important due to its status as one of the most significant films in a cycle that looked to capitalise on the monumental success of *Jaws* (Spielberg, 1975). These films often involved reworking *Jaws's* animal attack plot with other animals or sea creatures, such as bears in *Grizzly* (Girdler, 1976) or piranhas in *Piranha* (Dante, 1978).

Orca's variation on the premise of *Jaws*, specifically its eco-friendly narrative which sympathises with the creature (in this case a killer whale) also has similarities with *Nessie*, which could be classified as an unrealised entry in this cycle of post-*Jaws* animal revenge films. The relationship between *Jaws* and *Nessie* is not only apparent in the basic 'sea-monster on the loose' premise, but permeates nearly all aspects of production, from references in the screenplay, to merchandise and marketing. Although I will provide a more detailed examination of the plot in the next chapter, it is worth at this stage noting how heavily *Nessie* wears its influences. *Jaws* is referenced twice by name in the screenplay itself. Two doomed lovers on a private yacht directly in Nessie's path of destruction watch *Jaws* on a television set (Forbes 1976: 68), then later, as Nessie travels through the ocean, she is confronted by a great white shark 'bigger than *Jaws*' (Forbes 1976: 95). These allusions to *Jaws* are apparent in the characters as well, most notably the big game hunter Channon. Channon is essentially a substitute for Quint (Robert Shaw), the grizzled shark hunter in *Jaws*, although Channon takes on a more antagonistic role, working against the two protagonists to try and kill Nessie instead of capturing her. Like Quint, Channon does not make it to the film's end, being beheaded by a tuna fish net early in the third act.

Outside of the screenplay, marketing companies had also begun to see the similarities between the two projects and looked to capitalise on them. After a meeting with Seinger and Associates Advertising Company, who did the promotional campaign for *Jaws*, Carreras was sent a detailed proposal by Tony Seinger outlining how his company would approach the marketing of *Nessie* (Seinger to Carreras: 28 July 1976). Lloyd replied thanking Seinger for his letter and noted that 'the fine campaign [Seinger] did on *Jaws* deserves praise which I gladly give' (Lloyd to Seinger: 18 August 1976). Hammer were also approached by Gateway Productions, a company responsible for the merchandising of *Jaws*. In their letter, Gateway was keen to stress the connection, noting that they cited *Jaws* as a reference 'because it is more comparable to your production of Nessie than the many TV properties we handle' (Charlton to Carreras: 24 June 1976). Charlton also suggested that, due to the similarities with *Jaws*, they could begin to merchandise *Nessie* straight away, instead of having to 'wait until after a massive worldwide promotion of the production had made its impact and the release of the film' (ibid.).

The referential screenplay, as well as the correspondence with the merchandise and marketing agencies that handled *Jaws*, underlines *Nessie*'s similarities with *Jaws*. Another key similarity was its budget, which, at over $7 million, was equal to *Jaws*' own (boxofficemojo.com). As such, the choice of Michael Anderson as the film's director was both astute and understandable, given that he had helmed *Orca*, a film that had a $6 million budget. As a result of Anderson signing on, Hammer entered production on what would have been the most expensive post-*Jaws* animal-revenge film of the entire cycle, with a director who had recently finished the production of another expensive project borne out of the success of *Jaws*.

Despite a tumultuous pre-production period up to that point, in September, when Hammer approached Columbia Pictures, the film was arguably at its most marketable. They had guarantees on a considerable portion of the budget, a completed screenplay, a well-suited director and advertising and merchandising companies with proven track records in the genre also showing interest. With this considered it is perhaps not surprising that Columbia opened talks with Hammer about financing and distributing *Nessie*, and eventually set out the terms of a potential deal.

These terms are laid out in two documents held in the Hammer Script Archive. One is a handwritten note by Carreras, dated 17 November 1976 and titled 'Nessie-Columbia', and the other is a separate undated memo written by Carreras which stated, in reference to Columbia, what 'they do not like', what 'they want', what 'they accept', and what 'they are considering' (Carreras undated). Together, these two documents give a detailed account of Columbia's terms.

Columbia offered to give Hammer the full amount of $2,650,000, a number which with Toho and the German tax shelter money would have taken the project to the $7 million target figure. However, Columbia also outlined several terms and conditions that would have potentially complicated Hammer's relationships with existing partners. On the handwritten notes' 'do not like' section is the name of the director, Michael Anderson. As previously stated, Hammer had a difficult time attaching a director to the project before Anderson signed on. Anderson had only been confirmed for the project for eight weeks, yet Hammer found itself in a position where it could seemingly only gain the financing from Columbia if it lost one of their primary assets in Anderson. Furthermore, Carreras's note made it clear that although Columbia accepted that Toho had the Japanese distribution rights to the project and that their 25 per cent cut of worldwide profits would exclude Japan, the American studio was less accepting of losing the German/Austrian market to Gierse's Constantin Films and the German tax shelter group. Carreras's note stated that Columbia had explicitly asked for the German/Austrian rights and, in addition, were also considering 'the value and viability' of the tax shelter deal already in place in Germany. These issues were exacerbated by the time pressures of the German tax shelter deal, something made clear by Carreras in his initial letter to Columbia: 'I apologize for the urgency in this matter, but it is a basic requirement of the German Tax Shelter group that distribution arrangements are completed before going to the market next week' (Carreras to Begelman: 27 October 1976). Although negotiations between studios in this kind of arrangement are not uncommon, the indication that the German tax shelter deal also rested on an agreement with Columbia (due to it being time-sensitive) put Hammer under immense pressure, and in the precarious position of potentially losing both Columbia and the tax shelter group as partners.

However, perhaps even more potentially damaging to the deal was Columbia's insistence on a quality clause in relation to Toho's special effects. In a fax from Lloyd to Carreras, Lloyd was clearly fearful of such a clause being discussed: 'Please avoid at all costs any question of quality clause with Columbia or major as this would in my opinion negate the deal totally' (Lloyd to Carreras undated). This message in itself suggests a lack of confidence in Toho's special effects by Lloyd, but perhaps also indicates a more serious issue. After Columbia had noted its wariness of Hammer's deal with Toho, Hammer went to Toho to seek assurances that would assuage Columbia's fears, by having a quality clause written into Hammer's own contract with Toho. This then led to tensions between Hammer and Toho, with Lloyd noting that 'the Toho revised contract states "to Hammer's reasonable satisfaction", however, I expect further argument on this as they are trying to insist that quality should not be inferior to King Kong Vs. Godzilla' (Lloyd to Carreras undated). The fact that Toho would only go so far as to say the effects would be on par with *King Kong vs. Godzilla* (Honda, 1962) would hardly have been reassuring for Hammer or Columbia. Released nearly fifteen years before *Nessie* began production, *King Kong vs. Godzilla* relied on Toho's patented 'suitmation' technique (Kalat 2017: 61), which featured actors in large suits moving through small-scale scenery to bring the titular monsters to life. As such, it is perhaps understandable that Columbia would be reticent to allow Toho to continue the effects on what was to be a large scale, big-budget production. To add further context, in 1976 Columbia were deep in production on Steven Spielberg's *Close Encounters of the Third Kind* (1977), a $19 million blockbuster that would prove ground-breaking in its use of special effects. With Columbia's expectations likely built on these very high standards, Toho's suitmation would struggle to impress.

Hammer were forced to intervene and defend Toho to Columbia, attempting to, in Carreras's own words to Columbia's Stanley Jaffe, 'ease your quality fears' (Carreras to Jaffe: 23 November 1976). In order to do this, Carreras put forward a plan to Columbia. First, he suggested increasing Toho's special effects budget by half a million dollars from $1,900,000 to $2,400,000. Second, Carreras proposed having a representative of Columbia in Japan at Toho to provide 'constant supervision of progress and quality' (ibid.). Both suggestions seem like practical and sensible solutions to the issue at hand, yet Carreras's next point in the letter suggests a less firm grasp of the situation. In an attempt to convince Columbia that Hammer could produce a project of *Nessie*'s scale, Carreras stressed his own experience producing effects-heavy films:

> I have been directly associated with the production of space-science-fiction, pre-historic and countless horror special effects, and I believe the reputation earned over the last twenty years for high quality production for minimal cost are accepted by both the industry and by world audiences. (ibid.)

Indeed, Hammer had in the past been involved with its own effects-driven films, and Carreras was keen to point out its experience with genre films, from the prehistoric creatures of *One Million B.C.* to the science fiction of *Moon Zero Two* (Ward Baker, 1969). Yet Carreras also made the point that the quality of the effects within these films was balanced by the 'minimal cost' in bringing them to the screen. These films did not necessarily offer good special effects, but rather good special effects within the parameters of their (often modest) budgets. As a result, despite Hammer and Carreras having always been shrewd in the budgeting of Hammer's films (for example by using Bray Studios as its home studio between 1951 and 1966, utilising tight filming schedules, shooting films back to back and reusing sets), Carreras was promoting himself as economical to an industry that was becoming increasingly more relaxed about producing films with large budgets.

This leads to perhaps the strongest argument that *Nessie*'s fate was truly out of Carreras, Lloyd and Hammer's hands. At the end of 1976, as Hammer began negotiating with Columbia, Hollywood stood on the precipice of a change that would significantly alter the industry for decades: the rise of the blockbuster. After the financial caution that had followed the fiscal crisis in Hollywood between 1969 and 1971, key shifts within the industry began to take place, namely the buying of film companies by multi-conglomerates and the move away from staggered releases to wide releases brought on by the success of *The Godfather* (Coppola, 1972) and *Jaws* (which opened simultaneously on 350 and 464 screens respectively (Hall 2006: 164–9)). As a result, Hollywood began to dramatically increase the budgets of its most prominent pictures. *Star Wars* was released in May 1977 on a budget of roughly $12 million and, by November 1977, had become the highest grossing film ever made (second when accounting for inflation, behind *Gone with the Wind* (Fleming, 1940)) (Kermode 2005: 173; Krämer 2005: 89). *Close Encounters of the Third Kind*, which followed in November 1977, proved to be an enormous hit for Columbia and, along with *Star Wars*, 'persuaded the major studios that science fiction could generate massive profits' (Hall 2006: 175). Therefore, in 1976, with Columbia deep in production on *Close Encounters of the Third Kind* and 20th Century Fox's *Star Wars* seven months from release, *Nessie*, in hindsight, seemed to be adrift in a changing film industry. It was a special effects-driven film designed to entice Hollywood studios, but with a budget simultaneously too large for Hammer to produce itself, and too small to convince the Hollywood majors that the effects could be done successfully.

Whereas Hammer could not have possibly foreseen the arrival of these blockbuster films, Carreras was fully responsible for the disastrous move he took in another effort to ease Columbia's quality concerns. In the previously mentioned letter to Columbia, Carreras suggested sending

Columbia footage from Toho's new film: 'I have shipped in from London the final reels of Toho's "Conflagration" which contain the destruction of Tokyo Harbour – similar to our destruction of Hong Kong, for you to see and judge the quality' (Carreras to Jaffe: 23 November 1976). The footage was sent to Bill Tennant, a former agent who was then production vice president at Columbia (McClintick 1982: 280) with a request by Carreras that he could also attend the screening as and when it took place (Carreras to Tennant: 24 November 1976). Carreras's request went unheeded and he received a reply from Stanley Jaffe, another vice president of production, less than a week later:

> While I admire the work [Toho] did, the quality of what we saw would not be acceptable to us and, therefore, as so much of NESSIE would depend upon the quality of the special effects, we must unfortunately inform you that we feel it necessary to pass on the project. (Jaffe to Carreras: 30 November 1976)

Carreras's gamble could not have gone worse, demonstrating a fundamental misunderstanding of Columbia's own expectations for the picture. It is not difficult to see why Columbia balked at the effects sequences in *Conflagration* (Ishida, 1975). It mainly relies on miniatures to stage its explosive set pieces, and reuses footage of an oil tanker explosion taken from *Godzilla vs. Hedorah* (Banno, 1971). Again, this perhaps showed Hammer's naivety with such a big budget production. Whereas Carreras had clearly not only seen, but been impressed by Toho's efforts on *Conflagration*, Columbia had immediately pulled out of the project on viewing it, highlighting the gulf (which would only widen in the coming year) between Hammer's idea of an effects-driven film and that of a Hollywood major such as Columbia. Despite Carreras's protestations that they had been producing genre pictures for 'the last twenty years', the industry had begun to change around Hammer, and the hope that *Nessie* could act as a bridge to a wider international audience and once again announce Hammer as major global players was sinking quickly.

To his credit, Carreras did manage to entice Columbia back onto the project, offering the studio assurances that included a visit to Toho to examine the storyboards of the effect sequences, an increase in the budget of the effects (as first proposed in his letter), and handing over to Columbia a complete production cross plot and budget breakdown (Carreras to Jaffe: 9 December 1976). The deal with Columbia stayed in place for six months, when a fax was sent by a nervous Carreras to Lloyd asking if Columbia was yet to 'make up their minds' (29 June 1977). However, once more the fate of the deal was taken completely out of Hammer's hands. Euphemistically referred to by Meikle as 'musical chairs in the Columbia boardroom' (2009: 221), 1977 saw Columbia Pictures engulfed in a scandal. The president of Columbia, David Begelman, was found to have embezzled close to $75,000 from the company (Dick 1992: 30). Columbia mishandled the issue, only suspending Begelman when 'generally, forgery and embezzlement mean termination' (ibid.). Making matters worse, Columbia reinstated Begelman until he resigned in February 1978 (ibid.). The scandal was labelled 'HollywoodGate' (Anon. 1978), and became synonymous 'as a symbol of greed-driven Hollywood' (Dick 1992: 32). The ensuing aftermath resulted in Alan Hirschfield, then CEO of Columbia, resigning from the company.

Although Hammer's own hand in *Nessie*'s misfortunes has been highlighted throughout the chapter (and will be dealt with further in the next chapter), this particular situation was utterly out of its control. The Begelman scandal saw the studio left in disarray, and Hammer's *Nessie* was cast aside by a company fighting to survive. Despite Lloyd and Carreras's best efforts, *Nessie* had lost the backing of Columbia by September 1977 and, by October, Hammer was in danger of losing Toho as well. In a letter dated 24 October 1977, president of Toho Isao Matsuoka, seemingly furious at the mounting expenses on the project over the eighteen months since Toho signed on (Matsuoka notes that Toho's 'credit has been greatly damaged by [Hammer's] failure' (Matsuoka to Lloyd: 24 October 1977)), offered Hammer an ultimatum. First stating how it 'is a matter of great regret' that commencement on the production of *Nessie* had been so delayed, Matsuoka gave Hammer until 1 December to demonstrate to Toho 'that you can procure financing necessary for immediate commencement of shooting' (ibid.). December and January came and went, and although Toho was still on board with the project in February (Netter to Matsuoka: 24 February 1978), *Nessie* was dead in the water by the summer of 1978.

Conclusion

As noted in the introduction, *Nessie* was perhaps the peak of Carreras's new strategy for Hammer, which would have moved away from low-to-mid-budget genre pictures and instead looked to entice American majors with big-budget films with cross-market appeal. However, although Carreras had offered a radical new Hammer to the American majors, not much had really changed. Hammer were still dependent on American financial backing, and when they lost the support of Columbia, despite continuing for another year in development, *Nessie* never regained momentum and stayed, to use Carreras's own term, 'in dry-dock' (Carreras in Skinn and Brosnan 1978: 21).

Hammer's relationship with Toho also foregrounds how Hammer's ambitions perhaps superseded its capacity to develop a picture such as *Nessie*. The two-year relationship was mired by Toho's constant frustrations with Hammer over the delays in production, and the constant confusion about the nature of their arrangement. Quite clearly originating as a co-production deal, Hammer's scaling up of the budget to $7 million from $3 million reduced Toho to a minor financial partner, but still a major factor in the film's potential success, due to the Japanese studio providing the special effects. This tension caused a rift between the companies, with Toho clearly doubting Hammer could provide the finance for the picture after the Columbia deal fell through.

However, despite Hammer's own faults during the production of *Nessie*, two points should be underlined. First, to its credit, Hammer approached Columbia with a strong, saleable project (partly financed, with a director attached and marketers interested) and secured a deal. That Hammer even managed to achieve this international deal within the weakened British film industry is impressive. Second, it is necessary to point out that what I argue was the true killing blow to *Nessie*, the withdrawal of Columbia, was out of Hammer's control. Although Hammer did initially lose Columbia's support due to the issue with Toho's effects, the British studio regained it, and it was ultimately the changes at Columbia brought on by the Begelman scandal that derailed any chance the project had. This, as well as the blockbuster's rise to prominence in 1977, ultimately demonstrates that despite Hammer's own faults when dealing with a project of this scale on the international stage, the true reason for *Nessie*'s failure was out of Hammer's hands.

6

Nessie in dry dock

Although examining Hammer's international deals can offer us a comprehensive picture of the company in relation to its partners and potential financiers, to examine Hammer internally and domestically can, as this chapter attests, answer the question as to whether Hammer were truly up to the task of producing Carreras's proposed slate of proto-blockbusters. Previous chapters highlighted how difficult Hammer's situation had become as the 1970s progressed, and Carreras's new 'shit or bust attitude' can at best be seen as an optimistic but risky strategy to combat Hammer's decline. Focusing on large-scale productions as a result of failing to get mid-budget films financed seems wilfully self-destructive, but as noted in the previous two chapters, Carreras was arguably quite prescient in predicting Hollywood's shift towards big-budget genre films.

However, the question of whether Hammer was in any state internally to pursue this strategy is a significant one, and one this chapter will explore. One key aspect of this chapter will be an examination of the screenplay, and how it was received by potential financiers and talent. The screenplay, unlike the film's special effects or the international partnerships discussed in the previous chapter, was Hammer's sole responsibility, having firstly been developed in-house at Hammer before later being developed further by Bryan Forbes. However, even with Forbes's involvement, the project was still managed intensively by Carreras, and therefore I argue that the screenplay is perhaps the best way to examine Hammer's approach to *Nessie* away from the influence of any international partners. Carreras and Forbes's relationship throughout the development of *Nessie* is key to understanding the issues with the screenplay that ultimately led to delays in it being sent to partners and financiers (one of the primary issues Toho had with Hammer). It also gives insight into how Hammer approached such a project and how a writer/director such as Forbes fit (or did not) within Hammer's method of production.

However, the archival gaps within this area should be acknowledged. The initial treatment by John Starr, mentioned by Carreras in his correspondence to Euan Lloyd on 6 January 1976, is missing, and in a letter sent out to Hammer staff dated 11 August 1976, Carreras referred to two similarly absent screenplays written before Forbes involvement, 'the first being from John Starr, the second being from Chris Wicking' (Carreras to Lloyd et al.). The archive is also not in possession of any unaltered drafts written by Bryan Forbes after he was signed to the project. In correspondence to Michael Carreras, Forbes noted that he had written 'three separate drafts' (Forbes to Carreras: 28 August 1976) of the script, suggesting that, with Starr and Wicking's other drafts, there are five drafts of *Nessie* not held in the Hammer Script Archive. The archive does hold two *Nessie* screenplays. One, dated August 1976, is described as the 'final Bryan Forbes Script Amended by Michael Carreras', and is 138 pages long. The second script is listed as being 'revised in March 1978' and is described as a 'screenplay by Christopher Wicking and John Starr, shooting script by Bryan Forbes'. At 120 pages, the script features less ambitious action and special effects sequences; this was the screenplay prepared, presumably by Carreras, for a trimmer, post-Columbia version.

Despite the limitations of the archive's script holdings, ancillary materials such as production correspondence and financial documentation still provide a detailed overview of *Nessie*'s production history, as demonstrated in the previous chapter. One such document, which will be a primary focus of this chapter, is the previously mentioned letter from Forbes to Carreras where he indicated the existence of 'three other drafts' he had produced for the project. The crux of Forbes's letter is his anger at Carreras for amending his script significantly while still crediting Forbes as the sole author. In the letter, Forbes also attached five pages that detailed the changes Carreras made to his draft, and why he felt these damaged the screenplay. Using these five pages it is possible to get a sense, although not definitively, of what material was written by Forbes and what were Carreras's additions in the amended 1976 screenplay. As well as this, having two different screenplays stills allows cross-referencing between both and, by looking at the similar elements apparent over the two screenplays dated nearly two years apart, it is possible to summarise the basic plot elements most likely consistent throughout the project's development.

In both screenplays, *Nessie* begins with a pre-credit sequence. A vat of steroids called Mutane 4 spill into Loch Ness after a truck crash. As a result, the 1 million-year-old Elasmosaurus Nessie suffers steroid-enhanced growth and, with the loch polluted, escapes into the ocean. This leads to a number of set pieces as Nessie embarks on a journey to her ancient home in the South China Seas. Meanwhile, a vast array of characters from around the world attempt to stop her: arrogant TV reporter Mark Stafford, the film's nominal lead; Susan, a female scientist who wants the creature studied in a humane environment; Channon, an ill-fated hard-bitten huntsman; and Comfort, scientist turned company man who is out to ensure Nessie's demise at the hands of the US and UK governments. Both screenplays are also structured around a handful of disaster sequences. Nessie gets entangled with a nuclear submarine and tuna boats, causes an oil rig disaster and finally meets her end in the sea some miles from Hong Kong harbour.

The global nature of the film's plot is by no means coincidental and reflects the scramble for international finance detailed in the previous chapter. Hammer attempted to use the travelogue nature of the screenplay in order to directly appeal to specific foreign markets, a point made apparent in the overt description of the lead character Stafford as an American journalist, a clear appeal to the United States markets and a tactic Hammer had utilised since the late 1940s through their deal with Lippert Productions.

With its clear exploitation plot and almost cynical attempt to cater to international markets, it is initially difficult to see what had attracted Bryan Forbes to *Nessie*. Although there is no specific reference to it in the Hammer Script Archive, a good assumption would be that it was Forbes's prior relationship with David Frost of Paradine Productions, who came onto the *Nessie* project in February 1976. Forbes had directed and co-written *The Slipper and the Rose* (1976), a Paradine co-production (Hawk 1976: 27) on which David Frost had served as executive producer. The film, a $4.5 million musical adaptation of Cinderella with songs by the Sherman Brothers (Davies 1976: 108), drew positive notices from critics (Anon. 1976c: 35) and decent numbers at the box office (Thomas 1976a: 2, Thomas 1976b: 2), thereby making it plausible that Frost would recommend Forbes for *Nessie*.

However, although reviews for *The Slipper and the Rose* noted that Forbes had an 'honorable record' as a director and producer of family films (with *The Railway Children* (Jeffries, 1970) and *The Tales of*

Beatrix Potter (Mills, 1971) all produced under Forbes's tenure as head of production at EMI), his previous directorial effort, *The Stepford Wives* (1975), showed a director comfortable with more adult fare. The plot of that film sees a couple move to the idyllic town of Stepford, only to discover that the eerily docile wives of Stepford are in fact robotic replacements made by their husbands. Causing controversy on its release due to claims of misogyny, the film was relatively well received by critics (Murf 1975: 28) but proved a difficult sell at the box office (Anon. 1975a: 18; Anon. 1975b: 14). Unlike with Michael Anderson, where it is possible to chart a clear path from *Orca* to *Nessie*, Forbes, despite having previously worked with Frost, was a less obvious choice for the project. Clearly not a director fixed to one genre, Forbes had also had a career as an actor (even starring in two Hammer Films, *Quatermass 2* (Guest, 1957) and *Yesterday's Enemy* (Guest, 1959)), and had worked at EMI as head of production from 1969 to 1971, resigning in the wake of several financial issues and failed projects. Forbes himself suggests that Hammer's production deal with EMI during his tenure was an 'old pals act' (in Meikle 2009: 185) between James Carreras and Bernard Delfont, which actually prohibited Forbes from making some of the films he wanted: 'the very slender resources at my disposal... meant that I had to cancel other films which I would have preferred and which, I think, might have more materially contributed to the commercial success of my programme' (Forbes in Meikle 2009: 185). However, whatever the reason, be it his prior dealings with Hammer as an actor and EMI production head, or his relationship with David Frost on *The Slipper and the Rose*, Hammer was keen to have Forbes both write and direct the picture.

This intention for Forbes to direct the film as well as write the script ultimately led to tensions between Forbes and Hammer. Forbes's contract was officially sent as a draft on 28 June 1976, but was summarised in a Hammer memo written on 11 June. Forbes was given four weeks to work on the screenplay at $10,000 a week (Anon: 11 June 1976). If the script was to Hammer's satisfaction, Forbes was then to be given first refusal to direct for a fee of $200,000 dollars for twenty-six weeks of production (Wesson and Williams to Carreras: 14 June 1976). Although this was only written as an 'option' to direct, there was a clear indication that Hammer fully expected Forbes to helm the picture. Even before the contract was drafted, Doug Netter, an associate of Euan Lloyd, wrote to potential financier Salah Hassanein and overtly stated that 'Forbes will direct the film'

(Netter to Hassanein: 23 June 1976). However, on 22 July 1976, while under contract to write *Nessie*, Forbes wrote to Carreras and Lloyd declining the offer to direct:

> In reaching and formally tendering my decision not to proceed with the Direction of the film, I felt that I must attempt some rational explanation for what you have been kind enough to say will be a great disappointment to you and is certainly a disappointment to me.

Forbes went on to say that he hoped the script proved that he had taken the project seriously, saying that he felt his draft offered a 'blueprint which could make an exciting and somewhat different film in this particular genre' (Forbes to Carreras and Lloyd: 22 July 1976). However, he also envisioned the film as needing 'a director who paints in broader strokes than [he] does' (Forbes to Carreras and Lloyd: 22 July 1976) referring to himself as a 'miniaturist' who had never 'lost sight of my own limitations' (Forbes to Carreras and Lloyd: 22 July 1976). Forbes, in his own way, essentially tells Carreras and Lloyd that the project is not within his capacity as a director. This seems a fair assessment as his work before had all been smaller budget fare, with even the grandiose *The Slipper and the Rose*, arguably Forbes's most mainstream and elaborate film, being in a totally different genre to *Nessie*, as well as significantly less expensive. However, one could also argue that Forbes was distancing himself from the project, feeling uncomfortable with *Nessie*'s exploitation roots. In the same letter, Forbes also seemed keen to distance himself from the script itself. He wrote:

> I think it would be very wrong for me ever to ask for sole authorship of the piece . . . I believe that full recognition should be accorded to those previous writers who provided the framework and basic construction of the script. (Forbes to Carreras and Lloyd: 22 July 1976)

In just this letter, Forbes withdrew as director and insisted on not being the screenplay's sole author. This suggests that perhaps Forbes was indeed enticed onto the project as a favour to his former producer David Frost, a notion compounded by a later letter from Forbes where he noted that 'it is a matter of fact that $40,000 is below my market rate for a rewrite' (Forbes to Carreras: 4 September 1976).

Although Forbes's true feelings about the project can only be speculated on, the tensions that this produced between him and Hammer demonstrate one way in which Hammer ultimately bears culpability for some of the issues that hindered the development of this project. Hammer had already told potential investors that Forbes was on board, and Forbes himself noted that Hammer had seemed particularly keen to have him. In his letter officially announcing that he will not direct the picture, when Hammer and Forbes were on more cordial terms, Forbes framed this as a flattering gesture, saying that he must explain his decision not to direct, a decision Hammer 'have been kind enough to say will be a great disappointment'. Yet by September, due to disputes over pay and screenplay alterations (which I will discuss later in this chapter), the relationship between Forbes and Hammer became less amicable, and Forbes offers insights which show just how much Hammer wanted him to direct the film. Forbes wrote that even on initially meeting with Hammer before the contracts were signed, Forbes had 'arrived at the decision ... the film was not my cup of tea as a director' (Forbes to Carreras: 4 September 1976). Forbes noted that making this decision so quickly should have benefited Hammer as he decided immediately as opposed to causing delay, allowing Hammer to begin searching for a new director immediately (ibid.). However, Forbes suggested that Lloyd and Carreras 'persuaded [him] to take a raincheck on the directorial assignment' (ibid.). This therefore suggests that Hammer had delayed the project by attempting to convince Forbes to direct the film, instead of taking his initial refusal and moving on to search for a new director. This is particularly significant since, as seen in the previous chapter, Hammer often cited time pressures as a key reason why the production was delayed, included the numerous postponements in sending the script to Toho and the time pressures Hammer stress to Columbia regarding the German tax shelter group. However, here it is clear that these time pressures were not merely a consequence of an independent company like Hammer trying to juggle several complex international deals but instead were, at least if we are to believe Forbes, largely of the company's own making.

Hammer's desperation to secure a writer/director of Forbes's standing was also already problematic due to the Toho deal. By this time, Hammer already had a longstanding deal with Toho to do the special effects, and Toho was already in production on these effects based on Starr's treatment and Wicking's drafts. As a result, Forbes was extremely limited in what he could change conceptually about the project, as he stated in the September letter to Carreras:

> You were at some pains to tell me that the basic conception could not be materially altered because of the arrangement with your Japanese partners and the fact that they had already commenced work and would be thrown by any drastic change. (Forbes to Carreras: 4 September 1976)

One must therefore question what Hammer felt it could offer Forbes. As writer/director, one would assume that he expected a fair amount of autonomy on any given project, being able to conceive and then execute his own work from page to screen. However, this was clearly not the case with *Nessie*. As a writer, Forbes's hands were tied by previous deals Hammer had made long before he joined the project, meaning he could only rewrite the screenplay around existing action set-pieces that could not be altered. Although perhaps cynical, one could suggest that where creative control was lacking, financial reward may also have been equally enticing. However, again this is clearly not the case in relation to *Nessie* since, as previously mentioned, Forbes was working below his market rate. Therefore, Hammer could not conceivably expect to attract a writer and director such as Forbes to *Nessie*, and by delaying the inevitable and refusing to look for other directors, Hammer stalled the project even further, causing additional pressure on Hammer's increasingly fractious relationships with existing partners.

As these international relationships became more and more strained, so too did Hammer's relationship with Forbes, primarily due to two factors. The first issue was the authorship of the screenplay itself. In a social visit to David Frost's house, Forbes had happened upon a script for *Nessie* on Frost's table and was angered by two things. One was that, despite Forbes making it clear that he had not wanted to be credited as the sole author of the script, he was in fact the only writer listed on the title page. Second, the script itself had been significantly amended without Forbes's knowledge, with no mention of this fact on the screenplay itself and no suggestion of who had made the amendments. Forbes was furious, and wrote to Carreras, noting that, although Hammer had the legal right to change Forbes script:

> What you <u>do not</u> have the right to do is to make such changes and, without reference to me, issue that script with a title page which

states I am the sole author. This I object to most strongly and will, if necessary, take legal action to prevent. (Forbes to Carreras: 28 August 1976)

Forbes is seemingly not angry about the changes made to the script, but instead that the amendments were made under his name. In the same letter, Forbes also noted that the reason he looked at Frost's copy of the script in the first place is that 'nobody had sent me a copy' (ibid.). This indicates a fundamental lack of communication between Hammer and Forbes, particularly when Carreras had sent a letter with his thoughts on Forbes's script on 11 August 1976 to Euan Lloyd, Chris Wicking, John Starr and Tom Sachs, but not Forbes himself. Carreras was clearly not fully content with Forbes's draft either, with his first point in the letter being that 'this is not a shooting script and a lot of very detailed work will have to be done before it becomes one' (Carreras to Lloyd et al.: 11 August 1976). Carreras then went on to list three pages of amendments he felt should be made to the script. Why Carreras did not tell Forbes about his grievances with the script is unknown, but it is clear that Carreras decided to change the script himself, amending it while still keeping Forbes listed as the sole author. This is confirmed by a letter from Carreras to Lloyd enclosing amendment pages (Carreras to Lloyd: 26 August 1976) for the script, sent two days before Forbes's letter to Carreras. The question of why Carreras would keep Forbes in the dark about these amendments is perplexing, as is the question of why Carreras would employ a writer of Forbes's talent only to alter his work without consultation. Forbes himself made this point:

On the purely practical and business level I find it odd that you employ somebody like me, and pay me high fees, presumably because you believe that I have shown evidence that I possess certain talents, and then proceed to change my work without further reference to me. (Forbes to Carreras: 28 August 1976)

He even noted that it was not an availability issue that stopped Carreras from consulting him, saying that 'I was also at some pains to tell you that I was available to do further work on the script, should my last revised version still require additional material' (ibid.). Along with the letter, Forbes also sent five pages of notes on the amended script, focusing primarily on why the changes made by Carreras actually made the script worse.

It is hard not to feel that this disagreement, in which Forbes threatened legal action against Hammer if the company did not alter the screenplay credit, could easily have been avoided if Hammer had approached Forbes directly with the issue, or even simply altered the script to reflect that it was no longer solely Forbes's work. This later point in particular also reflected badly on Hammer, given that in the correspondence where Forbes passed on directing the picture, he specifically asked that he would not be solely credited for the film.

What is also noteworthy is the dates in which this correspondence takes place, well after Forbes's initial four-week contract had ended. This was first brought up by Forbes's agent in a letter to Carreras on 10 August 1976, where he noted that not only was Forbes not fully paid in line with his contract (Forbes was still owed $20,000 of the original $40,000 (Williams to Carreras: 10 August 1976)), but he believed that Forbes was owed another $10,000 due to additional services rendered. It is worth emphasising that Hammer had failed to pay a client under contract their agreed fee, a fact that could potentially get lost in the numerous other issues between Hammer and Forbes. Although the $10,000 extra asked for by Williams was under special circumstances (which Carreras debated later), the blame for the fact that Hammer had simply not paid Forbes 50 per cent of his contracted fee laid squarely with them. Again, this calls into question Hammer's own conduct when putting together a film such as *Nessie*. The factors outside of the company's control were documented in the previous chapter, but paying the writer of the project on time rests solely with Hammer, and whatever the reason, be it disorganisation or simply not having the capital, it suggests once again Hammer was significantly out of its depth with *Nessie*.

This issue was exacerbated when Carreras replied to Williams's request saying that he 'feels strongly that Bryan has yet to complete his assignment' (Carreras to Williams: 31 August 1976). Here Carreras's clear frustration at Forbes for not accepting the role of director became blatantly apparent. He noted that the figure of $40,000 was agreed as it was presumed that Forbes would not only write the initial script, but 'as director Bryan would have accepted the screenplay that was delivered at the end of that period and then would have continued to re-write it until satisfied' (Carreras to Williams: 31 August 1976). Carreras suggested that the $40,000 offered to Forbes was not supposed to be just for the four weeks, but would have covered other writing/rewriting duties he would have taken during production of the film as director. Carreras finished his

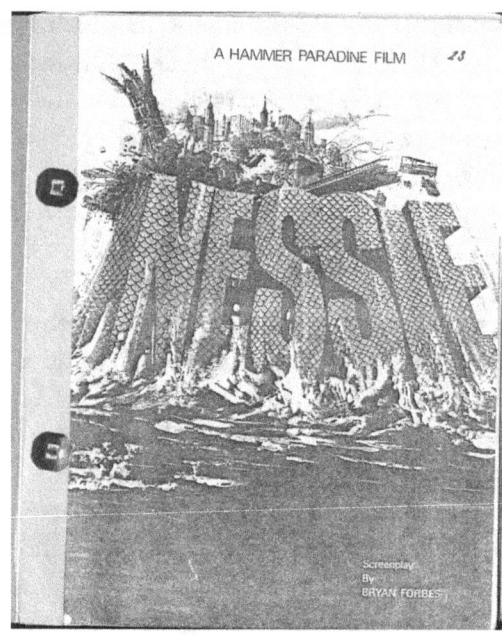

Figure 6.1 The title page of the screenplay *Nessie*. Credited solely to Bryan Forbes, despite alterations by Michael Carreras

response to Williams by clarifying what he meant when he says he feels Forbes had yet to complete his assignment: 'No major changes or thought are involved, only the refining and polishing of what is a major screenplay for a major film, for which we now have to attract a major director of Bryan's own calibre' (ibid.). This reaffirms the point made earlier within this section, that by Hammer assuming Forbes would direct, only for him to turn them down, the relationship between the two was irreversibly damaged. Forbes sent his own reply to Carreras noting that he handed in a first draft of his screenplay on 16 July, the second draft on 26 July and after a meeting on 3 August, 'went away and wrote a third draft, again incorporating the pooled suggestions' (Forbes to Carreras: 4 September 1976). In total, Forbes told Carreras that Hammer had his services for 'a total of seven weeks and two days' (Forbes to Carreras: 4 September 1976).

As noted in the previous chapter, one of the fundamental issues Toho had with Hammer was the company's failure to deliver the script on time, and the constant sending of changes and amendments, which made it impossible for Toho to actually begin designing the set pieces. With a treatment drafted on 6 January 1976, the fact that the script was still not finalised eight months later was clearly a huge issue for the project, and, unlike many of the issues that came from the international deals, the blame again lay solely with Hammer. Unlike the rest of the production, which truly was an international affair, the script was developed exclusively by Hammer, and their failure to secure a final screenplay after eight months of development, and writers such as John Starr, Christopher Wicking, Bryan Forbes and Carreras himself all having tackled the project, suggests again that regardless of the issues with financiers, Hammer was in no position to develop these big-budget projects.

Even after Carreras's amendments (or perhaps, Forbes would argue, because of these amendments) the script was still not enticing to potential investors. Martin Wragge, one of the potential investors that Hammer approached, bluntly itemised the script's problems in a letter to Carreras:

> I think the story is thin, the dialogue functional at best, the characters (with the exception of the girl) unsympathetic, and therefore, it seems to me, the success of the projects turns on the expertise of the sp fx people in Japan. IS THAT ENOUGH? (Wragge to Carreras: 31 August 1976)

Hammer therefore found themselves, even after the protracted disagreement with Forbes, without a script that could secure investment.

Carreras eventually agreed to pay Forbes the extra $10,000 for his additional work on the script (Williams to Carreras: September 1976), and Williams even offered Carreras Forbes's services to the eventual director: 'subject to his availability Bryan Forbes Ltd. could supply his services to consult with the director of the film and if requested to render further screen writing services' (Williams to Carreras: September 1976). However, by this point, it is hard to believe that the damage was not already done. Hammer had not only lost a potential ally of some standing in Forbes due to both financial issues and through questioning his commitment to the film, but in doing so had also caused multiple delays to a project that Carreras was always keen to stress was under immense time constraints.

This again emphasises the point that Hammer was really in no fit state to attempt to expand production to the level of *Nessie*. In trying to negotiate the tricky financial packaging overseas, Carreras was often slow in responding to letters, delaying the process further. For example, after Forbes's furious response to Carreras's letter which stated that Forbes had not fully completed his assignment, it took Carreras ten days to respond, saying that he had just 'returned from a week in Berlin' (Carreras to Forbes: 14 September 1976), which corresponds with a period when Carreras was attempting to secure the German tax shelter deal. After multiple letters from Williams to Carreras demanding to know why Forbes had yet to be paid his final $10,000 (letters dated 23 November and 16 December 1976), Carreras apologised for the delay and gave the explanation that he 'has just returned after three months in sunny California' (Carreras to Williams: 23 December 1976), which corresponds with the Columbia deal. Therefore, it seems that Hammer simply did not have enough staff to cover for Carreras's absences and to keep a project such as *Nessie* on schedule. There is no doubt that international deals were essential to the project, but to only be able to deal with each potential collaborator individually was quite clearly not sustainable on a project this size.

This issue was compounded as other projects began to take priority over *Nessie*. In 1977, Euan Lloyd began developing *The Wild Geese* (McLaglen, 1978), a $12 million production starring Richard Harris, Richard Burton and Roger Moore, which was to shoot in South Africa for eight weeks, and was 'probably the biggest British production since the days of *Lawrence of Arabia* and *The Guns of Navarone*' (Anon. 1977b: 13). Naturally this project had a long production process which took up a great deal of Lloyd's time, something that put him at odds with Carreras. In a letter to Lloyd in June 1977 which began 'whilst I'm always hopeful "no news is good news"' (Carreras to Lloyd: 29 June 1977), Carreras asked Lloyd for urgent updates regarding the Columbia deal and a potential television deal with the ABC Network. At the end of the letter Carreras signed off by telling Lloyd: 'I trust all goes well with the Wild Geese, but please understand that both Paradine and Hammer are totally concerned with the launching of "Nessie"' (Carreras to Lloyd: 29 June 1977). This (not particularly subtle) reference to Lloyd's other commitments impeding the progress of *Nessie* was even more pronounced when, as demonstrated throughout these chapters, it was primarily only Carreras and Lloyd who attempted to broker deals on *Nessie*. However, under similar circumstances, Lloyd also questioned Carreras's commitment to the project. As Hammer's last ever film under Carreras, *The Lady Vanishes* was given the greenlight and having, in his own words, 'sweated blood' (Lloyd to Carreras: 2 November 1977) over the Toho deal, Lloyd wrote to

Carreras asking him to confirm his commitment to the project: 'You have one helluva job to do at production level and I would not go to further trouble unless you personally commit wholeheartedly' (Lloyd to Carreras: 2 November 1977). Carreras replied with just four words: 'I am committed wholeheartedly' (Carreras to Lloyd: 4 November 1977). While it is difficult to dispute Carreras's own enthusiasm for the project, *Nessie* ultimately stands as a clear example of Hammer's domestic and international problems. At home, Hammer failed to keep collaborators such as Forbes on board, leading to a protracted development process that also affected international partners like Toho. Meanwhile, the project's enormity made it extraordinarily difficult for producers such as Lloyd to find finance or distribution. *Nessie* was undoubtedly an incredibly ambitious project, but ultimately, Hammer were in no position in the mid-to-late 1970s to be able to fulfil the project's potential.

Nessie sinks

In his chapter 'The End of Hammer', Wheeler Winston Dixon suggests that the key factor in Hammer's decline was that the company 'failed to understand the cultural shift that the end of the 1960s represented' (Dixon 2008: 14). This idea that Hammer, a major innovator of the British horror film in the late 1950s and 60s, gradually lost touch with its fan base is a pertinent one. In the 1970s in particular, Hammer relied on domestic comedy spin-offs such as *On the Buses* (Booth, 1971) and remakes such as *The Lady Vanishes*, while even the company's horror fare, such as *To the Devil a Daughter*, were influenced heavily by the success of American horror cinema such as *The Exorcist* (Friedkin, 1973). While these points could be used to argue that Hammer were in a financial and creative rut, this chapter's case study shows that the few pictures Hammer produced in this period do not tell the whole story. Instead, one must examine a project like *Nessie*, vast in scope and ambitious by almost any measure, to fully understand Hammer's downfall in the late 1970s.

Nessie in fact stands as the perfect microcosm of Hammer's decline, with myriad factors resulting in its eventual failure, some of Hammer's own doing and others entirely out of the company's hands. Whereas Hammer's produced films show a company in a creative rut, *Nessie* shows Hammer and its managing director Michael Carreras at their most self-destructively ambitious. Clearly aware that Hammer had to innovate not just in regard to what films the company produced but how these films were financed, Carreras embarked on an ambitious financial strategy. Seemingly taking some inspiration from the Shaw Brothers deal which saw Hammer and Shaw Brothers synthesise their particular genre expertise in an attempt to innovate their respective film cycles (horror and kung fu), Hammer turned to special effects veterans Toho to help develop *Nessie*. Although the Hammer/Shaw Brothers deal proved a harrowing experience for both parties, it at least saw two films produced and released.

Yet the Toho deal was also beset with problems and, emblematic of *Nessie* itself, these were both of Hammer's own doing and symptomatic of the broader film industry at the time. Carreras's tempestuous relationship with Bryan Forbes, which saw Forbes threaten to refer Hammer to the Writers Guild of America and take legal action, resulted in crucial delays which frustrated Toho and put time pressures on the entire project. Due to the piecemeal financing of *Nessie*, Hammer also found itself put in difficult situations as a result of previous deals. For example, Hammer could not offer Forbes the creative freedom necessary to entice him onto the project as both writer and director due to Toho having already begun work on specific effects sequences in the pre-existing script, limiting his ability to substantially change the screenplay. Hammer's existing relationship with Toho also impacted the proposed Columbia deal, with the Hollywood major reluctant to back the project with Toho on board. Although not Hammer's fault directly, the attempt to appease several different parties across multiple continents highlights the mammoth task the studio had set themselves.

This in turn leads to another key question when examining *Nessie*: was the project ever feasible? Hammer at this stage was 'reduced to a handful of executives and a few office staff' (Meikle 2009: 215) and this often led to numerous delays in responding to financial and creative partners on *Nessie*, with Lloyd and Carreras spread thin across other projects as well. The examination of Hammer's relationship with Forbes, as well as the screenplay itself, also suggests that Hammer's ambitions did not match the reality of its own situation. Yet, the project did provide Hammer with some short-term benefits. Despite *Nessie* never making it into production, Hammer did manage to secure some initial financing for the project. With Hammer's own finances in a dire state by late 1976 this *Nessie* pre-production money, according to Hammer board member Tom Sachs, did not only go towards launching the film, but was also used to 'bolster the company's finances as well' (cited in Meikle 2009: 222).

Nessie is an unmade production which had serious and tangible consequences for Hammer. On the one hand, its tortured near four-year development inevitably had a significant impact on Hammer's meagre resources, and significant consequences for other Hammer projects. *Nessie*, as well as Chapter 4's *Vampirella* and *Vlad the Impaler*, also no doubt contributed to Hammer's once fast-moving production slate shuddering to a halt. On the other hand, the project also demonstrates that although Hammer's late 1970s filmography depicts a studio suffering from chronic creative stagnation, Carreras was not only aware of Hammer's need to innovate but had a plan on how to do so. The detailed production file held in the Hammer Script Archive demonstrates that *Nessie* was not just erroneous wishful thinking, but the apex of a strategy which targeted international finance with big-budget productions.

Nessie's fate as an unmade $7 million Hammer blockbuster was sealed through Hammer's own faults, as well as a number of wider industrial factors that proved impossible to predict. The feeble state of the British film industry, as well as the American majors' weariness of Hammer's once efficacious brand of gothic horror, meant Hammer had to resort to creative piecemeal financing. However, as the project ballooned to $7 million it became almost inevitable that Hammer would be unable to sustain its myriad complex financial and creative relationships. As a result, *Nessie* stands as perhaps the most significant example of Carreras's doomed ambitions for a new era of Hammer.

Conclusion

With the failure of projects such *Nessie* throughout the 1970s, Michael Carreras's position at Hammer eventually became untenable, and he was removed as managing director in April 1979, after buying the company from his father James Carreras in 1973. It is difficult to compare father and son in regard to their success as chairman. Michael undoubtedly was operating at a fraught time for the industry, whereas James Carreras presided over Hammer at a time of prosperity and close Anglo-American industrial relations. However, despite the production contexts in which the two operated within being wildly different, some comparisons can be extracted. As noted in Chapter 1, Freddie Francis suggested that James Carreras 'loved the business side, the wheeler-dealing and the glamor' (Francis with Dalton 2013: 115) as opposed to the production of the films themselves. James Carreras, a former car salesman, was a pragmatic businessman not wedded to one genre of film. Porter, in his chapter 'The Context of Creativity: Ealing Studios and Hammer Films' in *British Cinema History* (Curran and Porter 1983), notes that James Carreras's primary goal as a producer was to simply 'produce films for the world market at a profit, without regard for the subject-matter of the films concerned' (193). Carreras himself freely admitted this, noting in an issue of *Variety* that, if the horror market were to collapse, 'I'm prepared to make Strauss waltzes tomorrow if they'll make money' (in Anon. 1958d: 7). Francis equated this pragmatism with a lack of interest in the films themselves, suggesting that as far as James Carreras was concerned, 'we could have been making furniture' (2013: 115). This may seem a dismissive comment from Francis, but on closer examination, by correctly identifying James Carreras's strengths as a businessman as opposed to a creative, Francis foregrounded an often-overlooked quality in the film producer. This trait is identified in the introduction to Spicer, McKenna and Meir's edited collection *Beyond the Bottom Line: The Producer in Film and Television Studies* (2014) as 'self-promotion and showmanship' (11). The authors go on to suggest that 'this showmanship need not always be outright self-promotion but includes an ability to promote and hence sell the "package"' (Spicer et al. 2014: 12). A crucial part of this is through the development of 'reputation networks' (ibid.), defined by Meir in a separate article as the 'ability to package and sell his products, first to financial backers then subsequently to distributors in order to stay in business' (Meir 2009: 470). Spicer and McKenna also elaborate on this trait in the conclusion to *The Man Who Got Carter: Michael Klinger, Independent Production and the British Film Industry 1960–1980* (2013), where they note in regard to Michael Klinger that his 'charisma was a vital if intangible asset in his producer's armoury' (194). Spicer, McKenna and Meir correctly identify this as an 'indispensable' (2014: 12) aspect of the producer, and it is undoubtedly where James Carreras's strengths lay as chairman, with his ability to nurture business relationships (often through his connections at the Variety Club) a fundamental component of Hammer's success in the 1950s and 1960s.

As intangible and immeasurable as this trait may be, an analysis of projects such as *Kali Devil Bride of Dracula*, *Nessie* and *Vampirella* suggests that this quality was not shared by Michael Carreras. As Hammer moved into the 1970s and the company's struggles began, James Carreras relied on prior relationships and old acquaintances to secure finance and distribution. This was noted in the previous section, with Bryan Forbes arguing that his tenure as head of production of EMI was marred due to the insistence by Bernard Delfont that Hammer were to have a place on their schedules (Meikle 2009: 185). However, the departure of James Carreras from the company saw the end of these 'old pal acts':

> Soon after [Michael bought Hammer] EMI support for future production (the development deal that was to have ensured Hammer's business continuity) was withdrawn. The reason was simple: cooperation between EMI and Hammer had been on a 'personal' basis, and as far as Bernard Delfont was concerned, Michael was *not* his father. (Meikle 2009: 205)

As well as the withdrawal of this existing relationship, an examination of Hammer's unmade projects shows Michael Carreras struggling to cultivate new ones. A crucial component in the failure of *Kali Devil Bride of Dracula* was the protracted writing process, exacerbated by the fractious relationship between Michael Carreras and Don Houghton. This inability to work productively with writers is emphasised even further in Carreras's relationship with Bryan Forbes on *Nessie*, which soured so dramatically that Forbes even threatened to take Carreras to court. Outside of these creative conflicts, Michael Carreras's Hammer also struggled to maintain any lasting international partnerships, with their deals with Shaw Brothers, Toho and Rank all ending acrimoniously. Despite his clear passion for the company, Michael Carreras simply seemed to lack the requisite charm and charisma often found in the most successful producers.

As emphasised previously, Michael Carreras's decisions and relationships as chairman of Hammer cannot be separated from the financial constraints he found himself working within. During James Carreras's time as chairman, *Variety* published an article that detailed his finance and distribution strategies: 'According to Carreras, the deals vary from picture to picture and include outright buys of Hammer financed pictures or involve co-production deals' (Anon. 1958d: 7). It is key here to note the 'outright buy' part of this strategy. Ever the pragmatist, James Carreras was seemingly more concerned with the immediate benefits of these international deals and less with the long-term implications of selling the entirety of the project's rights to a financier or distributor. This was a lesson that Michael Carreras was to learn the hard way when he inherited the company from his father, noting that '80 percent of what I thought was there wasn't there at all' (in Meikle 2009: 207).

The failure of later projects such as *Nessie* undoubtedly contributed to Hammer's closure, yet even at the time Michael Carreras took over the company, Hammer was by no means at the height of their success. In the *Fangoria* interview in 1987, Michael Carreras positioned the buyout as an emotional and irrational business move:

> I discovered my father was secretly negotiating to sell Hammer to EMI... I was bloody cross, and may have made some rather hasty, regrettable decisions. I knew I didn't want him to do what he was doing, so I set about preventing him and captured Hammer for myself... I was pissed off that I hadn't been told what was happening. Perhaps I overreacted. (Carreras in Swires 1987: 61–2)

Whereas James Carreras 'quit while the going was good' (Brian Lawrence in Meikle 2009: 207), Michael had made a rash decision based not only on his anger at his father, but on his affection for a company which had originally been his grandfather's. James Carreras, who had never displayed any affection for the film business in particular nor the horror films Hammer had become most notable for, clearly gauged that Hammer were exhausting the financial and distribution networks they had depended on in the 1950s and 1960s and left Hammer as the decline began. Michael Carreras had always been heavily involved in the creative process of filmmaking as a writer and director, with the lack of creative freedom being one of the key reasons he left Hammer in 1961, frustrated in his role as executive producer and wanting to get back 'to the floor' (Carreras in Swires 1987: 61).

These creative instincts saw Michael Carreras produce a bold and innovative strategy for the declining company, with the purpose of reigniting interest in the Hammer brand. Projects such as *Kali Devil Bride of Dracula*, *Vampirella*, *Vlad the Impaler* and *Nessie* demonstrate the scale of ambition Michael Carreras had for the company, and refute any claims of creative stagnation at Hammer in the mid-to-late 1970s. As I examined in this chapter (and Chapter 3) these creative instincts are the key reason Carreras's relationship with writers such as Houghton and Forbes broke down, with Carreras often trying to impose his own ideas onto writers despite often extremely limiting production contexts (such as Houghton on *Kali Devil Bride of Dracula*) or causing conflict due to meddling with others work uncredited and without their permission (such as with Forbes on *Nessie*).

Ultimately, Michael Carreras's tenure as chairman of Hammer was fundamentally undermined from its inception, due to the short-term pragmatism of its former owner James Carreras. Michael Carreras's passion for the film industry stood in stark contrast to his father's but proved both a blessing and a curse for Hammer. As these chapters have shown, Michael Carreras's creative instincts offered new ways for the company to potentially innovate its production slate and gain international recognition, but they also often frustrated creative and financial partners, and isolated Hammer when they were in desperate need of new financial and distribution networks. This was the end of the Carreras era at Hammer, but it was not the end of Hammer Films.

7

High stakes: the Roy Skeggs years

This chapter will examine the transition from the era of Michael Carreras to Roy Skeggs and Brian Lawrence, and Skeggs's subsequent two decades as the sole managing director of Hammer. In order to examine Skeggs's time at the company as managing director, the unmade projects do not only become essential tools but in fact the only way to get any semblance of the company's planned output, as no films were produced under Skeggs's tenure. As such, the majority of studies on Hammer do not cover Skeggs's directorship in any depth.

Despite the attempts detailed in previous chapters, Carreras failed to keep Hammer afloat and in April 1979 Hammer was put into the hands of an official receiver at the Insolvency Service, with Carreras removed as managing director. Skeggs and Lawrence were invited by the ICI (the creditors of Pension Fund Services (PFS) who by 1979 technically owned Hammer) to continue collecting the royalties from the Hammer library, as the ICI 'clearly had no use for a film production company or library' (Hearn and Barnes 2007: 171). As such, 1979 was 'the year the that Hammer changed hands for the first time since its inception in 1934' (Walker 2016: 111).

However, it would be difficult to define Skeggs's tenure at Hammer as the start of a new era. Skeggs had been a fixture at Hammer since October 1963, initially serving as production accountant on *The Evil of Frankenstein* (Francis, 1964) before being promoted to the company's accountant two years later (Kinsey 2010: 73). Michael Carreras's return to the company in 1971 saw Skeggs promoted to production supervisor and, by November 1974, he had taken the place of the recently resigned Brian Lawrence on the board of directors at Hammer (Kinsey 2010: 73).

Less than one year later, however, he also tendered his resignation: 'Skeggs' resignation was formally noted by a despondent Carreras at a meeting held on Wednesday 17 December 1975' (Hearn and Barnes 2007: 169). Despite Skeggs and Lawrence resigning from the board, both continued to manage Hammer's film library and collect royalties, and were the clear candidates to take over Hammer from the ICI after Carreras's forced departure (Kinsey 2010: 73; Hearn and Barnes 2007: 16).

Early in his term as co-managing director with Brian Lawrence, Skeggs produced two television series under the Hammer banner, *Hammer House of Horror* (1980) and *Hammer House of Mystery and Suspense* (1984–5), and these are often noted or analysed in works such as *The Hammer Vault* (Hearn 2011) or *Hammer on Television* (Hallenbeck 2018). However, Skeggs's time at Hammer is more often cited as just a footnote, with most histories or analyses of the company ending in 1979. This is almost certainly down to the complete lack of produced films during the period of 1980 to 2000. Yet this does not mean Skeggs was not trying to get projects produced in his two decades in charge.

One project that was developed for nearly Skeggs's entire term as managing director was *Vlad the Impaler*. As noted in Chapter 4, the Dracula origin story originally began development under Carreras in 1974 as an adaptation of Brian Hayles's Radio 4 drama, *Lord Dracula* (1974). *Vlad the Impaler* would have been an important project in Carreras's attempts to produce larger scale, big-budget productions for international markets, yet the project outlasted Michael Carreras's tenure and became a stalwart of the Skeggs era. Under Skeggs, *Vlad the Impaler* underwent a tremendous amount of developmental and pre-production work. As such, *Vlad the Impaler* clearly demonstrates that Skeggs was not merely content with Hammer's sporadic television output, but had clear plans to move Hammer back into theatrical production.

This chapter will trace the development of Hammer's unmade *Vlad the Impaler* during Skeggs's tenure primarily utilising the Hammer Script Archive and contemporaneous trade magazines. As well as the previously discussed *Dracula the Beginning*, there are four other *Vlad the Impaler* scripts credited to Brian Hayles, but with one separate credit for additional material on each script. These are accredited to Arthur Ellis (Ellis undated), John Peacock (Peacock undated) and Jonas McCord, with McCord being credited on one script with the title *Vlad the Impaler* (McCord undated) and an identical but renamed version called *Vlad Dracul*. *Vlad the Impaler* will therefore act as a through-line throughout the managerial changeover and the following decades. In effect, this chapter will present a comprehensive timeline on an unmade film in order to gain an understanding of a twenty-year period where Hammer were, in terms of produced films at least, seemingly entirely inactive.

Vlad the Impaler 1980–90

This point in Hammer's history is where almost every study of the company ends. The removal of Carreras in 1979 is in some respects a natural end point. It marks the last time a Carreras or Hinds would ever work at the company, and more importantly no feature films were released by Hammer for almost three decades after. One of the few studies to examine Hammer post-1979 appears in Johnny Walker's *Contemporary British Horror Cinema* in the chapter 'Let the Quiet Ones in' (2016: 109–29), which covers Hammer's revival in the twenty-first century, their development as a brand and their recent filmic output. Walker gives a brief analysis of Hammer from 1979 to 2005, before primarily focusing on their return to film production. However, despite briefly contextualising the company's thirty-year hiatus, the period between 1980 and 2000 is outside the scope of the chapter, and is not given detailed consideration. In fact, Hammer in the years 1979 to 2000 has received no consideration in any industrial or production history of the company. No films were produced, but the company remained active, and an examination of their unmade projects reveals a number of attempts to close several international production finance deals. The following chapter therefore looks to present a detailed examination of a lost period of Hammer history, illuminate the production methods of Roy Skeggs and draw comparisons between this iteration of Hammer and the one that preceded it.

With Carreras removed as managing director in 1979, Roy Skeggs and Brian Lawrence were brought on quickly by the creditors. As well as their associations with Hammer, Skeggs and Lawrence had a separate production company called Cinema Arts International. Through this production company, Skeggs and Lawrence focused on adapting British sitcoms for theatrical release such as *Rising Damp* (McGrath, 1980) and *George and Mildred* (Frazer-Jones, 1980). Through the revenue gained by these television spin-offs and the success of the television series produced by Skeggs and Lawrence – *Hammer House of Horror* – Skeggs and Lawrence cleared Hammer's debts with the ICI and bought back Hammer for $100,000

(Kinsey 2007: 417; Meikle 2009: 225; Hearn and Barnes 2007: 171). Hammer's debt was cleared and Skeggs and Lawrence were the outright owners of Hammer, and they began in earnest to consider production under the Hammer banner.

With Skeggs and Lawrence definitively in charge, one could see how this could be seen as a new era of Hammer Films. It was the first time Hammer had ever been owned by someone outside of the Carreras family and the decision to have *Hammer House of Horror*, a television series, as their first project suggested a new creative focus and market for the reborn company. While its immediate focus on television would prove to be an indicator of where Skeggs's and Lawrence's priorities lay in the early to mid-1980s, the idea that this was in any way a new iteration of Hammer would ultimately prove to be false. As noted in the introduction to this chapter, Skeggs had been associated with Hammer since 1963, holding various roles at the company for over twelve years. Lawrence himself joined Hammer 'mere months after James Carreras' (Kinsey 2010: 18) in 1945, working primarily as a sales manager before eventually also joining Hammer's board of directors. These intrinsic links back to the old Hammer were also compounded by the reliance on screenwriter John Peacock as the key creative liaison within this period. Peacock had worked at Hammer as a screenwriter in the 1970s under Carreras, writing *Straight on Till Morning* (Collinson, 1972) and *To the Devil a Daughter* (Sykes, 1976) for the company. Peacock's role at Hammer under Skeggs and Lawrence would be a significant one. After initially being brought on as a story editor for the television show *Hammer House of Mystery and Suspense*, Peacock became the driving creative force at Hammer in this period, not only producing his own draft of *Vlad the Impaler* in the late 1980s (discussed further in this section), but also acting as the key 'go between' for Hammer and Arthur Ellis, a British writer and the first drafted by Skeggs and Lawrence to rewrite *Vlad the Impaler*.

This section will examine Ellis and Peacock's work on *Vlad the Impaler* to argue two key points about Hammer in the 1980s. First, Skeggs and Lawrence's decision to prioritise television over Hammer's potential theatrical output fatally impeded any potential progress on *Vlad the Impaler* due to the company's limited creative and financial resources at the time. Second, this section will posit that viewing Skeggs and Lawrence's takeover of Hammer as a new phase for the company is a misnomer, with it still firmly in the grasp of Hammer's old guard. As a result, key creative decisions on pre-existing projects such as *Vlad the Impaler*, which had been held in such reverence by key figures at Hammer in the 1970s, are left in a state of inertia which ultimately prevented them from moving into production.

Skeggs and Lawrence's immediate focus on television production at Hammer is not particularly surprising. Hammer had always been interested in gaining a foothold in the television market, as noted in Chapter 1's discussion of *Tales of Frankenstein* in 1958. Whereas Michael Carreras in the 1970s had primarily tried to combat the popularity of television by attempting to mount bigger and more bombastic blockbusters, Skeggs and Lawrence simply seemed to acknowledge the shift noted by Sarah Street in her examination of the decline of British cinema in the 1970s, that one of the primary reasons for the collapse was that 'cinema admissions were declining at the same time as the popularity of television and other amusements increased' (Street 2009: 105). By 1983, Skeggs and Lawrence had produced two television shows under the Hammer banner.

As noted, *Hammer House of Horror* allowed Skeggs and Lawrence to clear Hammer's debts with the ICI and buy back Hammer. The second show, *Hammer House of Mystery and Suspense*, gave an indication of their long-term strategy. Skeggs and Lawrence enlisted American studio 20th Century Fox to produce *Hammer House of Mystery and Suspense*. This deal and Hammer's shift to television in the early 1980s suggest that Skeggs and Lawrence had learned a valuable lesson from Carreras's failures. Despite complex co-production deals on films such as *To the Devil a Daughter* and *Legend of the 7 Golden Vampires* (Ward Baker, 1974), as well as attempts to raise international finance outside of America for projects such as *Nessie*, Carreras did not manage to keep the company afloat after the withdrawal of American finance. Skeggs and Lawrence diversifying away from theatrical production immediately, as well as their courting of 20th Century Fox, suggests that they were keen to set out a new strategy for Hammer going forward. However, despite their short-term success in the early eighties in television production, theatrical film production would prove more difficult.

The first attempt by Skeggs to redevelop *Vlad the Impaler* is with British writer Arthur Ellis, with a script held within the Hammer Script Archive listed as being written by Brian Hayles with additional material by Arthur Ellis. There is another draft of *Vlad the Impaler* also with the same credit, which is an identical draft but with pencil annotations and deletions (Ellis undated). In an interview I conducted with Ellis on 30 April 2016, Ellis dated his work on the script to 'around 82/83' (Ellis 2016), after Skeggs and Lawrence had bought Hammer back from the creditors. Ellis noted that he was approached by John Peacock, who 'was working fairly full time at Hammer' (ibid.) as the script editor on the project and 'go-between' (ibid.) for Ellis, Skeggs and Lawrence. The fact that it was John Peacock who approached Ellis on behalf of Hammer certainly aligns with the '82/83' timeframe given by Ellis. Don Houghton was initially 'appointed head of Hammer's script and story department' in 1981 (Kinsey 2007: 421) but fell ill during the production of *Hammer House of Mystery and Suspense* (which began development in 1983). Peacock was brought in to finish the television series, and stayed on with Hammer after its completion (Kinsey 2007: 421). It is therefore likely that Ellis was developing the *Vlad the Impaler* script parallel with the production of *Hammer House of Mystery and Suspense* in 1983, a point discussed later in this section.

Despite being early in Skeggs and Lawrence's tenure, Ellis's time working on *Vlad the Impaler* suggests a tension at Hammer between wanting to engage new writers to rework and modernise projects, and holding existing work on *Vlad the Impaler* in an almost reverential state, ultimately impeding any major alterations or departures from the old Hammer model. Ellis noted in the interview that he received a brief from Peacock on how Hammer were looking to reimagine the project, with Ellis noting that 'the way I understood it they wanted it to be modernised ... a bit less period gothic and more *Omen*-y type gothic' (Ellis 2016). This brief was quite broad and lacked any detail on specific changes Skeggs and Lawrence were looking for in the new draft. As such, Ellis's draft remains largely the same as Hayles's original screenplay.

However, despite this similarity, the draft does feature additional material by Ellis, which can be seen as a response to Peacock's brief. The screenplay is literally modernised by Ellis through the creation of a contemporary prologue and epilogue. The prologue features an action set-piece that sees a vampire-hunter clearing out a nest of vampires in a dilapidated house, before his ruminations on the origin of the vampire sees the narrative shift back to the time of Vlad the Impaler, where Hayles's original story begins. The epilogue is on the last page of the script and takes us back to present day as the vampire hunter leaves the house. It seemingly teases a present-day sequel, with the last words spoken by the hunter being: 'oh where shall we meet, my sad Lord Dracula ... that we may duel once again' (Ellis undated: 139).

Although Ellis recounted this structural change as his primary alteration to Hayles's script, he also infused his draft with several overtly supernatural sequences which arguably have a greater effect on the narrative as a whole. In Hayles's screenplay it is not until page 42 of the 118-page draft that the witch Militsa appears, the first acknowledgment of the supernatural within the script. However, not only does Ellis immediately set up the script as a supernatural drama by adding a prologue featuring vampires, he also introduces supernatural elements much earlier in the narrative's main timeline. For example, on page 6 of Ellis's script a demonic horse named Salmander (who Vlad later takes as his own) is birthed from Hell, said to be sent by Satan himself: 'we are left in no doubt that the Devil has given birth to a plan of awesome evil . . . ' (Ellis undated: 7). Clearly Ellis's inclusion of supernatural material from the very start of the script marks his as a very different take on the project to Hayles.

Yet the second copy of Ellis's screenplay held in the Hammer Script Archive is annotated, and shows that it was these sequences that Skeggs and Lawrence were dissatisfied with. Many of the more overt supernatural sequences, such as the demonic horse at the beginning of the screenplay, are crossed out in pencil, leaving the modern prologue and epilogue as the only significant additions by Ellis to Hayles's original draft. Ellis himself expressed confusion as to why he was drafted in to work on what was clearly a revered script: 'according to John . . . the script was very, very much appreciated. They [Hammer] liked the script' (Ellis 2016). As a result, Ellis felt that the changes he made were incremental and added little to the screenplay:

> I said to John I don't know why I'm doing this, I'm only doing this because it's different, and that's my only criteria for doing it. I don't understand why I'm . . . I'm only putting a modern bookend type thing in it so I can say I've done a rewrite on it. There didn't seem to be any logic to it that I could work out. (Ellis 2016)

This suggests an indecisiveness on the part of Skeggs and Lawrence. By bringing on Ellis, Skeggs and Lawrence are clearly acknowledging that Hayles's original screenplay needed to be updated. Yet the contemporary scenes added by Ellis are set in a dilapidated manor, an intrinsically gothic setting with no real temporal attachment to the present day (similar to the issues with the portrayal of Dracula in *Dracula A.D. 1972* discussed in Chapter 3). Skeggs and Lawrence's reluctance to allow anything more than a small structural change suggests that they were unsure what ultimately needed altering in Hayles's original screenplay.

However, when considering *Vlad the Impaler*'s protracted and often convoluted development in this period, it is pertinent to note that it comes at a time when Skeggs and Lawrence were clearly far more concerned with Hammer's television enterprise as opposed to theatrical production. During Ellis's work on *Vlad the Impaler*, Hammer's limited resources were stretched with regards to the deal with 20th Century Fox to produce *Hammer House of Mystery and Suspense*. This ambitious co-production for television saw Hammer having to find the capital to produce the first two episodes, as well as find a way to extend the scripts from their original runtime of sixty minutes to ninety at the behest of Fox (Ilott 1984: 13). Although Fox had insisted on the 90-minute runtime (ibid.), the limited budget and 'extremely tight schedules' (ibid.) made the anthology series an extremely pressured process for Skeggs and Lawrence. As a result of this, and the fact the first two episodes were fully funded by Hammer, *Hammer House of Mystery and Suspense* undoubtedly became a priority, with all potential theatrical productions put on hold.

Ellis's time on *Vlad the Impaler* ultimately came to an end with the project no closer to production. Despite this lack of success, Ellis was recruited by Hammer again in the late 1980s (through Peacock) to work on an adaptation of the unpublished novel *Charlie* by R. P. Blount. The Hammer Script Archive holds an undated 'confidential report' from Peacock to Skeggs, which includes a story breakdown and locations for *Charlie*, and potential ways Hammer could adapt it as a television series. Sometime after this, Ellis is approached by Peacock to adapt it as a feature film entitled *Black Sabbath* (Ellis 2016). At least three years seem to have passed since Ellis's worked on *Vlad the Impaler*, as the *Black Sabbath* (Ellis undated(c)) screenplay rights were not acquired by Hammer until 16 April 1986 (Anon. 2000a). Ellis worked much longer on this project than he did *Vlad the Impaler*, writing the screenplay (he is listed as sole author on the script) and also doing a number of revisions on his first draft. In my interview with him, Ellis recalls working on the project for 'a number of months' (Ellis 2016).

Hammer's reasoning for rehiring Ellis after the unsuccessful work on the *Vlad the Impaler* project is difficult to ascertain. As noted in earlier chapters, Hammer had initially risen to prominence in the mid-to-late 1950s through the refining of a recurring Hammer style, which came through a reliance on previous contacts and recurring workers to craft a consistent style and tone. Yet these contacts and workers only became recurring figures after the success of *The Curse of Frankenstein* (Fisher,

1957). There is a clear logic in procuring the same cast and crew after a successful picture, but Ellis is rehired by Hammer only after the relative failure of the *Vlad the Impaler* rewrite, suggesting that Hammer was simply utilising Ellis due to their relatively limited resources. This is perhaps best reflected by the late Denis Meikle, in an interview I conducted in November 2016, where he spoke about a visit to Hammer under Skeggs in the 1980s: 'I went to see him at Elstree, he had one girl, one secretary girl outside, and him at his big desk, that was Hammer' (Meikle 2016). Despite being listed on a production slate for Hammer in the 4 July edition of *Screen International* in 1987 (Falks: 2), *Black Sabbath* ultimately never moved past the scripting stage. This inertia again calls into question why Skeggs and Lawrence looked to Ellis to develop the project after the issues on *Vlad the Impaler*. The examination of *Vlad the Impaler*'s development under Ellis and Meikle's above quote suggests it was out of necessity, with the company having lacked the creative resources it once had.

With Ellis's draft of *Vlad the Impaler* not moving forward at Hammer, the project stalled once more. Brian Lawrence would retire from Hammer in May 1985 following the end of *Hammer House of Mystery and Suspense* (Meikle 2009: 225; Kinsey 2007: 423), selling his stake in the company and leaving Skeggs as the sole owner of Hammer. The end of *Hammer House of Mystery and Suspense* would also ultimately signal the end of Hammer's television output as well. Skeggs noted that despite the difficult production, the show was initially renewed by Fox due to the studio being 'pleased with foreign sales, and delighted with the low cost of production' (Skeggs to Klemensen 2016: 47). However, Skeggs's primary contact at the studio, Steve Roberts, left Fox, leading to the studio cancelling Robert's future portfolio (Skeggs in Klemensen 2016: 47). This was the end of Hammer's television output under Skeggs (not including retrospectives or documentaries such as *Flesh and Blood: The Hammer Heritage of Horror* (Newsom, 1994)).

However, the late 1980s did see a potential revival in Hammer's hopes of restarting theatrical production. An article in *Screen International* in July 1987 tells of a deal being brokered between Skeggs and American producer Steve Krantz. The deal, which came 'following two years of intensive financial planning and packaging' (Falks 1987: 2) on Skeggs's part, lists five films on Hammer's slate, ready to begin theatrical production: *The House On The Strand*, *The Haunting of Toby Jugg*, *Vlad the Impaler*, *Black Sabbath* and *The White Witch of Rose Hall*. The announcement that

Hammer was back in active production with *Vlad the Impaler* coincides with another draft of the script held in the archive, with this iteration being bought by Hammer in December 1988 (Anon. 2000a). Brian Hayles is still listed as the sole writer, but revisions have this time been completed by John Peacock.

The script discards all of Ellis's changes (including the prologue and epilogue), with Peacock instead revising Hayles's original draft. The first and second act are extremely similar to Hayles's script, with only formatting issues being the key difference. There is, however, a significant change in the third act of the script. In Hayles's original draft (also maintained by Ellis in his revisions), Vlad and Militsa hold a black mass to turn Vlad into the vampire Dracula. Vlad dies but through the ceremony is later reborn. When Vlad is declared dead in the Hayles draft, Vlad and Militsa concoct a plot to retain his fortune and estate by leaving it to his estranged younger brother Vlaachim, whom no one previously knew existed. Vlaachim arrives to take over the estate and is welcomed by most as the new heir to Vlad's fortune. However, after the monk Benedek and Vlad's son Istvan inspect Vlad's grave and find his body missing, they realise that Vlaachim is in fact a revitalized and newly youthful Vlad, now a vampire. It is a convoluted twist, but works sufficiently enough in the radio play, where the slight change in the vocal performance of the lead actor makes the characters of Vlad and Vlaachim distinguishable. Yet on screen the artifice of characters not recognizing Vlaachim as Vlad (who, if like the radio play, would be played by the same actor), would perhaps impact the spectator's suspension of disbelief. Peacock rectifies this, by altering the narrative so that Vlad has left all his estate and fortune to Militsa, making her the ruler of Tirgoviste. This simplifies the narrative while also circumventing the complications of realising the Vlaachim twist on camera.

This was by far Peacock's greatest change to Hayles's original screenplay, emphasising the lack of revisions to a now fifteen-year-old script. Like Ellis before him, Peacock seems to have been restricted by the changes he could make to the script. Whereas Ellis was a freelancer working for Hammer, Peacock had an extensive background with the company and is effectively their in-house script editor at this stage. The fact that the revisions were done by Peacock also seems to compound the notion that Hammer were reluctant or unable to seek new writers and talent. Nine years into his tenure as chairman of Hammer, Skeggs still seemed gripped by the same issues apparent when Ellis was brought on to revise *Vlad the Impaler*.

Despite this, there is some evidence which suggests this latest draft of the screenplay by Peacock moved *Vlad the Impaler* the closest it had been to production since the 1970s. The Hammer Script Archive holds a shooting schedule which corresponds with Peacock's revisions. The schedule takes into account whether a scene will be interior or exterior, whether it is set at day or night, how many actors or stunt actors will be necessary and any other potential 'special requirements' for the sequence. The careful planning of each scene suggests a move forward in the writing process, as they begin to break down each scene into its component parts in preparation for potential production. It could therefore be presumed that, if this document was being produced, the script had been finalised and that Hammer was now putting the film into pre-production. The fact that Hammer had also announced a co-production deal with Krantz for *Vlad the Impaler* only a year before also supports the idea it was the closest it had been to production under Skeggs.

However, despite this promising sign the schedule is missing some information which would have been crucial if the production was in fact close to filming. The information given in the schedule is exclusively based on the script, with no details of filming locations, dates or crew featured at all. The question of why a schedule even exists at this stage could perhaps be tied to Peacock's position at Hammer. If Peacock was working closely with Skeggs as a script editor, he would have been aware of the need to have a schedule prepared for the film once the script was written, and therefore could have produced it concurrently with the script, as opposed to sometime after.

Despite the revised screenplay, schedule and the announcement of possible American finance through the deal with Steve Krantz, neither *Vlad the Impaler* nor any of the mooted projects made a significant step into production. Whereas one could see the inclusion of a schedule for *Vlad the Impaler* which correlates with the screenplay as a comparatively positive step forward from Ellis's draft, the fact that it is Peacock who has revised the script also potentially presents a step backwards. With the project being developed by Peacock with Skeggs overseeing it, *Vlad the Impaler* was effectively in the hands of two people who had been working with Hammer since 1963 and 1972 respectively. Although the installation of Skeggs and Lawrence in 1979 seemed to signal a new iteration of Hammer, removed from both James and Michael Carreras's tenures, nearly a decade later it was still very much the Hammer old guard developing a project that, in this instance, had also been in development for over a decade at the time.

Hammer International: *Vlad the Impaler* 1990–2000

By the advent of the 1990s Skeggs had been in charge of the company for a decade with no feature films produced. However, while the 1980s saw the prioritising of television production and a growing reliance on a small circle of writers such as Peacock and Ellis, in the 1990s Skeggs altered his strategy for Hammer. With Hammer's original gothic horror successes such as *The Curse of Frankenstein* and *Dracula* now over thirty years old, the notion that Hammer was a respectable company with a legacy of innovation in the genre was beginning to take hold. Wayne Kinsey specifically dates the moment this change occurs, noting that 'in August 1996, Hammer became respectable again when the Barbican celebrated 40 years of Hammer Horror' (2007: 424). Yet as this section will go on to detail, Skeggs recognised this shift towards nostalgic respectability for Hammer's former films even earlier, and began to focus on the potential of Hammer's existing library of films.

As this section will detail, Skeggs made a number of American finance and production deals at this time based solely on the option to remake past Hammer productions. Yet despite this change in approach, *Vlad the Impaler* remained a consistent fixture on Hammer's production slate throughout the period. A new draft was written by American writer Jonas McCord and will be analysed in relation to the other drafts of the script later in this section. Tracing the development of *Vlad the Impaler* will also illuminate by far the biggest production deal Skeggs made as managing director of Hammer, which was a long-term deal with Warner Bros. Skeggs's new strategy saw a focus on pre-existing properties and a clear attempt to garner American finance, tactics which were much more in line with Hammer's previous iterations under both James and Michael Carreras.

The beginning of the 1990s presented the best opportunity yet for *Vlad the Impaler*. Stacey Abbott suggests that the Oscar winning success of *The Silence of the Lambs* (Demme, 1992) 'renewed Hollywood's interest in the horror genre in the 1990s, with the main studios returning to classic horror tales ... but now reinvented through the lens of the high concept movie' (Abbott 2009: 29). A key example of this new blockbuster horror trend of the 1990s was Francis Ford Coppola's *Bram Stoker's Dracula*, released in 1992 to significant commercial success, grossing over $200 million from a $40 million budget. Although there is no material held within the Hammer Script Archive that suggest Skeggs took particular notice of *Bram Stoker's*

Dracula, the film's prologue, which sees Vlad Tepes's transformation into Dracula and the circumstances in which it happens (immediately following the death of his wife), draw clear similarities with Hammer's then near twenty-year-old *Vlad the Impaler* project. The box office receipts for the film also clearly demonstrated that a Dracula project could still do significant international business.

The link between *Bram Stoker's Dracula* and *Vlad the Impaler* is merely speculative, but a more concrete move forward for the project (and Hammer generally) occurred only a year later. The July 30 1993 edition of *Screen International* ran an article entitled 'Hammer back from the Dead' (Bateman 1993: 2), detailing a new deal between Hammer and Warner Bros. (specifically Schuler and Donner Productions) to produce 'a major slate of titles in 1994, including a series of remakes of classic Hammer titles' (ibid.). This information alone indicated a more auspicious arrangement than the one six years before with Krantz, with a studio co-production deal as opposed to the finance of one producer. The co-production deal was also indicated to be long term, with Hammer intending to 'make five films with Warner for the next year and 15 more over the following three years' (ibid.). The deal seemed to focus mainly on remaking Hammer titles, naming '*The Quatermass Experiment* [sic], *Stolen Face* and *The Devil Rides Out*' (ibid.). The idea to move away from new projects and perhaps exploit the existing Hammer titles from the 1950s and 1960s seems to have been a deliberate effort from Skeggs to move Hammer back into active production, and, as posited at the beginning of this section, seems to be a deliberate shift away from Skeggs's strategy in the 1980s to develop original titles under the Hammer name. Ellis's work for Hammer in the early eighties on *Vlad the Impaler* and *Black Sabbath* may have been adaptations (a radio play and an unpublished book respectively), but they were not remakes of old Hammer films. Similarly, the 1987 Krantz deal listed five properties ready to put in to production and while some were adaptations, none were Hammer remakes.

It did not necessarily seem to be the Warner deal that instigated this shift in Hammer's production strategy. As mentioned in the *Screen International* article, Hammer had a 'separate deal' (ibid.) to remake Val Guest's *The Day the Earth Caught Fire* (1961), working with the 'UK's Winchester Films for Twentieth Century Fox' (ibid.). Despite the original *The Day the Earth Caught Fire* not being a Hammer film, a script for the proposed remake by Kevin Quinn is held within the Hammer Script Archive and although undated, three drafts of this project were registered with the Writers Guild of America, the first on 1 June 1992. As with the Warner Bros. deal, Hammer's relationship with Winchester Films (also referred to as Winchester Productions) seems to have been focused specifically on remaking old Hammer properties. The Hammer Script Archive holds a script dated 25 June 1992 entitled *Legacy* (Sidaway and Sidaway) which, despite having 'Winchester Productions' written on its cover, has no writer listed on the screenplay itself. The Script Archive also holds a document from 29 February 2000, which is an exhaustive audit of all of Hammer's unmade projects past and present, with the key goal seemingly being to understand who holds the underlying screen rights for these projects (Anon. 2000a). *Legacy* is listed on this document, and the writers are listed as Robert and Ashley Sidaway (founders of Winchester Pictures). Furthermore, the project is described as a 'remake of Quatermass and the Pit using just the plot-line, to avoid legal issues' (Anon. 2000a). The Sidaways also appear as writers on another unmade Hammer script held in the Archive: *The Four Sided Triangle*. A remake of the 1953 Terence Fisher science fiction film of the same name, this script is not dated, but is listed as 'a work in progress' (Anon. 2000a). A second draft of *The Four Sided Triangle*, written by Christopher Wicking, is dated July 1992. These projects show that the idea to explore remakes of existing Hammer films was not necessarily put forward by Warner Bros., but potentially by Skeggs himself, as the same strategy seemed to be in place between Hammer and several different producers and studios. Therefore, in terms of developing screenplays of Hammer remakes, 1992 saw a flurry of activity, particularly in the months of June and July, which seemed to culminate the following year with the Warner Bros. deal.

The one outlier of this strategy is *Vlad the Impaler*, which was also listed as preparing to begin production in the *Screen International* article. Although it is not listed in the slate of remakes Warner Bros. was looking at developing, it is mentioned towards the end of the article: 'Hammer also has a $12m remake of Vlad the Impaler set to shoot in Romania early next year, possibly in a deal with Rank Film Distributors' (Bateman 1993: 2). Romania had been the proposed shooting location for Carreras's initial iteration of *Vlad the Impaler*, though Carreras noted that, when asking permission from the Romanian government, they 'turned [Hammer] down flat' due to Vlad still being considered a 'national hero' (Carreras in Skinn and Brosnan 1978: 21). What is telling about this 1993 announcement (despite erroneously referring to the project as a 'remake') is the specificity of it in comparison with the 1987 article, with a budget, location and distributor all seemingly in place. Unlike the 1987 Krantz announcement, this new slate of Hammer films also gained traction outside of the initial press release in *Screen International*. On 5 August 1993 the British newspaper *The Independent* ran the headline 'Hammer Films Returns to Revamp Horror Classics' (Connett 1993). The article repeated much of the information given in the *Screen International* article, but offered other insights as well. Namely Skeggs, interviewed for the article, suggested that Warner Bros. were financing the production costs of the films: 'we are scripting five films at the moment, which Warner Brothers will bankroll' (Skeggs in Connett 1993). He also noted that Vlad was very much still in production: 'we are making a new film called Vlad the Impaler, who inspired the Dracula story, which will be shot in Romania next year' (Skeggs in Connett 1993). A week later in the August 12 issue of *The Stage and Television Today*, another article on the deal was published, entitled 'Warner Snaps Up Hammer Classics'. This seemed to confirm the nature of the deal:

> The agreement has been signed with Hammer and Donner/Schuler-Donner Productions to develop film and television productions based on classic Hammer films and new material acquired by the British company. Warners will also have exclusive rights to develop and produce properties from the Hammer library. (Anon. 1993: 20)

These articles together seem to create a clearer picture of this co-production deal. Warner Bros. were prepared to finance the pictures, in exchange for the rights to produce and remake some of the classic horror titles in Hammer's catalogue.

Like the Krantz deal before it, the announcement of a new production deal led simultaneously to a new revision of *Vlad the Impaler* (with screenplay credit still being given solely to Hayles). This time writer Jonas McCord revised a draft, with Hammer purchasing the screen rights to his script on 30 November 1993 (Anon. 2000a). The Hammer Script Archive holds two exact copies of McCord's script, with the only difference being the title and the title page. One is entitled *Vlad the Impaler* and is listed as a first draft. The second is entitled *Vlad Dracul* (McCord undated). Although the actual scripts are identical, the title page for the *Vlad the Impaler* version of this script also features another interesting detail in the form of an American address for 'Hammer International'.

The script's listing of Hammer's American address (situated opposite the Warner Bros. lot), is the only document in the archive that confirms that Hammer had a physical presence in Hollywood as part of the Warner co-production deal, a significant development for a company who had relied heavily on the American film industry since the 1950s. The draft retitled *Vlad Dracul* does not feature this address, only that of Hammer's UK base in Borehamwood.

McCord is an American writer/director who, by 1993, had mainly served as executive producer for television shows such as *Dirty Dozen: The Series* (1988) and *The Young Riders* (1989–92). McCord's involvement was almost certainly a by-product of the Warner co-production deal, which, as well as providing financial support to new feature films, also opened up a new network of writers and directors to Hammer through Warner Bros.' status as one of the largest film production companies in

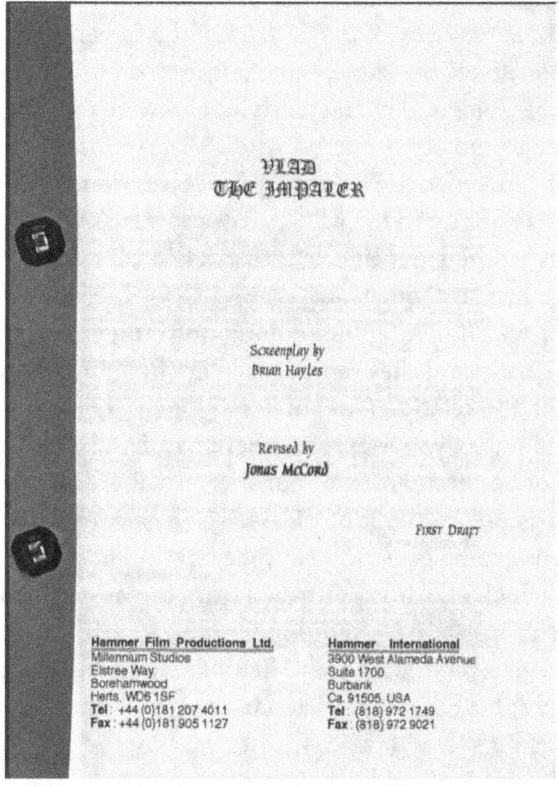

Figure 7.1 The title page of Jonas McCord's *Vlad the Impaler* screenplay, which gives an address for Hammer's American office near the Warner Bros. lot

Hollywood. It was with these new American allies that Skeggs finally sought support in order to get *Vlad the Impaler* into production.

In email correspondence on the 6 May 2016, McCord noted that he 'did quite an extensive rewrite' on *Vlad the Impaler*, with his usual method being to 'base everything on historical fact'. Although McCord's draft does not offer the historical detail mentioned by McCord, it is an extensive rewrite of the project, with significant changes to the narrative. First of note is that the Vlaachim twist, which was removed entirely from Peacock's draft of the script, was once again featured. Although this casts doubt as to whether McCord had read Peacock's revisions, there is definitive evidence that he had seen Ellis's version, as McCord also included a point-of-view possession sequence added by Ellis, where Vlad is 'imbued by the devil himself' (Ellis undated; McCord undated) after the death of his wife. However, this is the only surviving piece of any of Ellis's revisions, with no modern prologue or epilogue included in McCord's script. McCord undid many of the changes made by Peacock in the film's third act, and completely altered the majority of the first act of the screenplay. The main plot points stayed relatively the same, but characters such as Vlad's wife Ilonya were given larger roles and character dynamics were radically altered.

These changes mostly occurred when Vlad returns to his castle after being initially 'redeemed' by Benedek. In Hayles's draft of the script (and subsequent revisions up to the McCord draft) Vlad's wife Ilonya does not feature heavily in the story and is ultimately a plot device whose death triggers Vlad's lust for vengeance against God. In the drafts by Hayles, Ellis and Peacock, Ilonya enters labour only three pages after arriving at Tirgoviste Castle and dies ten pages later (nine in Peacock's draft). In McCord's draft, the relationship between Vlad and Ilonya was developed further, with nineteen pages between her arrival and death.

The cause of her premature labour was also altered. Whereas in previous drafts it was due to the long ride to the castle, McCord's draft has it take place during a major action set piece in the first act (entirely added by McCord), which sees Ilonya thrown from the horse Salmander during a boar hunt she insists on attending with Vlad. McCord also uses this sequence to revive the theme that Vlad's fate may be predestined (originally developed by Ellis). It is Salmander (the horse the devil birthed from Hell in Ellis's draft) who throws her to the ground, and afterwards Ilonya sees a 'girl, with the face of an angel and the heart of stone' (McCord undated: 35) standing next to the boar after she falls. The script later insinuates that this young girl was the witch Militsa in another form.

This sequence, as well as the previously mentioned possession scene, suggest that Vlad is chosen by the Devil to become Dracula, a thematic sentiment that, until this screenplay, had only appeared in Ellis's revisions of *Vlad the Impaler*. However, despite the extra sequences featuring Ilonya, after her death the script strays very little from the original Hayles draft. McCord's two main contributions were ultimately to give a stronger focus on the relationship between Vlad and Ilonya and to reinstate elements of the supernatural first added by Ellis.

Although there are no notes from anyone working at Hammer regarding this script, there is evidence that Skeggs was sufficiently satisfied with it to put the film in pre-production. In the 3 February 1995 issue of *Screen International*, *Vlad the Impaler* appeared on a list of projects in active production by European film companies under Hammer's name, with a production credit for Skeggs and the screenplay credit listed as 'Jonas McCord based on a screenplay by Brian Hayles' (Anon. 1995: 37). The listing also reveals the budget as $18 million, up from the $12 million first mentioned in the 1993 *Screen International* article. Hammer's production slate also appeared the following year in *Screen International* in the 26 July 1996 issue (Anon.: 31). *Vlad the Impaler* was listed again, this time with McCord receiving sole credit as writer and Hayles's story credit reduced to a mention in the brief one-line synopsis.

However, there was one crucial change since the previous listing. The film at this point had a director attached. Xavier Koller was listed as the director for the project in 1996 and also in the 28 March 1997 issue one year later (Anon. 1996; Anon. 1997), signalling his long-term involvement with the project. Koller, who originally hailed from Switzerland, had recently directed the Disney adventure film *Squanto: A Warriors Tale* (1994), his first English language production. *Squanto: A Warrior's Tale* tells the story of a seventeenth-century Native American who, after initially being kidnapped and sold into slavery, helped bring about peaceful liaisons between a group of English settlers and the Pokanoket tribe in America. More notably, however, Koller had also directed *Journey of Hope* in 1990, which told the story of a Turkish family who, after hearing of the promise and financial security of a life in Switzerland, sell their land and livestock and set off on a treacherous journey across multiple countries in an effort to find a better life. The film would go on to win the Best Foreign Language Film at the 1990 Academy Awards. There is seemingly no other documentation of Koller's involvement with *Vlad the Impaler* other than these production slates, but both *Journey of Hope* and *Squanto: A Warrior's*

Tale indicate a director not bound by a particular genre or style. It would be overly speculative to suggest how he would have brought *Vlad the Impaler* to the screen, but soon after Koller's announcement, *Vlad the Impaler* once again stalled, this time for good.

Two articles in 1996 seem to offer two primary reasons why Hammer, under Skeggs, failed to produce *Vlad the Impaler* or any other feature film in the 1990s. The first of these reasons was that, after over thirty years working for Hammer and sixteen years in charge, Skeggs was considering retirement. The second reason stemmed from the complex legal issues surrounding who owned the rights to existing Hammer films. In an interview printed in the 30 June edition of *The Observer*, Skeggs, while promoting the current crop of Hammer films he was hoping to get into production, revealed that the Warner deal with Donner had expired without producing any films: '[me and Donner are] still very good friends but he's so busy doing other things ... the deal ran out a year ago but it was a good start. It got Paramount and Fox interested' (Skeggs in Gilbert 1996: 137). Skeggs did still tout a slew of titles Hammer had in production (including *Vlad the Impaler*), and also seemed more committed to a strategy of exploiting Hammer's pre-existing properties: 'all the American majors want to remake Hammer films. We've signed five deals with companies like Fox, New World and Warner' (ibid.). In a particularly prescient comment, Skeggs went on to note the shift in Hollywood towards projects based on existing intellectual properties, including sequels and remakes: 'they have so little original material that's worthwhile. A few years ago they didn't want to do remakes. Now everybody wants to' (ibid.).

However, in the same article Skeggs also strongly hinted that he was considering reducing his involvement as owner of Hammer, and possibly even considering retirement: 'I'm 60 and it's time I relaxed a bit. I shall stay on as chairman. If I'm not enjoying it after a couple of years, I can sell my holding' (ibid.). With no overarching production deal in place and Skeggs seemingly sensing that his time at Hammer was coming to an end, it seemed Hammer's chances of going back into active production were becoming increasingly unlikely.

This is compounded by a more technical detail which potentially indicates why Hammer, after adopting an approach that heavily relied on remaking many of their existing properties, failed to move these projects into production. In an article in *Billboard* magazine dated 8 June 1996, entitled 'Demand for Reclaiming Foreign C'rights Less Frenzied Than Expected' (91), Seth Goldstein writes on section 104A of the Copyright

Act, which took effect on 1 January 1996, and the impact this copyright law will have on the film and music industry. The Act restored 'ownership of foreign works ... that had passed into the public domain here [in America]' (ibid.), and it was assumed that, when the Act came into place, the US copyright office would see 'a flood of applications from overseas rights holders who want to reclaim their herds of video cash cows' (ibid.). However, this wasn't the case, and relatively few applications were received. The exception to this lack of demand was Hammer Films, which applied for '141 features' (ibid.) from the US Copyright Office. This was suggested as a positive for the company by Goldstein in the article, who saw Hammer's reclamation of these titles as 'a new lease on life for still [sic] feisty inventory that stands a chance at being rediscovered by a '90s audience' (ibid.). However, it also suggests a wider problem at Hammer as they began to focus on their own existing properties, namely, which properties they actually owned the rights to. After officially taking over Hammer in 1973, Michael Carreras had found himself in similar circumstances regarding the rights to many of Hammer's most recognised films. Due to 'the way Sir James Carreras had done business, the rights to most of Hammer's Films were owned by the companies that had financed them' (Meikle 2009: 207). As noted in the previous chapter, this ultimately meant that Michael Carreras bought a company which did not own many of its most famous titles. Nearly twenty-five years later, Skeggs found himself in a similar position. One notable example is the previously mentioned *Legacy*, a remake of *Quatermass and the Pit* (Ward Baker, 1967), which had to be retitled by Hammer due to rights issues. Affirming this evidence is the document of literary materials owned by Hammer, dated 29 February 2000, which lists the unmade titles in Hammer's catalogue and who owns the specific rights to them. That this document even exists suggests Hammer knew that this was a prevailing issue, but the findings of the document also illustrate the often-complex issues surrounding many of their properties.

Despite this undoubtedly being a major issue for Skeggs during his tenure, particularly in the 1990s as he shifts towards exploiting Hammer's existing properties, it is difficult to definitively suggest that this was the key to *Vlad the Impaler*'s undoing. The literary document itemising Hammer's projects and their rights status lists separately the Ellis, Peacock and McCord drafts, noting on each that the project was 'last optioned 24/10/93 (now lapsed)' (Anon. 2000a). With *Vlad the Impaler* listed on *Screen International*'s European production slates in the 28 March 1997 issue, one can presume that the rights lapsed somewhere between 1997 and 2000. The loss of the rights to the project offers a possible explanation for why it seemed to disappear from Hammer's schedules after 1997. After twenty-three years of production, two managing directors and four screenwriters, *Vlad the Impaler* had finally been struck a killing blow.

Conclusion

By following the trajectory of *Vlad the Impaler* under Skeggs, a number of insights into how Hammer operated under his tenure can be established. For example, it becomes clear that defining Skeggs's and Lawrence's appointments as managing directors in 1980 as the start of a new phase of Hammer is incorrect. Although this was the first time in the company's history a Carreras was not working at Hammer, Skeggs had been working under both James and Michael Carreras since the early 1960s. Therefore, Skeggs's reluctance to move outside of the relatively small circle of contacts Hammer had in the late 1970s, and his utilisation of people like John Peacock, who worked under Carreras most notably on *To the Devil a Daughter*, was unsurprising given the context.

Although Skeggs's tenure was marred by the lack of any theatrical films being produced, it is important to contextualise this in relation to Hammer's financial precariousness in the early 1980s. As discussed earlier within the chapter, the success of the *Hammer House of Horror* television series had allowed Skeggs and Lawrence to purchase Hammer from ICI, but although they had control of the company, it was a far cry from the internationally recognised powerhouse it had once been. In addition, Hammer's limited resources were stretched with regards to the deal with 20th Century Fox to produce *Hammer House of Mystery and Suspense*, with Hammer having to find the capital to produce the first two episodes, as well as find a way to extend the scripts from their original runtime of one hour to ninety minutes at the behest of Fox.

With both creative and financial resources strained by *Hammer House of Mystery and Suspense*, it is perhaps no wonder that Ellis's initial brief for *Vlad the Impaler* was both vague and contradictory. Asked to modernise a historical drama, Ellis updated the script with a modern prologue and epilogue, and a demonic possession narrative that gave the script more overt supernatural sequences. However, as the annotated version of Ellis's revised script attests, Hammer was only interested in a superficial change to the narrative structure. As Ellis's own quotes emphasised this added nothing to the main narrative crux, but Hammer seemed disinterested in the more drastic changes made by Ellis. Whether hiring Ellis again for *Black Sabbath* was considered a second chance by Hammer or merely the result of desperation due to the few contacts the company had in the industry at this time is impossible to say. Be it down to the growing pains of new ownership or the pressures of their television production, Hammer in the early 1980s seemed completely inert in regard to their theatrical output.

Hammer's overreliance on contacts established in the 1970s was perhaps at its most blatant towards the end of the 1980s, with Peacock himself revising Hayles's script. This came off the back of a co-production deal with American producer Steve Krantz, which lined up five Hammer films for production. Peacock's script did alter the narrative more drastically than Ellis by removing the 'Vlaachim' twist, but it is remarkable how little Peacock altered a now fourteen-year-old script. Carreras's quote, in which he reverentially calls *Vlad the Impaler* his most 'prized possession', demonstrates how highly regarded Hayles's script was by Hammer under Carreras. This admiration for the script clearly continued into Skeggs's tenure, as not only was he persevering with the project nearly a decade and a half after its initial inception, but the changes made to it were so minimal that Hayles retained sole screenwriting credit on both Ellis's and Peacock's revised drafts. At this stage, Hammer seemed uncertain what to do with the script, even after hiring two writers to revise it. Skeggs clearly did not deem it fit for active production, yet he also seems reticent to alter the script in any meaningful way. Although it is speculative to make any causal links between Skeggs's background in the industry and this lack of development, it is worth noting his initial and most significant role at Hammer was as an accountant as opposed to any creative role. Whereas Michael Carreras had experience as both producer and director, Skeggs, although having fairly regular success brokering American co-production deals with Fox in 1983, Krantz in 1987 and Warner Bros. in 1993, seemed to lack creative intuition, failing to take the next step and put projects such as *Vlad the Impaler* (which had already had significant developmental work), into production.

Although Skeggs seemed to lack the creative instincts of either James or Michael Carreras, he was quick to latch onto a shift in Hammer's reputation in the early 1990s, securing a significant co-production deal with Warner Bros. based solely on the films Hammer had in its back catalogue.

As Hammer Films had slowly grown in stature critically, directors who had watched these films when younger had now risen to prominence in the industry. Skeggs capitalised by shifting his entire production strategy to pre-existing Hammer properties. Skeggs himself noted how influential Hammer Films had been on contemporary directors, saying that Joe Dante, who at this juncture was signed up to direct a remake of *The Devil Rides Out* (Fisher, 1968), was a 'Hammer buff', and that 'Martin Scorsese knows more about Hammer Films than I do. He's got a library of all the films' (Skeggs in Gilbert 1996: 137). Adapting properties with pre-existing audiences had been a facet of Hammer since *Dick Barton: Special Agent* (Goulding) in 1948. Skeggs, however, looked to utilise this strategy with Hammer's own properties, relying on past successes to open up deals for Hammer's future theatrical output. Lauren Schuler-Donner, one of the key proponents of the Warner deal, suggested that this not only offered Hammer the chance to bring in existing audiences, but also to bring the films into the mainstream: 'American audiences aren't so familiar with the Quatermass pictures. They only had cult appeal initially. But if we do *The Quatermass Xperiment* right, the whole world will embrace the character' (Schuler-Donner in Jones 1994: 4).

This seemed to be an expansion on Hammer's policy throughout the 1950s, '60s and '70s. Whereas American distribution (and often finance) had always been integral to Hammer's strategy, Skeggs, through this co-production deal, looked to utilise American funding, locations, directors and actors. This is best encapsulated through the American office address featured on Jonas McCord's script for *Vlad the Impaler*. Hammer was not only looking to utilise the funding and distribution options available through American partnerships, but was looking in effect to make Hammer an American production arm.

This strategy by Skeggs basically to assimilate Hammer into Warner Bros. through this deal, as well as his background in finance as opposed to film production, perhaps also contributes to the image of Skeggs as someone happy to just gain a profit from Hammer's name and legacy. This is suggested by Meikle in the quote presented earlier in this chapter, where he notes that Hammer was merely Skeggs sat 'at his big desk' (Meikle 2016). This certainly comes across in Wayne Kinsey's account of the Warner Bros. deal, where he states that 'this was not the Hammer we had come to love and the Hammer logo residing in what otherwise looked like a big Warner Bros movie did little to excite the more loyal fans' (2007: 424). Ultimately, Skeggs's ambitions did not come to fruition and, in 2000, Skeggs sold Hammer to a consortium led by Charles Saatchi (Kinsey 2007: 424; Meikle 2009: 226).

With no previous ties to Hammer's old guard, this new consortium was undoubtedly a new era for the company. However, while many accused Skeggs of exploiting Hammer's legacy for profit with no real plans for film production (a charge dispelled by this chapter), this new consortium made it explicit; exploiting the brand, not theatrical production, was the real priority. The announcement of the consortium's buyout in the 14–20 February weekly issue of *Variety* made this clear. A conciliatory mention of resuming active film production was made, but a quote from Larry Chrisfield, one of the members of the consortium, made no mention of it:

> Not only are the new opportunities in digital television and the Internet multiplying the value of Hammer's existing assets, but digital production and distribution techniques enable us to add to those assets at low cost and low risk. (Chrisfield in Dawtrey 2000: 25)

This was also apparent in the 11 February issue of *Broadcast*, where Terry Ilott, creative head of this new Hammer outfit with his partner Peter Naish, described the purchase as 'an investment in the brand' (Ilott in Anon. 2000b: 2), with Hammer 'not planning to build up a TV or film production business itself' (Anon. 2000b: 2). Skeggs may never have had any films released theatrically, but the deals he made and the amount of developmental work he authorised on a project such as *Vlad the Impaler* suggest this was not through a lack of trying. At this point, however, Hammer was clearly not prioritising film production.

Hammer, after changing hands once more in 2007, resumed theatrical production in September 2008 with *Wake Wood* (Keating, 2009). However, *Vlad the Impaler* seemed to have died in the 1990s. Despite current Hammer owner Simon Oakes suggesting in an interview in *The Independent* in 2012 that Hammer was working on a 'modern-day version of Dracula' (Oakes in Clark 2012), Universal's *Dracula Untold* (Shore, 2014) seems to have put paid to any speculation that *Vlad the Impaler* might see the light of day. A Dracula origin story released in 2014, *Dracula Untold* sees Vlad, having already repented for his evil past by the beginning of the film, desperate to save his kingdom from Turkish forces. He is given temporary powers by a Nosferatu-like creature (as opposed to a Witch), but after the death of his wife, decides to keep his new vampiric powers to take vengeance on her killers. The plot sounds similar to *Vlad the Impaler*, but the tone is remarkably different to Hammer's historical drama, adapting the story as more of a superhero origin story, with Vlad portrayed as an anti-hero rather than a villain (Louis 2017: 249–62).

The case study of *Vlad the Impaler* takes us through two iterations of Hammer, and comparisons between Michael Carreras and Roy Skeggs can consequently be made. The focus towards the end of their respective tenures on large scale productions that would necessitate international co-production finance is perhaps the most blatant, with Carreras looking to get big-budget films like *Vlad the Impaler* and *Nessie* off the ground and Skeggs, through the Warner deal, looking to remake older Hammer films as big-budget blockbusters.

Both Carreras and Skeggs also found themselves in difficult positions immediately after taking control of Hammer. In 1973, Michael Carreras inherited a depleted company from his father, with key figures like Tony Hinds long since retired and many of the rights to former Hammer projects residing with the American majors who had distributed them. Skeggs also struggled to move outside of a small circle of former Hammer employees, seemingly relying solely on John Peacock and young British writers such as Arthur Ellis.

As stated in the introduction, *Vlad the Impaler* is a pertinent case study of Skeggs's years in charge. Its inception as a Carreras project allows comparisons in how both Hammer managers developed the project. The sheer amount of developmental work that went into *Vlad the Impaler* also acts as a robust rebuttal of Skeggs's characterisation as someone more interested in Hammer's financial assets than film production. In effect, the project seems to perfectly embody the tensions of Skeggs as a member of the old guard relying on older Hammer properties, American co-productions and former Hammer staff, and someone aware of the shift in the film industry towards established properties and remakes, cleverly utilising Hammer's library to garner interest from major American studios. *Vlad the Impaler* may have come to nothing, but Skeggs's time in charge at Hammer is an interesting and important chapter in Hammer's history.

Conclusion

As I finish writing this book in August 2022, one of the biggest stories coming out of Hollywood is the cancellation of Warner Bros. *Batgirl*. The news was first broken by the *New York Post* on the 2 August (Oleksinski), before *Variety* provided a full breakdown on what had happened (Vary and Lang 2022). *Batgirl*, despite being completed and in the test screening phase of production, was the victim of a regime change at Warner Bros. and a subsequent shifting of priorities for the company. Originally put into production as a film made exclusively for Warner Bros. streaming service HBO Max, the $90 million project was viewed by Warner Bros. new CEO David Zaslav as too expensive for streaming, and not 'big enough to feel worthy of a major theatrical release' (ibid.). As a result, the film was used as part of a complex tax write-down as a way to guarantee a recoupment of some of the film's budget. *Variety* notes that a condition of this kind of tax write-off is that Warner Bros. can never monetise the film. As a result, *Batgirl*'s chances of ever seeing the light of day are small.

What this story has foregrounded is the loss felt when a project like this is cancelled. Both the directors of *Batgirl* Adil El Arbi and Bilall Fallah and its star Leslie Grace released statements which noted their shock at the decision (Couch 2022; Gajewski 2022), and the story picked up mainstream attention outside of the Hollywood trades as well. The key focus of the outcry seemed to stem from the huge loss of the time and creative energies of all involved. The hard work and effort of the cast and crew being squandered due to the project's cancellation was seen as a devasting blow. Yet as this book has argued in relation to unproduced projects, whether a film sees the light of day or not, the creative and economic labour poured into them is still vital to understanding how the film and television industry operates.

In relation to Hammer, an examination of their early unmade projects shows that the company's initial international success was forged in fights with the censor and American television executives, and these issues form the crux of the first two chapters. But perhaps the key element of the whole book is the foregrounding of Michael Carreras as managing director, and his ambitious but ultimately doomed strategy to create large, big-budget genre films utilising piecemeal international finance deals. With only two films produced between 1975 and 1979, the unmade projects are crucial in contextualising his attempts at revitalising an ailing company in innovative but ultimately costly ways.

This book has underlined the essential nature of unmade projects to film history and is the first ever production study to use them as primary case studies. James Fenwick's *Unproduction Studies and the American Film Industry* (2021) was the first monograph to focus solely on unmade projects, with Fenwick utilising the Production Code Administration (PCA) records held at the Margaret Herrick Library to examine twenty-eight unmade films and the traces they had left within the archive. As perhaps the closest in nature to this study, the commonalities and differences are an interesting way to draw out what makes this examination of Hammer Films significant. One key similarity is, to quote Fenwick, 'focusing attention on their [unmade films] existence within the archive and... amplifying the category of the unmade, unseen, and unreleased within other archives around the world' (114). Simply by using unmade case studies and examining their tangible impact on production companies such as Hammer throughout the decades, attention is drawn to how vital they are in presenting a holistic overview of the company's history, and consequently how important all unmade projects should be to every production study.

However, perhaps the biggest diversion from Fenwick's work is a methodological one. Fenwick opted in his study to focus solely on material held in the Margaret Herrick Library, and deliberately did not consult any material on these unmade films outside of the library's holdings. This was done to 'circumvent attempts at resolving these frustrations and absences, bringing to the fore the fact that there are gaps in empirical evidence' (114). While this is a sound methodological approach for Fenwick's study, which focuses on the materiality of the archive itself, a production study such as the one within this book necessitated a wider breath of sources. While a vast majority of this study has relied on materials from a variety of archives, in all cases a mixed approach has been utilised to supplement archival sources and present a more accurate and detailed analysis. This is apparent in the three interviews utilised in the study and the contemporaneous articles in the trades and fan magazines utilised alongside archival material. This results in triangulation, where what one cannot learn from one particular project (because specific archival materials such as correspondence are not available) can be learned from another. This ensures a rich and detailed study, and giving a greater veracity to the book's findings.

For example, an exclusive focus on the Hammer Script Archive would not have provided all the necessary information when examining *Frankenstein*, *Tales of Frankenstein*, or Richard Matheson's *The Night Creatures*. For the two chapters these case studies appear in the majority of the material was held in other archives, namely the BFI Archive, the BBFC Archive, the Margaret Herrick Library and the USC Warner Bros. Archive. These materials helped give essential context to Hammer's path to *The Curse of Frankenstein*, as well as the notable missteps on their way to crystalising their iconic gothic formula. As the book progressed, the archival materials used were sourced more frequently from the Hammer Script Archive, and while these were reinforced by interviews and secondary sources, several methodological shifts were necessary in order to adapt to the variety of material available. For example, Chapter 3's focus on screenwriter Don Houghton's Dracula in India project hinged largely on correspondence, with no script seemingly completed for *Kali Devil Bride of Dracula*. As such the relationship between Michael Carreras and Houghton takes precedence within the chapter. In way of contrast, Chapter 5 examines a significant amount of financial documentation on Hammer's *Nessie* project, and as such a closer look at the company's attempts to broker international production and distribution details comes more sharply into focus. In the final chapter, Roy Skeggs's tenure at Hammer is measured through the longevity of the *Vlad the Impaler* project, and with no archival material available except for six separate screenplays held in the archive, the scripts act as a roadmap through a period of Hammer where no films were produced theatrically for decades.

Though the need to adapt a pragmatic methodological framework is necessary when studying both produced and unproduced films, I would argue that it leads to a greater (and ultimately less consistent) variety of methodological practices within unmade films. No matter how a produced film's history is approached, each study will be anchored by the text itself. The film's narrative, time in development, director and cast are not suppositions or rumours, but fixed points for study. Without these, unmade film studies must look for other fixed points, which, as this study attests, can vary depending on the material available to the researcher.

Vampirella: a live script reading and future study

So, with these methodological questions in mind, what is the scope for further work within unmade film studies? This is a key question for the end of a study such as this, but it is slightly more complex in relation to unmade production studies. This is because the endgame for this particular study is to effectively render 'unmade production histories' obsolete. The central argument of this book is that unmade projects offer us key insights into the creative and financial labour of production companies, and as such they should not be cordoned off as failed productions, but be integrated into production histories and studied alongside produced work, to offer a holistic picture of the company being examined. Yet while the biggest sign of success in this case would mean the end of books like this one, this is not to say unmade film studies itself cannot still offer indispensable insights into vital areas of study.

For example, the lack of access and opportunity for women and ethnic minorities within the film industry is an indisputable fact, and is borne out in essential work such as in Clive Nwonka's 'Race and Ethnicity in the UK Film Industry' report (2020) and Shelley Cobb, Linda Ruth Williams and Natalie Wreyford's 'Calling the Shots: Women in Contemporary Film Culture' project (2016). The structural inequalities within the film industry means that the creative and financial efforts of, for example, black filmmakers, are far less likely to be rewarded and a significant amount of projects from black creators are not produced. As Whitney Strub notes in relation to black film history, 'recent scholarship has begun to construct something of a counterfactual canon of lost or unmade films' (2015: 273), and this is apparent not only in Strub's own article on the lost, unmade and unseen work of LeRoi Jones/Amiri Baraka, but also in Brian Norman's article in the *African American Review* examining James Baldwin's unmade *Malcolm X* project (2015: 103–18). In a similar attempt to foreground marginalised figures in the industry, Shelley Cobb's blog post 'Women Directors and Lost Projects' examines the huge gaps in female filmmakers' filmographies and the difficulties women filmmakers face in getting films produced. Cobb suggests that unmade projects developed by filmmakers such as Lynne Ramsay and Jocelyn Moorhouse are 'intriguing for their gendered power battles and their stand-offs over scripts' and that 'just writing about the films women filmmakers do make leaves out whole portions of women's film history' (Cobb 2014). These examples demonstrate that marginalised figures within the industry can be foregrounded by focusing on unproduced projects, and again underlines how essential these projects are in giving a fuller account of film history.

As well as these crucial areas, a developing field such as unmade film studies will only begin to properly formulate through amplification. Though often works focusing on unmade projects are diverse (either in their case studies, their methodologies, or both), edited collections have proven a good way to highlight important work within the field. To this end, I co-edited a collection entitled *Shadow Cinema* with James Fenwick and David Eldridge which brought together a number of essays that featured unmade projects as key case studies. Off the back of this collection, James Fenwick and I co-hosted a conference at Sheffield Hallam University in May 2022 entitled 'Shadow Screens', which not only looked to again amplify the existing work on unmade film and television, but also begin the early stages of creating a research network around the topic. On a pragmatic level though, we realised that amplification is not enough, and that in order to ensure unmade film studies continued to thrive as a nascent field, a self-reflexive look at exactly how the area can be studied was needed. This idea has led to another co-edited collection entitled *Studying the Unmade* which, when released, will look to tackle some of the key ways unmade film and television are examined, and the methodological challenges that have yet to be addressed within the field.

However, while I would contend that this work in the last five years on unmade film and television has been significant, its significance is only limited to within academia. While as an academic this is where a lot of my attention is focused, one of the key points of this book's introduction was how fandom, not just academia, is crucial to the success and longevity of unmade film histories. In regard to the Hammer Script Archive, there have been a number of public events that looked to foreground the company's unmade films in innovative ways that reach outside academic work. The first to actively engage with the archival materials was orchestrated in 2015 by Steven Sheil and Chris Cooke, the co-founders of the Broadway Cinema's annual horror, cult and science fiction film festival Mayhem.

Notably, Sheil and Cooke decided to utilise the unmade Hammer screenplay *The Unquenchable Thirst of Dracula* for a live script reading event that saw actor and film historian Jonathan Rigby narrate the script, with other actors portraying the characters on stage. The script, discussed previously in Chapter 3, was a well-considered choice due to the focus on the iconic Dracula character, and the fact it was written by former Hammer producer Tony Hinds (under his pseudonym John Elder). It is arguably Hammer's most well-known unmade project, with BBC Radio 4 adapting it in 2017 as part of their 'Unmade Movies' series, directed by Mark Gatiss and narrated by Michael Sheen.

Also in 2017, Mayhem would adapt another unmade Hammer film for a live reading, which would prove even more conceptually interesting than its predecessor. Sheil and Cooke decided to adapt another infamous Hammer project – *Zeppelins v Pterodactyls*. As noted in the book's introduction, *Zeppelins v Pterodactyls* has in many ways become one of the key projects in the canon of unfilmed Hammer, with its enticing imagery and title proving extremely tantalising to fans of the company. However, this intrigue is less to do with the project's narrative and more to do with the dissemination within fan circles of Tom Chantrell's artwork for it, created for Hammer in 1970.

Chantrell's *Zeppelins v Pterodactyls* artwork has become so iconic in part due to it being one of the few produced elements of the project, with there being no script ever written for it. The fact that a poster was developed before a script is hardly an anomaly in regard to Hammer's usual development process. Marcus Hearn notes that James Carreras struck a deal with every major American studio, and 'was often able to do this without a script or the promise of major stars, but he rarely went into negotiations without provisional poster artwork' (2010: 6). In lieu of a script, Sheil adapted a detailed fourteen-page treatment held in the Hammer Script Archive written by David Allen, dated 4 June 1970. While *The Unquenchable Thirst of Dracula* was a complete reading of an actual Hammer script which had archival correspondences to add further contextualisation, *Zeppelins v Pterodactyls* only had a treatment, with the script being written by Sheil nearly fifty years after the project's initial conception. This adaptation into a different medium itself is a fascinating use of archival materials, and was an inspiration for producing my own live script reading of *Vampirella*.

After completing my PhD in May 2019, I began a six-month postdoctoral project that would utilise the Hammer Script Archive to produce a live script reading of one of the company's unmade projects. *Vampirella* was chosen as the centrepiece of the project for two key reasons. The first was that it had not been a case study within my research up to that point, due to the Hammer Script Archive not possessing a script for *Vampirella* until I procured two draft screenplays from Hammer in August 2018. Secondly, the addition of these two screenplays to the *Vampirella* file made it one of the most detailed files the archive held. As such, its notable impact on Hammer at the time of its initial development and the Hammer Script Archive's inclusion of two scripts on the project made it an ideal case study for the live script reading.

External funding for the project allowed for an ambitious reading to take place at the Regent Street Cinema in London, and Jonathan Rigby was hired to both direct the piece and star as *Vampirella*'s mentor/sidekick Pendragon, the role designated to Peter Cushing when the project was originally in production. Rigby, as well as being an accomplished director and actor, has also written extensively on the subject of British horror in his book *English Gothic* (2000), and is a regular contributor to Hammer Blu-ray releases (such as the BFI's 2013 release of *Dracula* and the Powerhouse/Indicator releases of Hammer boxsets since 2017). This meant that he was a creative partner on the project who had a pre-existing and detailed understanding of the project's history at Hammer in the 1970s.

One of the first issues apparent when developing the reading was which script to adapt. The archive held two scripts and, as noted in Chapter 4, Carreras suggested there were '25 different versions' of the project throughout its development. Ultimately, a decision was made to utilise Christopher Wicking's October 1975 draft. The script immediately preceded Hammer taking the project to the Famous Monsters Convention in New York that November, and Barbara Leigh and Cushing attended the convention already cast in the film. As such, while it is impossible to deem any draft of an unmade project 'definitive', this screenplay was likely the one that was the closest to being produced by Hammer, and as such was chosen to be adapted for the 2019 live script reading.

Chapter 4 outlined how Wicking's self-referential screenplay had many intertextual elements that directly referenced Hammer's own history, and there were even more to consider when it came to adapting the screenplay for the live script reading in 2019. For example, when it came to casting, one of the first people who was approached for this production was Caroline Munro. Munro had worked with Hammer in the 1970s on two films, *Dracula A.D. 1972* (Gibson, 1972) and *Captain Kronos – Vampire Hunter* (Clemens, 1974). As well as these two appearances, Munro was also heavily linked to the role of *Vampirella*, and this link between Munro and the project has remained since. There are several reasons for the connection. Outside of the resemblance between Munro and Vampirella on the page, Munro did have initial talks with Hammer for the role. However, Munro noted during the 2019 show that these had never progressed past informal conversations. The Hammer Script Archive holds an undated typed list titled 'Possible Vampirellas: From T.V. to A List', with stars such as Julie Newmar, Charlotte Rampling and Diane Keaton all listed, but not Munro. While this list is undated, a casting memo dated 30 September 1975 confirms the casting of Barbara Leigh with the statement 'Hammer's new discovery . . . Barbara Leigh, the sex sensation of the seventies!' Yet despite Leigh's official casting, Munro is still often tied to the role. Nowhere is this more apparent than in Executive Replicas and TB League's release in December 2019 of a special edition Caroline Munro Vampirella action figure. The description notes that 'in 1976 [*sic*], 7 years after Vampirella's first appearance, Hammer Films opted the rights to produce the Vampirella Film and their first choice to star in the lead role was the beautiful Caroline Munro'. The figure, retailing at $249.99, cements how intrinsically tied to the property Munro still is. Munro would join the live script reading as 'the Chief', a character who runs the 'SODS' spy agency and a role gender-flipped for the production. Actor Georgina Dugdale, Caroline Munro's daughter, would join the production as Vampirella.

The casting of Munro in relation to her previous links with the project again brings up the role of the archive in these kinds of live script adaptations. If archival documents including correspondence, marketing plans, financial documentation, cast lists and scripts are to be considered the legitimate or authentic history of the *Vampirella* project, Munro's casting is arguably inauthentic, or at least is in opposition to evidence, as there are no archival traces of Munro in relation to the project. However, like Wicking's own references to the company throughout his screenplay in 1975, Hammer's own legacy, as well as its fandom, were also important elements to be considered in the lead up to the live script reading. This is notable in further casting decisions such as Jason Morell, an accomplished actor who is the son of André Morell, who had appeared in several Hammer Films including *The Hound of the Baskervilles* (1959), *She* (1965) and *The Plague of the Zombies* (1966). An animation detailing the origins of *Vampirella* was also commissioned for the project, with Judy Matheson – who had featured in Hammer's *Twins of Evil* (1971) and *Lust for a Vampire* (1971) – providing the voiceover. Like Munro, Morell and Matheson had no direct ties to the *Vampirella* project but are intrinsically linked to Hammer as a company. *Vampirella* as a live script reading may have been a relatively unknown entity for audiences, but these connections create a tangible link between the unproduced project and the produced Hammer canon for established fans.

Vampirella – A Live Script Reading, was performed on 17 October 2019. It had an original soundtrack written by composer Luke Jackson, an introductory animation by Karlton Dolo, and an opening and closing credit sequence (using images from the original comic, much like Wicking's script), by Adam Fox. The promotional poster for the event was designed by Graham Humphreys, with the brief given to design a poster based on Wicking's script. As such, it features Cushing as Pendragon and Munro as Vampirella (again privileging fan expectations over archival evidence). However, although the poster operates visually as a 'what-if' for Hammer's *Vampirella*, the text on the poster, which lists the cast and crew

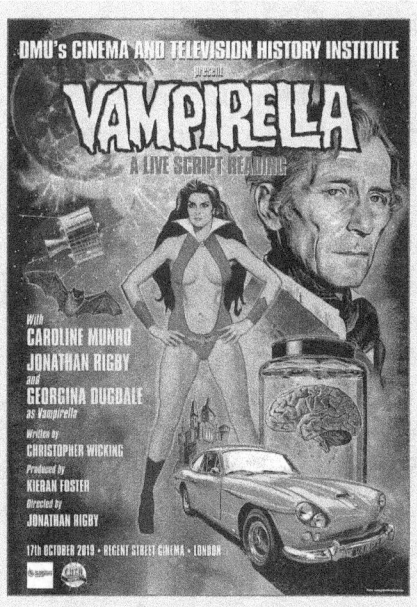

Figure C.1 The *Vampirella*: the live script reading poster designed by Graham Humphreys

of the live script reading, arguably weakens this concept. The poster therefore acts as an acute reflection of the adaptation itself. While the poster, casting and credit sequences all look to align the reading directly with the unmade film itself, it is undoubtedly left to the audience to bridge the gap between the project that could have been and the live reading of the script they saw.

Conclusion

This book has argued that although many projects may not make it to the screen, they can have sizeable impacts on directors, producers, stars and studios. As such, they should be studied with the parity of produced projects in order to fully understand the inner workings of global film production. The role of the archive in both non-academic and academic work on unmade projects is central to this. With no completed film to work from, any exploration of an unmade production will be reliant on material such as screenplays, story outlines, studio correspondence, financial documentation, articles and interviews to name only some. As such, archives are often the sole repository of information on thousands of unproduced films. This conclusion has focused solely on the public events centred on Hammer's unmade works, but other projects such as the 'Unfolding the Aryan Papers' exhibition, which took one of Kubrick's most well-known unmade films – *The Aryan Papers* – and created a work 'as much about a film that never happened as it is a portrait of the chosen lead actress Johanna ter Steege'. This fascinating project utilised materials from the Kubrick Archive held at the University of the Arts London, again stressing the importance of archives and their material. While these readings and exhibits ultimately can never directly show what could have been, the archival material used does create a clear link between the unmade project's history and the contemporary works themselves.

While academic work, readings and exhibitions use and repurpose archival materials to create new projects that relate in some way to the original unproduced work, the central relationship between the archive and unmade productions remains as it would for any work that uses them – to offer key insights into the significant creative and financial labour of unmade productions, and in doing so make these supposed shadow films all the more tangible.

On the subject of labour, it should be noted here the essential work done across the globe by archivists, librarians and many other staff within the archives themselves. Archival materials are very rarely 'discovered' or 'unearthed' by researchers such as myself. They are in fact already discovered and are waiting to be seen; procured, filed away meticulously and kept safe from the wear and tear of everyday life by dedicated teams of professional and highly qualified individuals. Without them so many films, produced and unproduced, would be lost to time. As a film researcher I have been (and remain) entirely reliant on their skills and expertise to conduct my work.

Hammer Films is a well-established studio which has received a great deal of attention within academic works. This book, however, has demonstrated that the study of unmade films can disrupt and embellish established production histories, as well as present new and original findings. As this project demonstrates, unmade films are not merely interesting 'what if' scenarios or archival curiosities, but important primary texts which are as much a part of film history as the films that make it through production.

Bibliography

Unpublished and archival sources

BBFC Archive

Anderson, P. to Trevelyan, J. [correspondence], 20 November 1957. BBFC Archive. Naked Terror/Last Man on Earth File.

Anon. (1957h), 'Examiner's Report', 1 December 1957. BBFC Archive. Naked Terror/Last Man on Earth File.

Anon. (1957i), 'Examiner's Report', 1 December 1957. BBFC Archive. Naked Terror/Last Man on Earth File.

Anon. (1958b), 'Examiner's Report', 26 February 1958. BBFC Archive. Naked Terror/Last Man on Earth File.

Anon. (1958c), 'Examiner's Report', March 1958. BBFC Archive. Naked Terror/Last Man on Earth File.

Carreras, J. to Nicholls, J. [correspondence], 26 February 1958. BBFC Archive. Naked Terror/Last Man on Earth File.

Carreras, J. to Trevelyan, J. [correspondence], 23 November 1964. BBFC Archive. Naked Terror/Last Man on Earth File.

Croft, F. (1956). 'Examiner's Report', 1956. BBFC Archive. The Curse of Frankenstein File.

Elwood, R. P. to Trevelyan, J. [correspondence], 24 August 1961. BBFC Archive. Naked Terror/Last Man on Earth File.

Elwood, R. P. to Trevelyan, J. [correspondence], 3 September 1961. BBFC Archive. Naked Terror/Last Man on Earth File.

Fields, A. (1956), 'Examiner's Report', 10 October 1956. BBFC Archive. The Curse of Frankenstein File.

Fields, A. (1957), 'Examiner's Report', 25 November 1957. BBFC Archive. Naked Terror/Last Man on Earth File.

Fields, A. to Nicholls, J. [correspondence], 3 December 1957. BBFC Archive. Naked Terror/Last Man on Earth File.

Nicholls, J. to Carreras, J. [correspondence], 11 March 1958. BBFC Archive. Naked Terror/Last Man on Earth File.

Nicholls, J. to Hinds, A. [correspondence], 12 December 1957. BBFC Archive. Naked Terror/Last Man on Earth File.

Trevelyan, J. (1961), 'Handwritten Note on Letter from R. P. Elwood', 16 September 1961. BBFC Archive. Naked Terror/Last Man on Earth File.
Trevelyan, J. to Carreras, J. [correspondence], 26 November 1964. BBFC Archive. Naked Terror/Last Man on Earth File.
Trevelyan, J. to Elwood, R. P. [correspondence], 28 August 1961. BBFC Archive. Naked Terror/Last Man on Earth File.

BFI National Archive

Anon. (1958a) [memo], 'General Information for Writers', 28 February 1958. BFI National Archive. Special Collections. Hammer Film Productions Collection. Item 19c.
Anon. to Carreras, J. [correspondence], 24 August 1956. BFI National Archive. Special Collections. Hammer Film Productions Collection. Item 1b.
Bryan, P. (1958), 'Tales of Frankenstein: Synopsis Five', 8 May 1958. BFI National Archive. Special Collections. Hammer Film Productions Collection. Item 19e.
Carreras, J. to Birking, I. [correspondence], 9 December 1957. BFI National Archive. Special Collections. Hammer Film Productions Collection. Item 18.
Carreras, J. to Hyman, E. [correspondence], 23 August 1956. BFI National Archive. Special Collections. Hammer Film Productions Collection. Item 1b.
Carreras, J. to Hyman, E. [correspondence], 21 November 1956. BFI National Archive. Special Collections. Hammer Film Productions Collection. Item 1b.
Carreras, J. to Hyman, E. [correspondence], December 1956. BFI National Archive. Special Collections. Hammer Film Productions Collection. Item 1b.
Carreras, J. to Hyman, E. [correspondence], 1 October 1957. BFI National Archive. Special Collections. Hammer Film Productions Collection. Item 1b.
Carreras, M. to Sangster, J. [correspondence], 15 October 1957. BFI National Archive. Special Collections. Hammer Film Productions Collection. Item 19a.
Dryhurst, E. (1958), 'Tales of Frankenstein: Synopsis Four', 10 April 1958. BFI National Archive. Special Collections. Hammer Film Productions Collection. Item 19e.
Hinds, A. to Bryan, P. (1958), 'Tales of Frankenstein: Synopsis Five', 8 May 1958. BFI National Archive. Special Collections. Hammer Film Productions Collection. Item 19e.
Hinds, A. to Rawlinson, A. R. (1958), 'Tales of Frankenstein: Synopsis One', 26 March 1958. BFI National Archive. Special Collections. Hammer Film Productions Collection. Item 19e.
Kersh, C. (1958), 'Tales of Frankenstein: Synopsis Three', 1958. BFI National Archive. Special Collections. Hammer Film Productions Collection. Item 19e.
Rawlinson, A. R. (1958), 'Tales of Frankenstein: Synopsis One', 26 March 1958. BFI National Archive. Special Collections. Hammer Film Productions Collection. Item 19e.
Sangster, J. to Carreras, M. [correspondence], undated. BFI National Archive. Special Collections. Hammer Film Productions Collection. Item 19a.
Woodhouse, H. (1958), 'Tales of Frankenstein: Synopsis Two', 1 April 1958. BFI National Archive. Special Collections. Hammer Film Productions Collection. Item 19e.

Hammer Script Archive

Anon. (1975a), 'Merchanising [sic] Promotional Concepts for the Trade Launch of "Vampirella"', 8 August 1975. Hammer Script Archive. De Montfort University.

Anon. (1975b), 'Vampirella Preliminary Unit List – Number 1', 7 October 1975. Hammer Script Archive. De Montfort University.
Anon. (1975c), 'Proposed Cast List', 30 October 1975. Hammer Script Archive. De Montfort University.
Anon. (1975d), 'Revised Budget', 10 September 1975. Hammer Script Archive. De Montfort University.
Anon. (1975e), 'Shooting Schedule', 15 September 1975. Hammer Script Archive. De Montfort University.
Anon. (1975f), 'Sets and Settings', 23 September 1975. Hammer Script Archive. De Montfort University.
Anon. (1975g), 'Preliminary Crew List', 7 October 1975. Hammer Script Archive. De Montfort University.
Anon. (1975h), 'Location Report', 15 October 1975. Hammer Script Archive. De Montfort University.
Anon. (1976a), 'Budget Summary', 26 March 1976. Hammer Script Archive. De Montfort University.
Anon. (1976b), 'Details of suggested Bryan Forbes contract as received from Penny Wesson and Tony Williams', 11 June 1976. Hammer Script Archive. De Montfort University.
Anon. (2000a), 'Literary materials held on Hammer Projects', 29 February 2000. Hammer Script Archive. De Montfort University.
Carreras, M. (undated), 'Columbia Terms of Agreement'. Hammer Script Archive. De Montfort University.
Carreras, M. (1976), 'Nessie-Columbia'. Hammer Script Archive. De Montfort University.
Carreras, M. to Begelman, D. [correspondence], 27 October 1976. Hammer Script Archive. De Montfort University.
Carreras, M. to Forbes, B. [correspondence], 14 September 1976. Hammer Script Archive. De Montfort University.
Carreras, M. to Frost, D. [correspondence], 5 February 1976. Hammer Script Archive. De Montfort University.
Carreras, M. to Gersh [correspondence], 22 September 1976. Hammer Script Archive. De Montfort University.
Carreras, M. to Gierse, H. [correspondence], 26 August 1976. Hammer Script Archive. De Montfort University.
Carreras, M. to Houghton, D. [correspondence], 14 October 1974. Hammer Script Archive. De Montfort University.
Carreras, M. to Jaffe, S. [correspondence], 23 November 1976. Hammer Script Archive. De Montfort University.
Carreras, M. to Jaffe, S. [correspondence], 9 December 1976. Hammer Script Archive. De Montfort University.
Carreras, M. to Lloyd, E. [correspondence], 6 January 1976. Hammer Script Archive. De Montfort University.
Carreras, M. to Lloyd, E. [correspondence], 10 February 1976. Hammer Script Archive. De Montfort University.
Carreras, M. to Lloyd, E. [correspondence], 15 March 1976. Hammer Script Archive. De Montfort University.
Carreras, M. to Lloyd, E. [correspondence], 2 April 1976. Hammer Script Archive. De Montfort University.

Carreras, M. to Lloyd, E. [correspondence], 26 August 1976. Hammer Script Archive. De Montfort University.
Carreras, M. to Lloyd, E. [correspondence], 29 June 1977. Hammer Script Archive. De Montfort University.
Carreras, M. to Lloyd, E. [correspondence], 4 November 1977. Hammer Script Archive. De Montfort University.
Carreras, M. to Lloyd, E. et al. [correspondence], 11 August 1976. Hammer Script Archive. De Montfort University.
Carreras, M. to Russell, K. [correspondence], October 1974. Hammer Script Archive. De Montfort University.
Carreras, M. to Tennant, B. [correspondence], 24 November 1976. Hammer Script Archive. De Montfort University.
Carreras, M. to Williams, A. [correspondence], 31 August 1976. Hammer Script Archive. De Montfort University.
Carreras, M. to Williams, A. [correspondence], 23 December 1976. Hammer Script Archive. De Montfort University.
Carreras, M. and Lloyd, E. to Toho [correspondence], 4 August 1976. Hammer Script Archive. De Montfort University.
Charlton to Carreras, M. [correspondence], 24 June 1976. Hammer Script Archive. De Montfort University.
Elder, J. [Hinds, T.] (undated), *Dracula High Priest of Vampires*, unpublished screenplay, undated c. 1970. Hammer Script Archive. De Montfort University.
Elder, J. [Hinds, T.] (1977), *The Unquenchable Thirst of Dracula*, unpublished screenplay, February 1977. Hammer Script Archive. De Montfort University.
Ellis, A. (undated), *Vlad the Impaler*, unpublished screenplay, undated c. 1982–3. Hammer Script Archive. De Montfort University.
Ellis, A. (undated), *Vlad the Impaler*, unpublished screenplay [annotated], undated c. 1982–3. Hammer Script Archive. De Montfort University.
Ellis, A. (undated), *Black Sabbath*, unpublished screenplay, undated c. 1986. Hammer Script Archive. De Montfort University.
Forbes, B. (1976), *Nessie*, unpublished screenplay, August 1976. Hammer Script Archive. De Montfort University.
Forbes, B. to Carreras, M. and Lloyd, E. [correspondence], 22 July 1976. Hammer Script Archive. De Montfort University.
Forbes, B. to Carreras, M. [correspondence], 28 August 1976. Hammer Script Archive. De Montfort University.
Forbes, B. to Carreras, M. [correspondence], 4 September 1976. Hammer Script Archive. De Montfort University.
Forbes, B., Wicking, C. and Starr, J. (1978), *Nessie*, unpublished shooting script, 28 March 1978. Hammer Script Archive. De Montfort University.
Hayles, B. (undated), *Dracula: The Beginning*, unpublished screenplay, undated c. 1974. Hammer Script Archive. De Montfort University.
Hayles, B. (undated), *Vlad the Impaler*, unpublished screenplay, undated c. 1974. Hammer Script Archive. De Montfort University.
Hinds, A. to Carreras, M. [correspondence], 31 January 1977. Hammer Script Archive. De Montfort University.
Hinds, A. to Carreras, M. [correspondence], 3 February 1977. Hammer Script Archive. De Montfort University.

Houghton, D. (undated), *A Devil Bride for Dracula*, unpublished screenplay, undated c. 1974. Hammer Script Archive. De Montfort University.
Houghton, D. (1972a), *Victim of His Imagination*, unpublished treatment, January 1972. Hammer Script Archive. De Montfort University.
Houghton, D. (1972b), *Victim of His Imagination*, unpublished treatment [annotated]. Hammer Script Archive. De Montfort University.
Houghton, D. (1974), *Dracula and the Curse of Kali*, unpublished treatment, May 1974. Hammer Script Archive. De Montfort University.
Houghton, D. (1974), *Dracula and the Blood Lust of Kali*, unpublished treatment [annotated], June 1974. Hammer Script Archive. De Montfort University.
Houghton, D. (1974), *Kali Devil Bride of Dracula*, unpublished treatment, June 1974. Hammer Script Archive. De Montfort University.
Houghton, D. (1974), *Devil Bride of Dracula*, unpublished treatment, November 1974. Hammer Script Archive. De Montfort University.
Houghton, D. to Carreras, M. [correspondence], 16 October 1974. Hammer Script Archive. De Montfort University.
Jaffe, S. to Carreras, M. [correspondence], 30 November 1976. Hammer Script Archive. De Montfort University.
Lawrence, B. to Carreras, M. [correspondence], 12 March 1974. Hammer Script Archive. De Montfort University.
Lloyd, E. to Carreras, M. [correspondence], undated. Hammer Script Archive. De Montfort University.
Lloyd, E. to Carreras, M. [correspondence], 12 March 1976. Hammer Script Archive. De Montfort University.
Lloyd, E. to Carreras, M. [correspondence], 30 August 1976. Hammer Script Archive. De Montfort University.
Lloyd, E. to Carreras, M. [correspondence], 2 November 1977. Hammer Script Archive. De Montfort University.
Lloyd, E. to Matsuoka, I. [correspondence], 9 August 1976. Hammer Script Archive. De Montfort University.
Lloyd, E. to Pierotti [correspondence], 18 August 1976. Hammer Script Archive. De Montfort University.
Lloyd, E. to Seinger, T. [correspondence], 18 August 1976. Hammer Script Archive. De Montfort University.
Lloyd, E. to Wragge, M. [correspondence], 18 August 1976. Hammer Script Archive. De Montfort University.
McCord, J. (undated), *Vlad the Impaler*, unpublished screenplay, undated c. 1993. Hammer Script Archive. De Montfort University.
McCord, J. (undated), *Vlad Dracul*, unpublished screenplay, undated c. 1993. Hammer Script Archive. De Montfort University.
Matheson, R. (1957), *The Night Creatures*, unpublished screenplay, November 1957. Hammer Script Archive. De Montfort University.
Matsuoka, I. to Lloyd, E. [correspondence], 13 September 1976. Hammer Script Archive. De Montfort University.
Matsuoka, I. to Lloyd, E. [correspondence], 24 October 1977. Hammer Script Archive. De Montfort University.
Matsuoka, I. to Lloyd, E. and Carreras, M. [correspondence], 4 August 1976. Hammer Script Archive. De Montfort University.

Netter, D. to Hassanein, S. [correspondence], 23 June 1976. Hammer Script Archive. De Montfort University.

Netter, D. to Matsuoka, I. [correspondence], 24 February 1978. Hammer Script Archive. De Montfort University.

Newman, P. R. (undated), *The Rape of Sabena*, unpublished screenplay, undated c. 1960. Hammer Script Archive. De Montfort University.

Peacock, J. (undated), *Vlad the Impaler*, unpublished screenplay, undated c. 1988. Hammer Script Archive. De Montfort University.

Quinn, K. (undated), *The Day the Earth Caught Fire*, unpublished screenplay, undated c. 1992. Hammer Script Archive. De Montfort University.

Russel, K. to Carreras, M. [correspondence], October 1974. Hammer Script Archive. De Montfort University.

Sachs, T. to Matsuoka, I. [correspondence], 30 July 1976. Hammer Script Archive. De Montfort University.

Seinger, T. to Carreras, M. [correspondence], 28 July 1976. Hammer Script Archive. De Montfort University.

Sidaway, R. and Sidaway, A. (undated), *The Four Sided Triangle*, unpublished screenplay, undated. Hammer Script Archive. De Montfort University.

Sidaway, R. and Sidaway, A. (1992), *Legacy*, unpublished screenplay, 25 June 1992. Hammer Script Archive. De Montfort University.

Starr, J. (1977), *Vampirella*, unpublished screenplay, February 1977. Hammer Script Archive. De Montfort University.

Subotsky, M. (undated), *Frankenstein*, unpublished screenplay [copy], undated c. 1956. Hammer Script Archive. De Montfort University.

Toho Draft Agreement [contract], With Hammer Film Productions and Euan Lloyd Productions, 11 March 1976. Hammer Script Archive. De Montfort University.

Toho Draft Agreement [contract], With Richmond Film Production (West) Ltd, 23 July 1976. Hammer Script Archive. De Montfort University.

Wesson, P. and Williams, A. to Carreras, M. [correspondence], 14 June 1976. Hammer Script Archive. De Montfort University.

Wicking, C. (1975), *Vampirella*, unpublished screenplay, October 1975. Hammer Script Archive. De Montfort University.

Wicking, C. (1992), *The Four Sided Triangle*, unpublished screenplay, July 1992. Hammer Script Archive. De Montfort University.

Williams, A. to Carreras, M. [correspondence], 10 August 1976. Hammer Script Archive. De Montfort University.

Williams, A. to Carreras, M. [correspondence], September 1976. Hammer Script Archive. De Montfort University.

Williams, A. to Carreras, M. [correspondence], 23 November 1976. Hammer Script Archive. De Montfort University.

Williams, A. to Carreras, M. [correspondence], 16 December 1976. Hammer Script Archive. De Montfort University.

Wragge, M. to Carreras, M. [correspondence], 31 August 1976. Hammer Script Archive. De Montfort University.

Margaret Herrick Archive

Anderson, P. to Shurlock, G. [correspondence], 20 November 1957. Margaret Herrick Library. MPAA Collection. The Night Creatures File.

Anon. to Carreras, M. [correspondence], 14 November 1974. Margaret Herrick Library. The Guy Green Papers. File 52.
Coleman, M. to Femme Fatales Magazines (1995) [correspondence], 13 September 1995. Margaret Herrick Library. MPAA Collection. The Night Creatures File.
Kelley, J. and Kelley, B. (1975) [interview], 'Cushing Interview', 1975. Margaret Herrick Library. Cinefantastique Magazine Records. File 2620.
Shurlock, G. to Elwood, R. P. [correspondence], 24 May 1961. Margaret Herrick Library. MPAA Collection. The Night Creatures File.
Shurlock, G. to Hinds, A. [correspondence], 4 December 1957. Margaret Herrick Library. MPAA Collection. The Night Creatures File.
Swires, S. (1975), 'Horror as a Family Business: Inside the House of Hammer', November 1975. Margaret Herrick Library. Cinefantastique Magazine Records. File 2522.
White, G. to Shurlock, G. [correspondence], 30 March 1961. Margaret Herrick Library. MPAA Collection. The Night Creatures File.

Unpublished material

Ellis, A. (2016), interviewed by Kieran Foster, 30 April.
Hearn, M. (2016), interviewed by Kieran Foster, 20 December.
Meikle, D. (2016), interviewed by Kieran Foster, 7 November.

Warner Bros. Archive

Subotsky, M. (undated), *Frankenstein*, unpublished screenplay, undated c. 1956. Warner Bros. Archives. University of Southern California.

Books, articles and reports

Abbot, S. (2009), 'High Concept Thrills and Chills: The Horror Blockbuster', in I. Conrich (ed.), *The Horror Zone*, London: I. B. Tauris, pp. 27–44.
Abbott, S. (2016), *Undead Apocalypse: Vampires and Zombies in the Twenty-First Century*, Edinburgh: Edinburgh University Press.
Anon. (1956), 'Kings of the Bogey Men!', *Variety (Archive: 1905–2000)*, 204 (10), p. 21.
Anon. (1957a), 'Stations Loves Those Chillers, SG's $2,500,000 Sales on U Pix', *Variety (Archive: 1905–2000)*, 207 (12), pp. 28, 40.
Anon. (1957b), 'SG's "Frankenstein"', *Variety (Archive: 1905–2000)*, 208 (4), p. 31.
Anon. (1957c), 'ABC, Screen Gems Set "Frankenstein"', *Variety (Archive: 1905–2000)*, 208 (8), p. 50.
Anon. (1957d), 'ABC-TV, SG Agree on "Frankenstein"', *Broadcasting (Archive 1957–1993)*, 53 (22), p. 90.
Anon. (1957e), 'Carreras Makes Vidpic Pilot on "Frankenstein"', *Variety (Archive: 1905–2000)*, 208 (13), p. 16.
Anon. (1957f), 'Diffring Coast-Bound for "Frankenstein"', *Variety (Archive: 1905–2000)*, 209 (2), p. 52.
Anon. (1957g), 'London', *Variety (Archive: 1905–2000)*, 208 (4), p. 74.
Anon. (1958d), 'Pictures: Horror Remains a Money Commodity; and James Carreras Oughta Know', *Variety (Archive: 1905–2000)*, 210 (13), p. 7.
Anon. (1972), 'Hammer's twenty-fifth Anniversary pull-out', *Films Illustrated*, December issue.

Anon. (1975a), '"Alice" Pleasant $28,300, Cleve; "Vrooder" Dim $3,300, "Spook" 4G', *Variety (Archive: 1905–2000)*, 278 (3), p. 18.

Anon. (1975b), 'Heatwave Nips Portland; "Ride" So-So 31/2G, "Wives" Pale £3,500, "Jaws" 141/2G', *Variety (Archive: 1905–2000)*, 280 (6), p. 14.

Anon. (1976a), 'Ready for World Release Easter 1977', *Variety (Archive: 1905–2000)*, 283 (2), p. 40.

Anon. (1976c), 'The Slipper and the Rose The Story of Cinderella', *Variety (Archive: 1905–2000)*, 282 (13), p. 35.

Anon. (1977b), '"Wild Geese" takes off', *Screen International (Archive: 1976–2000)*, (107), p. 13.

Anon. (1977c), 'Certain Things are Regulated', *Der Spiegel* [online], (48), <http://www.spiegel.de/spiegel/print/d-40680598.html> [TRANSLATED] (last accessed 24 February 2019).

Anon. (1978), '"Hollywoodgate" Issue Steamy', *Variety (Archive: 1905–2000)*, 291 (6), p. 4.

Anon. (1993), 'Television News: Warner snaps up Hammer classics', *The Stage and Television Today (Archive: 1959–1994)*, (5861), p. 20.

Anon. (1995), 'Production European', *Screen International (Archive: 1976–2000)*, (993), pp. 28–32, 34–8, 40.

Anon. (1996), 'European Production', *Screen International (Archive: 1976–2000)*, (1067), pp. 19–20, 22–32, 34–5.

Anon. (1997), 'European Production', *Screen International (Archive: 1976–2000)*, (1101), pp. 34–8, 40, 42–6.

Anon. (2000b), 'Programming and Production: Hammer Mulls Indie Deals', *Broadcasting (Archive: 1973–2000)*, (6), p. 2.

Anon. (2013), 'Getting Movies Made is a "Miracle" Says Oblivion Director', BBC News Online (last accessed 12 September 2022).

Armstrong, R. (2008), '"To Get Things Done … " Jarman, Bowie and *Neutron*', in D. North (ed.), *Sights Unseen: Unfinished British Films*, Newcastle: Cambridge Scholars Publishing, pp. 105–20.

Atkins, T. R. (1976), *Ken Russell*, New York: Monarch Press.

Baillieu, B. and J. Goodchild (2002), *The British Film Business*, New Jersey: Wiley.

Barnett, V. (2014), 'Hammering Out a Deal: The Contractual and Commercial Contexts of The Curse of Frankenstein (1957) and Dracula (1958)', *Historical Journal of Film, Radio and Television*, 34 (2), pp. 231–52.

Barthes, R. (1967), 'Death of the Author', *Aspen 5–6: The Minimalism Issue*, Fall/Winter.

Bateman, L. (1993), 'Hammer Back from the Dead', *Screen International (Archive: 1976–2000)*, (918), p. 2.

BBC Online (2013), 'Getting movies made is a "miracle" says Oblivion director', <https://www.bbc.co.uk/news/av/entertainment-arts-22113842> (last accessed 9 January 2023).

Bettinson, G. (2011), 'The Shaw Brothers Meet Hammer: Coproduction, Coherence and Cult Film Criteria', *Asian Cinema*, 22 (1), pp. 122–37.

Blurton, R. (1993), *Hindu Art*, Cambridge, MA: Harvard University Press.

Box Office Mojo, *1984 Domestic Grosses*, https://www.boxofficemojo.com/yearly/chart/?yr=1984&p=.htm (last accessed 18 December 2018).

Box Office Mojo, *Bram Stoker's Dracula*, <https://www.boxofficemojo.com/movies/?id=bramstokersdracula.htm> (last accessed 18 December 2018).

Box Office Mojo, *Jaws*, <https://www.boxofficemojo.com/movies/?id=jaws.htm> (last accessed 31 March 2023).
Brock, J. (2014), *Disorders of Magnitude: A Survey of Dark Fantasy*, Lanham, MD: Rowman & Littlefield.
Carringer, R. (1985), *The Making of Citizen Kane*, Berkeley: University of California Press.
Casper, D. (2012), *Hollywood Film 1963–1976*, Chichester: Wiley-Blackwell.
Castle, A. (2009), *Stanley Kubrick's Napoleon: The Greatest Movie Never Made*, Cologne: Taschen.
Chapman, J., M. Glancy and S. Harper (2007), 'Introduction', in J. Chapman, M. Glancy and S. Harper (eds), *The New Film History: Sources, Methods, Approaches*, Basingstoke: Palgrave MacMillan, pp. 1–10.
Chibnall, S. and R. Murphy (1999), *British Crime Cinema*, London: Routledge.
Clark, N. (2012), 'Simon Oakes: "It's a welcome return, We've managed to fire people's imaginations"', *The Independent*, <https://www.independent.co.uk/arts-entertainment/films/features/simon-oakes-its-a-welcome-return-weve-managed-to-fire-peoples-imaginations-7216693.html> (last accessed 24 February 2019).
Cobb, S. (2014), 'Women Directors and Lost Projects', [Blog] *Women's Film & Television History Network*, <https://womensfilmandtelevisionhistory.wordpress.com/2014/03/21/women-directors-and-lost-projects/> (last accessed 23 February 2019).
Cobb, S. (2015), *Adaptation, Authorship, and Contemporary Women Filmmakers*, New York: Palgrave MacMillan.
Cobb, S., L. R. Williams and N. Wreyford (2016), *Calling the Shots: Women and Contemporary UK Film Culture*, [report], University of Southhampton.
Collins, F. (2016), 'A Tale of Unspeakable Cravings' [Blu-ray booklet], *The Count Yorga Collection*, Arrow Video, United Kingdom.
Connett, D. (1993), 'Hammer Films Returns to Revamp Horror Classics', *The Independent*, <https://www.independent.co.uk/news/uk/hammer-films-returns-to-revamp-horror-classics-1459372.html> (last accessed 24 February 2019).
Conrich, I. (2008), 'The Divergence and Mutation of British Horror Cinema', in R. Shail (ed.), *Seventies British Cinema*, London: British Film Institute/Palgrave MacMillan, pp. 25–35.
Couch, A. (2022), '"Batgirl" Directors "Saddened and Shocked" After Movie Is Shelved', *The Hollywood Reporter*, <https://www.hollywoodreporter.com/movies/movie-news/batgirl-directors-hbo-max-canceled-1235191936/> (last accessed 13 September 2022).
Cripps, T. (1975), 'The Future Film Historian: Less Art and More Craft', *Cinema Journal*, Winter, 14 (2), pp. 42–6.
Curran, J. and V. Porter (1983), *British Cinema History*, London: Weidenfeld and Nicolson.
David, S. (2002), *The Indian Mutiny: 1857*, London: Penguin Books.
Davies, B. (1976), 'Slipper and the Rose, The', *Monthly Film Bulletin*, 43 (504), pp. 107–8.
Dawtrey, A. (2000), 'Film/International: New Owners Hammer our Strategy for Horror Brand', *Variety (Archive: 1905–2000)*, 377 (131), p. 25.
Dick, B. (1992), 'The History of Columbia, 1920–1991', in B. Dick (ed.), *Columbia Pictures: Portrait of a Studio*, Lexington, KY: University Press of Kentucky, pp. 2–65.
Dickinson, M. (1983), 'The State and the Consolidation of Monopoly', in J. Curran and V. Porter (eds), *British Cinema History*, London: Weidenfeld and Nicolson, pp. 74–98.

Dickinson, M. and S. Street (1985), *Cinema and the State: The Film Industry and the British Government 1927–1984*, London: British Film Institute.

Dixon, W. W. (2008), 'The End of Hammer', in R. Shail (ed.), *Seventies British Cinema*, London: British Film Institute/Palgrave MacMillan, pp. 14–24.

Ede, L. N. (2012), 'British Film Design in the 1970s', in S. Harper and J. Smith (eds), *British Film Culture in the 1970s: The Boundaries of Pleasure*, Edinburgh: Edinburgh University Press, pp. 50–61.

Elgood, H. (2000), *Hinduism and the Religious Arts*, London: Bloomsbury.

Eyles, A., R. Adkinson and N. Fry (1994), *House of Horror: The Complete Hammer Films Story*, London: Creation Books.

Falks, Q. (1987), 'News: Hammer Heads Back to Cinema', *Screen International (Archive: 1976–2000)*, (607), p. 2.

Fenwick, J. (2017), 'The Eady Levy, "the Envy of Most Other European Nations": Runaway Productions and the British Film Fund in the Early 1960s', in I. Q. Hunter, L. Porter and J. Smith (eds), *The Routledge Companion to British Cinema History*, London: Routledge.

Fenwick, J. (2021) *Unproduction Studies and The American Film Industry*, London: Routledge.

Fenwick, J., K. Foster and D. Eldridge (eds) (2020), *Shadow Cinema: The Historical and Production Contexts of Unmade Films*, New York: Bloomsbury Academic and Professional.

Forshaw, B. (2013), *British Gothic Cinema*, London: Palgrave Macmillan.

Foster, K. (2017), 'Dracula Unseen: The Death and Afterlife of Hammer's *Vlad the Impaler*', *Journal of Adaptation in Film & Performance*, 10 (3), pp. 203–15.

Francis, F. with T. Dalton (2013), *The Straight Story from Moby Dick to Glory*, Plymouth: Scarecrow Press.

Frank, A. (1978), 'Today and Tomorrow', *Little Shoppe of Horrors*, (4), pp. 30–3.

Gajewski, R. (2022), ''Batgirl' Star Leslie Grace Responds After Film Is Shelved, Calls Herself "My Own Damn Hero"', *The Hollywood Reporter*, <https://www.hollywoodreporter.com/movies/movie-news/batgirl-star-leslie-grace-responds-film-shelved-1235192379/> (last accessed 13 September 2022).

Gilbert, S. (1996), 'They live again', *The Observer*, 30 June 1996, p. 137.

Goldstein, S. (1996), 'Demand for Reclaiming Foreign C'rights Less Frenzied Than Expected', *Billboard*, 108 (23), p. 91.

Hall, S. (2006), 'Blockbusters in the 1970s', in L. R. Williams and M. Hammond, *Contemporary American Cinema*, Maidenhead: McGraw-Hill Education, pp. 164–84.

Hallenbeck, B. (2010), *British Cult Cinema: The Hammer Vampire*, Hailsham: Hemlock Books.

Hallenbeck, B. (2018), *Hammer on Television*, Hailsham: Hemlock Books.

Harper, S. and V. Porter, (2003), *British Cinema of the 1950s: The Decline of Deference*, Oxford: Oxford University Press.

Harper, S. and J. Smith, (2012), *British Film Culture in the 1970s: The Boundaries of Pleasure*, Edinburgh: Edinburgh University Press.

Hawk (1976), 'Film Reviews: The Slipper And The Rose', *Variety (Archive: 1905–2000)*, 282 (10), p. 27.

Hearn, M. (2010), *The Art of Hammer: Posters from the Archive of Hammer Films*, London: Titan Books.

Hearn, M. (2011), *The Hammer Vault: Treasures from the Archive of Hammer Films*, London: Titan Books.

Hearn, M. and A. Barnes (2007), *The Hammer Story: The Authorised History of Hammer Films*, 2nd edn, London: Titan Books.
Higson, A. (1993), 'A Diversity of Film Practices: renewing British cinema in the 1970s', in B. Moore-Gilbert (ed.), *The Arts in the 1970s: Cultural Closure?*, London: Routledge, pp. 216–39.
Houston, P. (1966), 'England, Their England', *Sight and Sound*, 35 (2), p. 54.
Hughes, D. (2008), *The Greatest Sci-Fi Movies Never Made*, 2nd edn, London: Titan Books.
Hughes, D. (2012), *Tales from Development Hell: The Greatest Movies Never Made*, 2nd edn, London: Titan Books.
Hutchings, P. (1993), *Hammer and Beyond: The British Horror Film*, Manchester: Manchester University Press.
Hutchings, P. (2002), 'The Amicus House of Horror', in S. Chibnall and J. Petley (eds), *British Horror Cinema*, London: Routledge, pp. 131–44.
Hutchings, P. (2004), *The Horror Film*, London: Pearson Education Limited.
Hutchings, P. (2008), 'American Vampires in Britain: Richard Matheson's *I am Legend* and Hammer's *The Night Creatures*', in D. North (ed.), *Sights Unseen: Unfinished British Films*, Newcastle: Cambridge Scholars Publishing, pp. 53–71.
Hutchinson, T. (1957), 'Stop, Look and Listen', *Picturegoer (Archive 1932–1960)*, 34 (1166), p. 16.
Ilott, T. (1984),'Hammer are Back in Business with 13 Features Produced in Under 35 Weeks', *Screen International (Archive: 1976–2000)*, (452), pp. 13–14.
Jones, A. (1994), 'The Return of Hammer Horror', *Cinefantastique*, 4 February 1994, pp. 4–5, 125.
Jones, C. and J. Ryan (2006), *Encyclopaedia of Hinduism*, New York: Infobase Publishing.
Kalat, D. (2017), *A Critical History and Filmography of Toho's Godzilla Series*, 2nd edn, Jefferson, NC: McFarland and Company.
Kermode, M. (1997), *The Exorcist*, London: British Film Institute.
Kermode, M. (2005), 'Star Wars', in L. R. Williams and M. Hammond, *Contemporary American Cinema*, Maidenhead: McGraw-Hill Education, pp. 172–4.
Kerrigan, F. (2010), *Film Marketing*, London: Routledge.
Kinsey, W. (2002), *Hammer Films: The Bray Studios Years*, Surrey: Reynolds and Hearn.
Kinsey, W. (2007), *Hammer Films: The Elstree Studios Years*, Sheffield: Tomahawk Press.
Kinsey, W. (2010), *Hammer Films: The Unsung Heroes*, Sheffield: Tomahawk Press.
Klemensen, R. (2016), '"Thank Goodness, It's Only For Two Weeks", Roy Skeggs – A Lifetime in Hammer', *Little Shoppe of Horrors*, 37.
Koetting, C. (1994), 'When the Set on Hammer', *Little Shoppe of Horrors*, (13), p. 52.
Krämer, P. (2005), *The New Hollywood: From Bonnie and Clyde to Star Wars*, London: Wallflower Press.
Krämer, P. (2016), 'Adaptation as Exploration: Stanley Kubrick, Literature and A.I. Artificial Intelligence', *Adaptation: The Journal of Literature on Screen Studies*, 18 (3), pp. 372–82.
Krämer, P. (2018), 'An Angel in Hell: Artur Brauner and the Attempt to Make a German Oskar-Schindler-Biopic', *sinecine: Sinema Araştırmaları Dergisi*, 9 (1), pp. 45–80.
Long, R. E. (2006), *James Ivory in Conversation: How Merchant Ivory Makes Its Movies*, Berkeley: University of California Press.

Louis, S. (2017), 'Twenty-first Century Vampires: From the Dracula Myth to New (American) Superheroes', *Journal of Adaptation in Film and Performance*, 10 (3), pp. 249–62.

McClintick, D. (1982), *Indecent Exposure: A True Story of Hollywood and Wall Street*, New York: William Morrow.

McFarlane, B. (1996), *Novel to Film: An Introduction to the Theory of Adaptation*, Oxford: Oxford University Press.

McKenna, A. T. (2012), 'Gaps and Gold in the Klinger Archive', *Journal of British Cinema and Television*, 9 (1), pp. 111–21.

Magor, M. and P. Schlesinger (2009), '"For this relief much thanks", Taxation, Film Policy and the UK Government', *Screen*, 50 (3), pp. 299–317.

Matheson, R. (1954), *I Am Legend*, New York: Gold Medal Books.

Meikle, D. (2009), *A History of Horrors: The Rise and Fall of the House of Hammer*, 2nd edn, Lanham, MD: Scarecrow Press.

Meir, C. (2009), 'The Producer as Salesman: Jeremy Thomas, Film Promotion and Contemporary Transnational Independent Cinema', *Historical Journal of Film, Radio and Television*, 29 (4), pp. 467–81.

Melia, M. (2022), 'The Shared History of Stanley Kubrick's A Clockwork Orange (1971) and Ken Russell's The Devils (1971)', *Historical Journal of Film, Radio and Television*, 42 (1), pp. 8–23.

Moore, S. (1976), 'Behind the Scenes at Hammer Studios', *The House of Hammer* (2), pp. 26–9.

Murf (1975), 'Film review: The Stepford Wives', *Variety (Archive: 1905–2000)*, 278 (1), p. 28.

Murphy, M. (1998), 'Interview with Anthony Hinds', *Dark Terrors*, 16, p. 11.

Murray, S. (2008), 'Phantom Adaptations: *Eucalyptus*, the Adaptation Industry and the Film that Never Was', *Adaptation*, 1 (1), pp. 5–23.

Myers (1957), 'Col '58 Brit, Pix Seen Getting 50% of its UK Gross', *Variety (Archive: 1905–2000)*, 208 (2), pp. 7, 12.

Norman, B. (2015), 'Reading a "closet screenplay": Hollywood, James Baldwin's Malcolms and the threat of historical irrelevance', *African American Review*, 39(1/2), pp. 103–18.

North, D. (2008), *Sights Unseen: Unfinished British Films*, Newcastle: Cambridge Scholars Publishing.

Nutman, P. (2008), 'Scream and Scream Again: The Uncensored History of Amicus Productions', *Little Shoppe of Horrors*, 20.

Nwonka, C. J. (2020), *Race and Ethnicity in the UK Film Industry: An Analysis of the BFI Diversity Standards* [report], LSE.

Oleksinski, J. (2022), '"Irredeemable" "Batgirl" Movie Gets "Shelved" by Warner Bros, Despite $70m Price Tag: Source', *New York Post* [online], <https://nypost.com/2022/08/02/batgirl-movie-gets-shelved-by-warner-bros-source/> (last accessed 13 September 2022).

Phelps, G. (1975), *Film Censorship*, Sussex: Littlehampton Book Services.

Picart, C. (2002), *The Cinematic Rebirths of FRANKENSTEIN: Universal, Hammer, and Beyond*, Westport, CT: Praeger Publishers.

Pirie, D. (1973), *Heritage of Horror: The English Gothic Cinema, 1946–1972*, London: Gordon Fraser.

Pirie, D. (2008), *A New Heritage of Horror: The English Gothic Cinema*, London: I. B. Tauris.

Porter, V. (1982), 'The Context of Creativity: Ealing Studios and Hammer Films', in J. Curran and V. Porter (eds), *British Cinema History*, London: Weidenfeld and Nicolson, pp. 179–207.
Ramachandran, N. (2021), '*Dracula* Producer Hammer Films Teams With Network Distributing to Form Hammer Studios', *Variety*, <https://variety.com/2021/film/global/dracula-hammer-films-network-distributing-1235117981/> (last accessed 13 September 2022).
Rigby, J. (2002), *English Gothic*, 2nd ed, Richmond: Reynolds and Hearn.
Sangster, J. (2001), *Inside Hammer*, Richmond: Reynolds and Hearn.
Sanjek, D. (1992), 'Twilight of the Monsters: The English Horror Film 1968–1975', *Film Criticism*, 16 (1), pp. 111–26, 135.
Shail, R. (2008), *Seventies British Cinema*, London: British Film Institute/Palgrave MacMillan.
Shelley, M. (1818), *Frankenstein*, London: Lackington, Hughes, Harding, Mavor and Jones.
Shiel, M. (2006), 'American Cinema 1965–70', in L. Williams and M. Hammond (eds), *Contemporary American Cinema*, Berkshire: Open University Press, pp. 12–40.
Skal, D. J. (2011) 'Introduction' – Dracula: Undead and Unseen', in J. E. Browning and C. J. Picart (eds), *Dracula in Visual Media: Film, Television, Comic Book and Electronic Game Appearances, 1921–2010*. Jefferson, NC: McFarland and Company, pp. 9–17.
Skinn, D. and J. Brosnan (1978), 'Hammerhead – An Interview with Michael Carreras', *The House of Hammer*, (17), pp. 20–4.
Spicer, A. (1999), 'The Emergence of the British Tough Guy: Stanley Baker, Masculinity and the Crime Thriller', in S. Chibnall and R. Murphy (eds), *British Crime Cinema*, London: Routledge, pp. 81–93.
Spicer, A. (2007), 'The Author as Author: Restoring the Screenwriter to British Film History', in J. Chapman, M. Glancy and S. Harper (eds), *The New Film History: Sources, Methods, Approaches*, Basingstoke: Palgrave MacMillan, pp. 89–103.
Spicer, A. (2008), 'Missing Boxes: The Unmade Films of Sydney Box, 1940–1967', in D. North (ed.), *Sights Unseen: Unfinished British Films*, Newcastle: Cambridge Scholars Publishing, pp. 87–105.
Spicer, A. (2010), 'Creativity and Commerce: Michael Klinger and New Film History', *New Review of Film and Television Studies*, 8 (3), pp. 297–314.
Spicer, A. and A. T. McKenna (2013), *The Man Who Got Carter: Michael Klinger, Independent Production and the British Film Industry 1960–1980*, London: I. B. Tauris.
Spicer, A., A. T. McKenna and C. Meir (2014), *Beyond the Bottom Line: The Producer in Film and Television Studies*, London: Bloomsbury.
Springhall, J. (2009), 'Hammer, House of Horror: The Making of a British Film Company, 1934 to 1979', *Historian*, (104), pp. 14–19.
Stoker, B. (1897), *Dracula*, London: Archibald Constable.
Street, S. (2002), *Transatlantic Crossings: British Feature Films in the USA*, New York: Continuum International Publishing Group.
Street, S. (2009), *British National Cinema*, 2nd edn, Abingdon: Routledge, pp. 87–9.
Strong, E. (1957), 'SG to "Program" Universal's 550', *The Billboard (Archive: 1894–1960)*, 69 (2), p. 18.
Strub, W. (2015), 'The Baraka Film Archive: The Lost, Unmade, and Unseen Film Work of LeRoi Jones/Amiri Baraka', *Black Camera: An International Film Journal* (The New Series), 7 (1), pp. 273–87.

Stubbs, J. (2009), 'The Eady Levy: A Runaway Bribe? Hollywood Production and British Subsidy in the Early 1960s', *Journal of British Cinema and Television*, 6 (1), pp. 1–20.

Swires, S. (1987), 'Michael Carreras – Inside the House of Hammer', *Fangoria*, (63), pp. 57–68.

Thomas, D. (1976a), 'Box Office: Having a Ball – That's "Cinders"', *Screen International (Archive: 1976–2000)*, (30), p. 2.

Thomas, D. (1976b), 'Box Office', *Screen International (Archive: 1976–2000)*, (67), p. 2.

Trevelyan, J. (1977), *What the Censor Saw*, 2nd edn, London: Michael Joseph.

Tsutski, W. (2004), *Godzilla on My Mind: 50 Years of the King of Monsters*, New York: St Martin's Press.

Tsutski, W. (2006), 'Introduction', in W. Tsutski and M. Ito (eds), *In Godzilla's Footsteps: Japanese Pop Culture Icons on the Global Stage*, New York: Springer, pp. 1–9.

Vary and Lang (2022), 'Why Warner Bros, Killed "Batgirl": Inside the Decision Not to Release the DC Movie', *Variety*, <https://variety.com/2022/film/news/batgirl-movie-why-not-releasing-warner-bros-1235332062/> (last accessed 13 September 2022).

Waldman, H. (1991), *Scenes Unseen: Unreleased and Uncompleted Films from the World's Master Filmmakers, 1912–1990*, Jefferson, NC: McFarland and Co.

Walker, J. (2016), *Contemporary British Horror Cinema: Industry, Genre and Society*, Edinburgh: Edinburgh University Press.

Wynorski, J. interviewed by M. Haberfelner (2013), 'An Interview with Jim Wynorski', January 2013, <http://www.searchmytrash.com/articles/jimwynorski(1-13).shtml> (last accessed 13 June 2020).

Filmography

20,000 Leagues Under the Sea, dir. Richard Fleisher. USA: Walt Disney Productions, 1954.
28 Days Later, dir. Danny Boyle. United Kingdom: DNA Films/UK Film Council, 2002.
A Thousand Acres, dir. Jocelyn Moorhouse. USA: Beacon Pictures, 1997.
Abbott and Costello Meet Frankenstein, dir. Charles Barton. USA: Universal Pictures, 1948.
The Abominable Snowman, dir. Val Guest. United Kingdom: Hammer Film Productions, 1957.
A.I.: Artificial Intelligence, dir. Steven Spielberg. USA: Amblin Entertainment, 2001.
All Monsters Attack, dir. Ishirō Honda. Japan: Toho, 1969.
Batman and Robin, dir. Joel Schumacher. USA: Warner Bros., 1997.
Blacula, dir. William Crain. USA: American International Pictures, 1972.
Blood from the Mummy's Tomb, dir. Seth Holt. United Kingdom: Hammer Film Productions, 1964.
Bram Stoker's Dracula, dir. Francis Ford Coppola. USA: American Zoetrope/Osiris Films, 1992.
Bride of Frankenstein, dir. James Whale. USA: Universal Pictures, 1935.
The Brides of Dracula, dir. Terence Fisher. United Kingdom: Hammer Film Productions, 1960.
The Camp on Blood Island, dir. Val Guest. United Kingdom: Hammer Film Productions, 1958.
Captain Clegg, dir. Peter Graham Scott. United Kingdom: Hammer Film Productions, 1962.
Captain Kronos: Vampire Hunter, dir. Brian Clemens. United Kingdom: Hammer Film Productions, 1974.
Casque d'Or, dir. Jacques Becker. France: Robert et Raymond Hakim, 1952.
Citizen Kane, dir. Orson Welles. USA: Mercury Productions, 1942.
The City of the Dead, dir. John Llewellyn Moxey. United Kingdom: British Lion, 1960.
Close Encounters of the Third Kind, dir. Steven Spielberg. USA: Columbia Pictures, 1977.
Conflagration, dir. Katsumune Ishida. Japan: Toho, 1975.
Count Yorga, Vampire, dir. Bob Kelljan. USA: Erica Productions Inc., 1970.

The Curse of Frankenstein, dir. Terence Fisher. United Kingdom: Hammer Film Productions, 1957.
The Curse of the Mummy's Tomb, dir. Michael Carreras. United Kingdom: Hammer Film Productions, 1964.
The Curse of the Werewolf, dir. Terence Fisher. United Kingdom: Hammer Film Productions, 1961.
The Day the Earth Caught Fire, dir. Val Guest. United Kingdom: British Lion Films, 1961.
Dead of Night, dir. Alberto Cavalcanti, Charles Crichton, Robert Hamer and Basil Dearden. United Kingdom Ealing Studios, 1945.
The Deceivers, dir. Nicholas Meyer. USA: Merchant Ivory Productions, 1988.
Demons of the Mind, dir. Peter Sykes. United Kingdom: Hammer Film Productions, 1971.
Destroy All Monsters, dir. Ishirō Honda. Japan: Toho, 1968.
The Devil Rides Out, dir. Terence Fisher. United Kingdom: Hammer Film Productions, 1968.
The Devils, dir. Ken Russell. USA: Warner Brothers, 1971.
Dick Barton at Bay, dir. Godfrey Grayson. United Kingdom: Hammer Film Productions, 1950.
Dick Barton: Special Agent, dir. Alfred J. Goulding. United Kingdom: Hammer Film Productions, 1948.
Dick Barton Strikes Back, dir. Godfrey Grayson. United Kingdom: Hammer Film Productions, 1949.
Dirty Dozen: The Series [TV series]. USA: Fox Broadcasting Company, 1988.
Dracula, dir. Tod Browning. USA: Universal Pictures, 1931.
Dracula, dir. Terence Fisher. United Kingdom: Hammer Film Productions, 1958.
Dracula A.D. 1972, dir. Alan Gibson. United Kingdom: Hammer Film Productions, 1972.
Dracula Has Risen From the Grave, dir. Freddie Francis. United Kingdom: Hammer Film Productions, 1968.
Dracula Prince of Darkness, dir. Terence Fisher. United Kingdom: Hammer Film Productions, 1966.
Dracula Untold, dir. Gary Shore. USA: Legendary Pictures, 2014.
Earthquake, dir. Mark Robson. USA: Universal Pictures, 1974.
Ebirah, Horror of the Deep, dir. Jun Fukuda. Japan: Toho, 1966.
El Conde Dracula, dir. Jesús Franco. Spain: Fénix Films, 1970.
The Evil of Frankenstein, dir. Freddie Francis. United Kingdom: Hammer Film Productions, 1964.
The Exorcist, dir. William Friedkin. USA: Warner Bros., 1973.
Fanatic, dir. Silvio Narizzano. United Kingdom: Hammer Film Productions, 1965.
Flesh and Blood: The Hammer Heritage of Horror, dir. Ted Newsom. United Kingdom: BBC, 1994.
Frankenstein, dir. James Whale. USA: Universal Pictures, 1931.
Frankenstein and the Monster from Hell, dir. Terence Fisher. United Kingdom: Hammer Film Productions, 1974.
Frankenstein Created Woman, dir. Terence Fisher. United Kingdom: Hammer Film Productions, 1967.
Frankenstein Meets the Wolf Man, dir. Roy William Neill. USA: Universal Pictures, 1943.

Frankenstein Must Be Destroyed, dir. Terence Fisher. United Kingdom: Hammer Film Productions, 1969.
The French Connection, dir. William Friedkin. USA: 20th Century Fox, 1971.
George and Mildred, dir. Peter Frazer-Jones. United Kingdom: Cinema Arts International Production, 1980.
Ghidorah, the Three-Headed Monster, dir. Ishirō Honda. Japan: Toho, 1964.
The Ghost of Frankenstein, dir. Erle C. Kenton. USA: Universal Pictures, 1942.
The Ghoul, dir. T. Hayes Hunter. United Kingdom: Gaumont British, 1933.
The Godfather, dir. Francis Ford Coppola. USA: Paramount, 1972.
Godzilla, dir. Ishirō Honda. Japan: Toho, 1954.
Godzilla, King of the Monsters!, dir. Ishirō Honda and Terry Morse. Japan/USA: Toho/Jewel Enterprises, 1956.
Godzilla Raids Again, dir. Motoyoshi Oda. Japan: Toho, 1955.
Godzilla vs. Gigan, dir. Jun Fukuda. Japan: Toho, 1972.
Godzilla vs. Hedorah, dir. Yoshimitsu Banno. Japan: Toho, 1971.
Godzilla vs. Mechagodzilla, dir. Jun Fukuda. Japan: Toho, 1974.
Godzilla vs. Megalon, dir. Jun Fukuda. Japan: Toho, 1973.
Gone with the Wind, dir. Victor Fleming. USA: Selznick International Pictures, 1940.
The Golden Voyage of Sinbad, dir. Gordon Hessler. USA: Morningside Productions, 1973.
The Gorgon, dir. Terence Fisher. United Kingdom: Hammer Film Productions, 1964.
Grizzly, dir. William Girdler. USA: Columbia Pictures, 1976.
Halloween, dir. John Carpenter. USA: Compass International Pictures, 1978.
Hammer Horror: The Warner Bros Years, dir. Marcus Hearn. United Kingdom: Diabolique films, 2018.
Hammer House of Horror [TV series]. United Kingdom: ITV Productions, 1980.
Hammer House of Mystery and Suspense [TV series]. United Kingdom: ITV Productions, 1984–5.
Horror of Frankenstein, dir. Jimmy Sangster. United Kingdom: Hammer Film Productions, 1970.
The Hound of the Baskervilles, dir. Terence Fisher. United Kingdom: Hammer Film Productions, 1959.
House of Dark Shadows, dir. Dan Curtis. USA: Metro-Goldwyn-Mayer, 1970.
House of Dracula, dir. Erle C. Kenton. USA: Universal Pictures, 1945.
The House of Frankenstein, dir. Erle C. Kenton. USA: Universal Pictures, 1944.
I Am Legend, dir. Francis Lawrence. USA: Warner Bros., 2007.
The Incredible Hulk [TV series]. United States: CBS, 1978.
Indiana Jones and the Temple of Doom, dir. Steven Spielberg. USA: Lucasfilm Ltd, 1984.
Invasion of Astro-Monster, dir. Ishirō Honda. Japan: Toho, 1965.
The Invisible Man Returns, dir. Joe May. USA: Universal Pictures, 1940.
Jaws, dir. Steven Spielberg. USA: Universal Pictures, 1975.
Journey of Hope, dir. Xavier Koller. Switzerland/Turkey: Miramax Films, 1990.
Journey to the Unknown [TV Series]. United Kingdom: Hammer Film Productions, 1968–9.
Junior Bonner, dir. Sam Peckinpah. USA: ABC Pictures, 1972.
King Kong vs. Godzilla, dir. Ishirō Honda. Japan: Toho, 1962.
The Lady Vanishes, dir. Alfred Hitchcock. United Kingdom: Gainsborough Pictures, 1938.

The Lady Vanishes, dir. Anthony Page. United Kingdom: Hammer Film Productions/Rank Films, 1979.
The Last Man on Earth, dir. Sidney Salkow. USA/Italy: Associated Producers Inc./Produzioni La Regina, 1964.
Legend of the 7 Golden Vampires, dir. Roy Ward Baker. United Kingdom: Hammer Film Productions, 1974.
Les Diaboliques (1955), dir. Henri-Georges Clouzot. France: Cinèdis, 1955.
Let Me In, dir. Matt Reeves. United Kingdom: Hammer Film Productions, 2010.
Logan's Run, dir. Michael Anderson. USA: Metro-Goldwyn-Mayer, 1976.
Lord Dracula, written by Brian Hayles. BBC Radio 4, 20:30, 27 April 1974.
Lust for a Vampire, dir. Jimmy Sangster. United Kingdom: Hammer Film Productions, 1971.
The Man Who Fell to Earth, dir. Nicolas Roeg. United Kingdom: British Lion Films, 1976.
The Man Who Knew Too Much, dir. Alfred Hitchcock. United Kingdom: Gaumont British, 1934.
Maniac, dir. Michael Carreras. United Kingdom: Hammer Film Productions, 1963.
Moon Zero Two, dir. Roy Ward Baker. United Kingdom: Hammer Film Productions, 1969.
Mothra vs. Godzilla, dir. Ishirō Honda. Japan: Toho, 1964.
The Mummy, dir. Terence Fisher. United Kingdom: Hammer Film Productions, 1959.
The Mystery of the Mary Celeste, dir. Denison Clift. United Kingdom: Hammer Film Productions, 1935.
Night of the Living Dead, dir. George Romero. USA: Image Ten, 1968.
The Night Stalker, dir. John Llewellyn Moxey. USA: Associated Broadcasting Company, 1972.
The Omega Man, dir. Boris Sagal. USA: Walter Seltzer Productions, 1971.
The Omen, dir. Richard Donner. USA: 20th Century Fox, 1976.
On the Buses, dir. Harry Booth. United Kingdom: Hammer Film Productions, 1971.
One Million Years B.C., dir. Don Chaffey. United Kingdom: Hammer Film Productions, 1966.
Orca, dir. Michael Anderson. USA: Dino De Laurentiis, 1977.
Paranoiac, dir. Freddie Francis. United Kingdom: Hammer Film Productions, 1963.
Peeping Tom, dir. Michael Powell. United Kingdom: Anglo-Amalgamated, 1960.
Piranha, dir. Joe Dante. USA: New World Pictures, 1978.
The Plague of the Zombies, dir. John Gilling. United Kingdom: Hammer Film Productions, 1966.
Posters of the Moulin Rouge, written by John Peacock [4 part series]. BBC Radio 4, December 1989.
The Proprietor, dir. Ismail Merchant. USA: Merchant Ivory Productions, 1996.
Psycho, dir. Alfred Hitchcock. USA: Paramount, 1960.
Quatermass 2, dir. Val Guest. United Kingdom: Hammer Film Productions, 1957.
Quatermass and the Pit, dir. Roy Ward Baker. United Kingdom: Hammer Film Productions, 1967.
The Quatermass Experiment [TV Series]. United Kingdom: BBC, 1953.
The Quatermass Xperiment, dir. Val Guest. United Kingdom: Hammer Film Productions, 1955.
The Railway Children, dir. Lionel Jeffries. United Kingdom: EMI Elstree, 1970.
The Return of Count Yorga, dir. Bob Kelljan. USA: Peppertree Productions Inc., 1971.

The Revenge of Frankenstein, dir. Terence Fisher. United Kingdom: Hammer Film Productions, 1958.
Revenge of the Stepford Wives, dir. Robert Fuest. United Kingdom: Edgar J. Scherick Associates, 1980.
Rising Damp, dir. Joseph McGrath. United Kingdom: Cinema Arts International Production, 1980.
Rock, Rock, Rock!, dir. Will Price. USA: Vanguard Productions, 1956.
Rosemary's Baby, dir. Roman Polanski. USA: Paramount, 1968.
The Satanic Rites of Dracula, dir. Alan Gibson. United Kingdom: Hammer Film Productions, 1973.
Savages, dir. James Ivory. USA: Merchant Ivory Productions, 1972.
Scars of Dracula, dir. Roy Ward Baker. United Kingdom: Hammer Film Productions, 1970.
Schindler's List, dir. Steven Spielberg. USA: Amblin Entertainment, 1993.
Shatter, dir. Michael Carreras. United Kingdom/Hong Kong: Hammer Film Productions/Shaw Brothers Studio, 1974.
The Silence of the Lambs, dir. Jonathan Demme. United States: Orion Pictures, 1991.
Slave Girls, dir. Michael Carreras. United Kingdom: Hammer Film Productions, 1967.
The Slipper and the Rose, dir. Bryan Forbes. United Kingdom: Paradine Co-Production, 1976.
The Snorkel, dir. Guy Green. United Kingdom: Hammer Film Productions, 1958.
Son of Dracula, dir. Curt Siodmak. USA: Universal Pictures, 1943.
Son of Frankenstein, dir. Rowland V. Lee. USA: Universal Pictures, 1939.
Son of Godzilla, dir. Jun Fukuda. Japan: Toho, 1967.
Soylent Green, dir. Richard Fleisher. USA: Metro-Goldwyn-Mayer, 1973.
Squanto: A Warriors Tale, dir. Xavier Koller. USA: Disney Studios, 1994.
Star Wars, dir. George Lucas. USA: 20th Century Fox, 1977.
Straight on Till Morning, dir. Peter Collinson. United Kingdom: Hammer Film Productions, 1972.
The Stepford Children, dir. Alan J. Levi. USA: Edgar J. Scherick Associates, 1987.
The Stepford Husbands, dir. Fred Walton. USA: Edgar J. Scherick Associates, 1996.
The Stepford Wives, dir. Bryan Forbes. USA: Palomar Pictures, 1975.
The Stepford Wives, dir. Frank Oz. USA: DeLine Pictures, 2004.
The Stranglers of Bombay, dir. Terence Fisher. United Kingdom: Hammer Film Productions, 1959.
Superman, dir. Richard Donner. United States: Warner Bros. 1978.
The Tales of Beatrix Potter, dir. Reginald Mills. United Kingdom: EMI Elstree, 1971.
Tales of Frankenstein [TV Pilot], dir. Curt Siodmak. United Kingdom/USA: Hammer Film Productions/Screen Gems, 1958.
Taste of Fear, dir. Seth Holt. United Kingdom: Hammer Film Productions, 1961.
Taste the Blood of Dracula, dir. Peter Sasdy. United Kingdom: Hammer Film Productions, 1970.
Terror of Mechagodzilla, dir. Ishirō Honda. Japan: Toho, 1975.
To the Devil a Daughter, dir. Peter Sykes. United Kingdom: Hammer Film Productions, 1976.
Top Gun: Maverick, dir. Joseph Kosinski. United States: Paramount Pictures, 2022.
Twins of Evil, dir. John Hough. United Kingdom: Hammer Film Productions, 1971.
The Unquenchable Thirst of Dracula, dir. Mark Gatiss. BBC Radio 4, 28 October, 2017.
Vampirella, dir. Jim Wynorski. USA: CineTel Films, 1996.

The Vampire Lovers, dir. Roy Ward Baker. United Kingdom: Hammer Film Productions, 1970.
The Viking Queen, dir. Don Chaffey. United Kingdom: Hammer Film Productions, 1967.
Von Ryan's Express, dir. Mark Robson. USA: 20th Century Fox, 1965.
Wake Wood, dir. David Keating. United Kingdom: Hammer Film Productions, 2009.
When Dinosaurs Ruled the Earth, dir. Val Guest. United Kingdom: Hammer Film Productions, 1970.
Whispering Smith Hits London, dir. Francis Searle. United Kingdom: Hammer Film Productions, 1952.
The Wild Geese, dir. Andrew V. McLaglen. United Kingdom: Richmond Film Productions (West) Ltd, 1978.
Wolfshead: The Legend of Robin Hood, dir. John Hough. Hammer Film Productions, 1969.
The Wolf Man, dir. George Waggner. USA: Universal Pictures, 1941.
X the Unknown, dir. Leslie Norman. United Kingdom: Hammer Film Productions, 1956.
Yesterday's Enemy, dir. Val Guest. United Kingdom: Hammer Film Productions, 1959.
The Young Riders [TV Series]. USA: American Broadcasting Company, 1989–92.

Appendix: Hammer Films – *The Quatermass Xperiment* to 1979

1955	The Quatermass Xperiment
1956	X the Unknown
1956	Women Without Men
1957	The Curse of Frankenstein
1957	The Abominable Snowman
1957	Quatermass 2
1957	The Steel Bayonet
1958	The Camp on Blood Island
1958	Murder at Site 3
1958	Dracula
1958	Up the Creek
1958	The Snorkel
1958	I Only Arsked!
1958	The Revenge of Frankenstein
1958	Further Up the Creek
1959	Don't Panic Chaps!
1959	The Hound of the Baskervilles
1959	The Mummy
1959	The Man Who Could Cheat Death
1959	The Phoenix
1959	The Ugly Duckling
1959	Yesterday's Enemy
1959	The Stranglers of Bombay
1960	The Brides of Dracula
1960	Hell Is a City
1960	Never Take Sweets from a Stranger
1960	Sword of Sherwood Forest
1960	The Two Faces of Dr. Jekyll
1960	Visa to Canton
1960	The Full Treatment
1961	Cash on Demand
1961	The Curse of the Werewolf

1961	*The Shadow of the Cat*
1961	*Taste of Fear*
1961	*The Terror of the Tongs*
1961	*Watch It, Sailor!*
1961	*A Weekend with Lulu*
1962	*Captain Clegg*
1962	*The Phantom of the Opera*
1962	*The Pirates of Blood River*
1963	*The Damned*
1963	*The Kiss of the Vampire*
1963	*Paranoiac*
1963	*Maniac*
1963	*The Old Dark House*
1963	*The Scarlet Blade*
1964	*The Curse of the Mummy's Tomb*
1964	*The Devil-Ship Pirates*
1964	*The Evil of Frankenstein*
1964	*The Gorgon*
1964	*Nightmare*
1965	*The Brigand of Kandahar*
1965	*Fanatic*
1965	*Hysteria*
1965	*She*
1965	*The Nanny*
1965	*The Secret of Blood Island*
1966	*Dracula Prince of Darkness*
1966	*The Plague of the Zombies*
1966	*Rasputin the Mad Monk*
1966	*The Reptile*
1966	*The Witches*
1966	*One Million Years B.C.*
1967	*A Challenge for Robin Hood*
1967	*The Viking Queen*
1967	*Frankenstein Created Woman*
1967	*The Mummy's Shroud*
1967	*Quatermass and the Pit*
1967	*Slave Girls*
1968	*The Anniversary*
1968	*The Vengeance of She*
1968	*The Devil Rides Out*
1968	*Dracula Has Risen From the Grave*
1968	*The Lost Continent*
1969	*Frankenstein Must Be Destroyed*
1969	*Moon Zero Two*
1970	*Taste the Blood of Dracula*
1970	*Crescendo*
1970	*Scars of Dracula*
1970	*The Horror of Frankenstein*
1970	*The Vampire Lovers*

1970	When Dinosaurs Ruled the Earth
1971	Vampire Circus
1971	Countess Dracula
1971	Lust for a Vampire
1971	Creatures the World Forgot
1971	Dr. Jekyll and Sister Hyde
1971	Blood from the Mummy's Tomb
1971	Twins of Evil
1971	Hands of the Ripper
1971	On the Buses
1972	Dracula A.D. 1972
1972	Fear in the Night
1972	Straight On till Morning
1972	Demons of the Mind
1972	Mutiny on the Buses
1972	Nearest and Dearest
1973	Holiday on the Buses
1973	Love Thy Neighbour
1973	Man at the Top
1973	That's Your Funeral
1973	The Satanic Rites of Dracula
1973	Wolfshead: The Legend of Robin Hood
1974	Captain Kronos – Vampire Hunter
1974	Frankenstein and the Monster from Hell
1974	Man About the House
1974	Shatter
1974	The Legend of the 7 Golden Vampires
1976	To the Devil a Daughter
1979	The Lady Vanishes

Index

20,000 Leagues Under the Sea, 118–19
20th Century Fox, 57, 123, 150, 153, 154, 166
28 Days Later, 41

A Clockwork Orange, 90
Abbott, Stacey, 3, 41, 157
Abominable Snowman, The, 44
Akerman, Forest J., 92
Allen, David, 176
American Broadcasting Company (ABC), 26, 64, 138
American International Pictures (AIP), 99, 100, 101–2, 104, 106, 110
Amicus Productions, 23, 60, 101
Anderson, Michael, 119, 120, 121, 130
Anderson, P., 50
Anglo-Amalgamated, 60
Arbi, Adil El, 171
Arkoff, Sam, 99, 102
Armstrong, R., 4
Aryan Papers, The, 180
Asher, Jack, 14
Associated Artists Pictures, 18–19
Associated British Picture Corporation (ABPC), 64, 77, 84

Atkins, T., 90
Atlas Comics, 102
Axelrod, George, 110

Baillieu, B., 59
Baldwin, James, 174
Banno, Yoshimitsu, 124
Baraka, Amiri, 174
Barnett, V., 24, 25
Bashar, Leon, 16
Bateman, L., 158, 159
Batgirl, 171
Begelman, David, 117, 121, 125, 126
Bernard, James, 14
Bettinson, Gary, 72, 109
Billboard, 25, 164
Birking, Irving, 33
Black Sabbath, 153, 154, 158, 167
Blasphemer, The, 91
Blood from the Mummy's Tomb, 94
Blount, R. P., 153
Blurton, R., 74
Booth, Harry, 139
Boyle, Danny, 41
Bray Studio, 10, 58, 61, 123
Briant, Shane, 65–6
British Board of Film Classification (BBFC), 6, 10, 22, 24, 25, 37–8, 42, 45, 46–8, 50–7, 173

British Film Fund Agency (BFFA), 15
British Film Institute (BFI), 6, 17–18, 21, 25–6, 27, 28, 94, 173, 177
Broadway Cinema, 5, 175
Brock, J., 119
Brosnan, J., 88, 89, 91, 92, 126, 160
Browning, Tod, 43
Bryan, P., 27, 28, 29
Burton, Richard, 92, 104, 138

Camp on Blood Island, The, 26, 102
Cannes Film Festival, 114
Capricorn Productions, 58
Captain Clegg, 58
Captain Kronos – Vampire Hunter, 178
Carlson, Richard, 16
Carnivore, 111
Carreras, Enrique, 13, 103, 149
Carreras, James, 10, 13, 15, 18, 19, 21, 22, 25–6, 27, 35, 45, 47, 52–8, 61–2, 64, 66, 69, 105, 108, 141–5, 149, 156, 157, 165, 166, 176
Carreras, Michael, 31–5, 41, 42, 47, 55, 56, 58, 61–2, 63–6, 69, 70, 72–5, 77, 79–92, 94–101, 111–15, 117–28, 130–50, 156, 157, 159, 165–7, 170, 172, 173, 177
Carringer, R., 4
Casper, D., 59
Castele, A., 4
Cavalcanti, Alberto, 39
CBS, 94
Chaffey, Don, 95, 111, 112
Chantrell, Tom, 5, 176
Chapman, J., 4
Charlie (novel), 153
Charlton, 120
Chiang, David, 81
Chrisfield, Larry, 169
Cinema and Television History Institute (CATHI), 3, 67
Cinema Arts International, 148
Clark, Dane, 16
Clark, N., 169

Clemens, Brian, 178
Clift, Denison, 39
Close Encounters of the Third Kind, 122, 123
Cobb, Shelley, 4, 174–5
Coleman, M., 104
Collinson, Peter, 149
Columbia, 8, 9, 11, 17, 25, 26, 32, 33, 46, 47, 48, 58, 102, 108, 111–25, 126, 128, 132, 138, 140
Conflagration, 124
Connett, D., 160
Conrich, I., 60
Constantin Films, 91, 92, 117, 121
Conte, Richard, 16
Cooke, Chris, 175–6
Coppola, Francis Ford, 123, 157
Copyright Act (17 US Code § 104A, 1996), 164–5
Corman, Roger, 104
Couch, A., 171
Count Yorga, Vampire, 70
creepy, 92
Crichton, Charles, 39
Croft, Frank, 45, 52
Curran, J., 142
Curse of the Mummy's Tomb, The, 58, 108
Curse of the Werewolf, The, 46, 48, 56, 106
Cushing, Peter, 14, 19, 23, 31, 33, 44, 60, 63, 72, 95, 97, 98, 101, 106, 177, 179

Daily Mail, 111
'Dalton Duty', 14
Dalton, Hugh, 14
Daltrey, Roger, 104
Danforth, Jim, 111–12
Dante, Joe, 119, 168
David, Saul, 77
Davies, B., 129
Dawtrey, A., 169
Day the Earth Caught Fire, The, 158

Dead of Night, 39, 40
Delfont, Bernard, 61, 130, 143
Demme, Jonathan, 157
Demons of the Mind, 94
Der Spiegel, 92
Detective Comics (DC), 94
Devil Rides Out, The, 158, 168
Devilina, 102–3
Devils, The, 90
Dick Barton (trilogy), 15
Dick Barton: Special Agent, 168
Dick, B., 125
Dickinson, M., 59
Diffring, Anton, 27, 32, 33
Dirty Dozen: The Series, 161
Disney, 163
Dixon, Wheeler Winston, 61, 139
Dolo, Karlton, 179
Donner, Richard, 94
Dracula
   Bram Stroker's Dracula, 157–8
   Brides of Dracula, The, 29, 63, 95
   Devil Bride of Dracula/A Devil Bride for Dracula, 83
   Dracula (1931), 43
   Dracula (1958), 25, 38, 42–4, 53, 63, 95, 106, 157, 177
   Dracula (character), 10, 65–6, 67–9, 72, 74–5, 79, 80, 101, 106, 110
   Dracula (Hammer series), 10, 62–3, 64, 65, 66, 69, 70, 71, 76, 77, 84, 85, 86, 95
   Dracula (novel), 17, 40, 43–4, 50, 68, 72
   Dracula AD 1972, 64, 65, 68, 70, 72, 84, 95, 152, 178
   Dracula Has Risen From the Grave, 63–4
   Dracula High Priest of Vampires, 67, 68, 69, 70, 71, 73, 74, 84
   Dracula Prince of Darkness, 63
   Dracula the Beginning, 89, 147
   Dracula Untold, 169–70
   Kali Devil Bride of Dracula/Dracula and the Curse of Kali, 10, 11, 67, 71–84, 85, 86, 87, 98, 142, 143, 144, 173
   Lord Dracula, 88, 89, 147
   Satanic Rites of Dracula, The, 64–5, 72, 84, 95
   Scars of Dracula, 64, 70, 84
   Son of Dracula, 33
   Taste the Blood of Dracula, 64
   Unquenchable Thirst of Dracula, 11, 66–71, 87, 92, 176
Dryhurst, Edward, 27, 31
Dugdale, Georgina, 178
Duryea, Dan, 16
Dynamite Entertainment, 109

Eady Levy, 15–16, 59
Ealing Studios, 39, 40, 142
Earthquake, 118
East India Trading Company, 76
Ede, Laurie N., 58, 62
Eerie, 92
Elder, John, 28, 67, 176
Eldridge, David, 175
Elgood, H., 74
Ellis, Arthur, 7, 147, 149, 150–4, 155, 156, 157, 158, 162–3, 165, 166–7, 170
Elstree Studio, 10, 58, 61, 71, 154
Elwood, R. Paul, 54–5, 56
EMI, 61, 64, 130, 143, 144
Exclusive Films, 13
Executive Replicas, 178
Exorcist, The, 90, 93, 99, 139
Eyles, A., 15

Falks, Q., 154
Fallah, Bilall, 171
Famous Monsters Convention, 74, 97, 177
Famous Monsters of Filmland, 93
fan/fanbase/fandom, 5, 7, 97, 139, 173, 175, 176, 178, 179

Fanatic, 108
Fangoria, 91, 101, 144
Femme Fatales, 104
Fenwick, James, 4, 15, 172–3, 175
Fields, Audrey, 45, 50, 51, 52
Fisher, Terrence, 1, 14, 16, 28, 29, 38, 63, 72, 73, 95, 102, 106, 153, 159, 168
Fleischer, Richard, 118–19
Fleming, Victor, 123
Flesh and Blood: The Hammer Heritage of Horror, 154
Forbes, Bryan, 8, 11, 107, 118, 119, 127–39, 140, 143, 144, 145
Forbes-Robertson, 72
Forshaw, B., 2, 40, 60
Foster, Kieran, 67, 68–9, 70
Four Sided Triangle, The, 159
Fox, Adam, 179
Foy, Bryan, 26, 27
Francis, Freddie, 18, 64, 141, 142, 146
Frank, Alan, 65, 99, 101, 102, 103
Frankenstein
  Blood of Frankenstein, The, 26
  Bride of Frankenstein, 19, 20, 22, 23
  Curse of Frankenstein, The, 1, 9, 10, 16–48, 53, 57, 97, 106, 108, 153, 157, 173
  Evil of Frankenstein, The, 28, 29, 146
  Frankenstein (1931), 19, 20, 21, 22, 23, 33, 35
  Frankenstein (character), 19, 23, 24, 25, 26, 27, 29, 30, 31, 32, 33
  Frankenstein (Hammer series), 9, 17, 28, 62, 63
  Frankenstein (novel), 19, 21, 40, 53
  Frankenstein (Subotsky), 9, 17, 18–25, 29, 34, 35, 37, 60, 173
  Frankenstein (Universal series), 20
  Frankenstein and the Monster from Hell, 90
  Frankenstein Created Woman, 28
  Frankenstein Meets the Wolf Man, 33
  Horror of Frankenstein, The, 64, 93

  Revenge of Frankenstein, The, 25, 26, 38, 102, 108
  Tales of Frankenstein, 7, 9, 17–18, 25–34, 35, 37, 40, 57, 150, 173
Frazer-Jones, Peter, 148
French Connection, The, 90
Friedkin, William, 90, 139
Frost, David, 111, 115, 129, 130, 131, 133, 134

Gajewski, R., 171
Gateway Productions, 120
Gatiss, Mark, 67, 176
George and Mildred, 148
German Tax Shelter Group, 91, 116, 117, 120, 121, 132
Gersh, 118–19
Ghoul, The, 39
Gibson, Alan, 64–5, 95, 178
Gielgud, John, 101
Gierse, Doctor Helmut, 91–2, 117, 121
Gilbert, S., 164, 168
Giling, Josh, 29, 46
Girdler, William, 119
Godfather, The, 123
Godzilla
  Godzilla, 112
  Godzilla vs. Hedorah, 124
  Godzilla, King of the Monsters!, 112
  King Kong vs. Godzilla, 122
Golden Voyage of Sinbad, The, 85
Goldstein, Seth, 164–5
Gone With the Wind, 123
Goodchild, J., 59
Gorgon, The, 106, 108
gothic horror (definition), 13–14
Governor General Dalhousie, 77
Grace, Leslie, 171
Green, G., 26, 102
Grizzly, 119
Guest, Val, 1, 16, 26, 41, 44, 46, 102, 111, 130, 158
Guns of Navarone, The, 138

Hall, S., 123
Hallenbeck, B., 65, 147
Hamer, Robert, 39
'Hammer Glamour', 97
Hammer House of Mystery and Suspense, 97, 147, 149, 150, 151, 153, 154, 166
Hammer International, 160–1, 168
Hammer Script Archive, 3, 5, 6, 12, 17, 19, 38, 42, 46, 67, 73, 84, 88, 89, 93, 98, 105, 107, 109, 114, 128, 129, 141, 147, 150, 152, 153, 156, 157, 158, 159, 160, 173, 175, 176–7, 178
Hammer, Will, 13
Harper, S., 2, 14, 15, 16, 40
Harris, Richard, 92, 104, 138
Harryhausen, Ray, 112
Hassanein, Salah, 130–1
Haunting of Toby Jugg, The, 154
Hawk, 129
Hayes Hunter, T., 39
Hayles, Brian, 88, 89, 92, 105, 110, 147, 150, 151, 152, 155, 160, 162, 163, 167
HBO Max, 171
Hearn, Marcus, 1, 2, 7, 10, 21, 27, 32, 44, 46, 47, 48, 58, 61, 63, 64, 67, 68–9, 70, 71, 82, 87, 109, 110, 146, 147, 148–9, 176
Hessler, Gordon, 85, 101, 102
Heston, Charlton, 41
Higson, A., 60
Hinds, Anthony/Tony, 10, 13, 14, 22, 23, 24, 25, 27, 28, 29, 30, 31, 32, 34, 47, 51, 52, 55, 56, 64, 67, 68, 69, 70, 71, 73, 84, 148, 170, 176
Hinds, William, 13
Hirschfield, Alan, 125
Hitchcock, Alfred, 27, 110
HollywoodGate/Begelman Scandal, 125, 126
Holt, Seth, 94
Honda, Ishiro, 112, 122

Hough, John, 69, 96–7, 101, 102, 106
Houghton, Don, 8, 10, 65, 66, 71, 73–84, 85, 86, 143, 144, 151, 173
Hound of the Baskervilles, The, 29, 178
House of Hammer, The, 7, 88, 92
House on the Strand, The, 154
Houston, Penelope, 59
Humphreys, Graham, 179
Hutchings, Peter, 2, 3, 4, 14, 23, 38, 39, 40, 41–2, 48, 56, 57, 60, 63
Hyman, Eliot, 9, 17, 18, 19, 21, 24, 25, 26, 35, 108

I am Legend (novel), 10, 37, 40, 41, 43, 50
I am Legend (film), 41
ICI, 146, 147, 148–9, 150, 166
Ilott, Terry, 153, 169
Incredible Hulk, The, 94
Independent, The, 160, 169
Indian authorities, 77, 80, 81, 82, 83, 84, 86
Indian government, 77, 78, 82, 84, 85, 86
Indian Rebellion, 76–7, 78, 83, 86
Indiana Jones and the Temple of Doom, 85, 86
Indicator, 177
Insolvency Service, 146
Invisible Man Returns, The, 33
Ireland, John, 16
Irving, Henry, 65–6
Ishida, Katsumune, 124
Ivory, James, 73

Jackson, Luke, 179
Jaffe, Stanley, 122, 124
Jaws, 119–20, 123
Jeffries, Lionel, 129
Jones, A., 168
Jones, C., 74
Jones, LeRoi, 174

Jones, Mervyn, 39
Journey of Hope, 163–4
Junior Bonner, 97

Kalat, D., 122
Karloff, Boris, 21, 26, 31, 39
Katz, Norman, 67, 69
Keating, David, 169
Keaton, Diane, 178
Kelley, B., 98
Kelley, J., 98
Kelljan, Bob, 70
Kermode, Mark, 90, 123
Kerrigan, F., 14
Kersh, Cyril, 27, 29
Kinsey, Wayne, 1, 18, 22, 24–5, 45, 46, 47, 48, 58, 63–4, 71, 81, 82, 84, 94, 97, 102, 103, 109, 110, 146, 147, 148–9, 151, 154, 157, 168–9
Klemensen, R., 154
Klinger, Michael, 142
Kneale, Nigel, 16
Koetting, C., 100
Koller, Xavier, 163–4
Kosinski, Joseph, 3
Kramer, Peter, 3, 4, 7, 90, 123
Krantz, Steve, 154, 156, 158, 160, 167
Kubrick Archive, the, 180
Kubrick, Stanley, 90, 180

Lady Vanishes, The, 2, 107, 110, 111, 138, 139
Lang, 171
Last Man on Earth, The, 40–1, 56
Lawrence of Arabia, 138
Lawrence, Brian, 12, 70, 73, 144, 146, 147, 148, 149, 150, 151, 154, 156, 166
Lawrence, Francis, 41
Lee, Christopher, 14, 23, 60, 63, 64, 66, 72, 74, 75, 97
Lee, Stan, 94
Legacy, 159, 165
Legend of King Kong, The, 112
Legend of the 7 Golden Vampires, 68, 71, 72, 73, 74, 79, 81, 82, 83, 84, 85, 86, 95, 109, 113, 150
Leigh, Barbara, 97, 98, 101, 104, 177, 178
Lippert, Robert, 15, 16, 56, 57
Little Shoppe of Horrors, 7, 101, 102
Lloyd, Euan/Euan Lloyd Productions, 111, 112, 113–18, 119–20, 121–2, 123, 125, 130–1, 132, 134, 138–9, 140
Logan's Run, 119
Long, R. E., 73
Louis, Stella, 170
Lucas Film, 103
Lucas, George, 103
Ludlam, Harry, 66
Lugosi, Bela, 39
Lust for a Vampire, 69, 179

Magor, M., 14, 15, 58
Malcom X, 174
Man Who Knew Too Much, The, 27
Maniac, 58
Margaret Herrick Library, 6, 38, 42, 54, 97, 104, 110, 172, 173
Marvel/Marvel Comics, 94
Matheson, Judy, 179
Matheson, Richard, 10, 37, 40, 41, 42, 43, 44, 48, 49, 51, 52, 56, 57, 173, 179
Matsuoka, Isao, 114, 115–16, 125
May, Joe, 33
Mayhem Film Festival, 5, 67, 175, 176
McClinktick, D., 124
McCord, Jonas, 147, 157, 160–3, 165, 168
McGrath, Joseph, 148
McKenna, A. T., 4, 105, 142
McLaglen, Andrew V., 138
McQueen, Steve, 97
Meikle, Denis, 1, 7, 16, 18, 19, 22, 34–5, 44, 45, 46, 47, 71, 82, 94, 99, 110, 125, 130, 140, 143, 144, 148–9, 154, 165, 168–9

Meir, C., 142
Melia, M., 90
MGM, 119
Mills, Reginald, 129–30
Moon Zero Two, 122
Moore, Roger, 138
Moore, S., 100
Moorhouse, Jocelyn, 175
Morell, Andre, 178
Morell, Jason, 178–9
Morley, Robert, 101
Morse, Terry, 112
Motion Picture Association (MPAA), 10, 42, 50, 51, 52, 53, 54, 56, 57
Munro, Caroline, 177–8
Murf, 130
Murphy, M., 69
Murray, S., 4
Myers, 26, 102
Mystery of the Mary Celeste, The, 39

Naish, Peter, 169
Nakano, Shokei, 112
Narizzano, Silvio, 108
National Film Finance Corporation (NFFC), 40
Neill, Roy, 33
Nessie, 11, 12, 91, 94, 103, 107–26, 127–41, 142, 142, 144, 145, 150, 170, 173
Netter, Doug, 125, 130–1
New World, 164
New York Post, 171
Newman, Peter R., 46
Newmar, Julie, 178
Newsom, Ted, 154
Nicholls, John, 51–2, 53
Night Creatures, The, 3, 7, 10, 37–60, 173
Night of the Living Dead, 41, 62, 90
Norman, Brian, 174
Norman, Leslie, 16
North, Dan, 4
Nutman, P., 60
Nwonka, Clive, 174

Oakes, Simon, 1, 169
Observer, The, 164
Olensinski, J., 171
Omega Man, The, 41
Omen, The, 151
On the Buses, 139
One Million Years B.C., 95, 112
Orca, 119, 120, 130

Page, Anthony, 2, 107
Paradine, 107, 111, 112, 129, 138
Paramount, 164
Peacock, John, 147, 149, 151, 153, 155–6, 157, 162, 165, 166, 167, 170
Pearden, Basil, 39
Peckinpah, Sam, 97
Peel, David, 63
Peeping Tom, 45, 55
Pension Fund Securities (PFS), 61, 146
Phelps, Guy, 38, 39, 69
Picart, C., 35
Pierce, Jack, 20, 33
Pierotti, 117
Piranha, 119
Pirie, D., 2, 18, 39, 45
Plague of the Zombies, The, 29, 178
Pleasance, Donald, 99
Porter, V., 2, 14, 15, 16, 40, 142
Powell, Michael, 45
Powerhouse, 177
Price, Vincent, 41
Production Code Administration (PCA), 172

Quatermass 2, 16, 18, 130
Quatermass and the Pit, 159, 165
Quatermass Experiment, The, 16, 158
Quatermass Xperiment, The, 1, 16–17, 34–5, 37, 40, 44, 168
Quinn, Kevin, 158

Railway Children, The, 129
Ramachandran, N., 1

Rampling, Charlotte, 178
Ramsay, Lynne, 175
Rank Film, 110, 143, 159
Rape of Sabena, The, 46, 47, 48, 56, 57, 58
Rawlinson, A. R., 27, 28, 29
Redgrave, Michael, 39
Reed, Michael, 14
Reynolds, Clarke, 111
Richardson, Ralph, 101
Richmond Film Production, 114, 115
Rigby, Jonathon, 2, 21, 22, 39, 45, 176, 177
Rising Damp, 148
Robert Lippert Productions/Lippert Deal, 15, 16, 18, 40, 56, 108, 129
Robert, Shaw, 119
Roberts, Steve, 154
Robinson, Bernard, 14
Robson, Mark, 118
Romero, Cesar, 16
Romero, George, 41, 62, 90
Rosemary's Baby, 90, 93, 99
Rosenberg, Max, 19, 23, 24, 60
Russell, Ken, 89, 90–1, 104
Ryan, J., 74

Saatchi, Charles, 1, 169
Sachs, Tom, 94, 114, 134, 140
Sagal, Boris, 41
Salkov, Sidney, 41
Sangster, Jimmy, 14, 16, 17, 18, 19, 22, 23, 24, 25, 26, 27, 29, 31, 32, 33, 34, 45, 64, 69, 72, 93
Sanjek, David, 62
Sasdy, Peter, 64
Satpathy, Nandini, 80
Schlesinger, P., 14, 15, 58
Schuler and Donner Productions/ Donner/Schuler-Donner, 158, 160, 164, 168
Scorsese, Martin, 168
Scott, Peter Graham, 58
Scott, Zachary, 16

Scream and Scream Again, 101
Screen Gems, 9, 17, 25, 26, 32, 33, 34, 35
Screen International, 154, 158, 159, 160, 163, 165–6
Searle, Francis, 16
Seinger and Associates Advertising Company, 119
Seinger, Tony, 119–20
Shadow Screens Conference, 175
Shail, R., 61
Shatter, 82, 109
Shaw Brothers, 71, 82, 85, 109, 108, 110, 112, 113, 116, 140, 143
Shaw, Robert, 119
Shaw, Run Run, 71
Shaw, Vee King, 109
She, 178
Sheen, Michael, 67, 176
Sheil, Steven, 175–6
Shelley, Mary, 9, 18–25, 17, 29, 34, 37, 60
Sherman Brothers, 129
Shiel, M., 90
Shiel, Steven, 5
Shock!/Shock Theatre, 25, 34
Shore, Gary, 169
Shortt, Edward, 39
Sidaway, Ashley, 159
Sidaway, Robert, 159
Silence of the Lambs, The, 157
Singh, Dharam Vir, 80
Siodmak, Curt, 27, 33
Skal, D., 66
Skeggs, Roy, 12, 100, 105, 146–170, 173
Skinn, D., 88, 89, 91, 92, 126, 159
Slaughter, Todd, 39
Slave Girls, 58
Slipper and the Rose, The, 129, 130, 131
Smith, Will, 41
Snorkel, The, 26, 102
Soto, Talisa, 104
Soylent Green, 119

Spicer, Andrew, 4, 142
Spielberg, Steven, 85, 119, 122
Springhall, J., 16
Squanto: A Warriors Tale, 163–4
Stage and Television Today, The, 160
Stranglers of Bombay, The, 73, 76, 78–9, 85
Star Wars, 103, 123
Starr, John, 100–1, 102, 104, 105, 107, 128, 132, 134, 137
Starr, Ringo, 99
Steege, Johanna ter, 180
Stepford Wives, The, 130
Stoker, Bram, 17, 43, 50, 65, 66, 72, 76
Stolen Face, 158
Straight on Till Morning, 149
Street, Sarah, 14–15, 59, 60, 150
Strong, E., 25
Strub, Whitney, 174
Stubbs, J., 14, 15
Superman, 94
Surlock, Geoffrey, 50, 51, 53, 54, 55
Swires, Steve, 74–5, 91, 92, 98, 99, 102, 144
Sykes, Peter, 2, 94, 99–100, 107, 149

Tales of Beatrix Potter, The, 129–30
TB League, 178
Tennant, Bill, 124
Tenser, Tony, 61
Thomas, D., 129
Thuggee Cult, 73, 75, 83
Tigon, 60, 61
To the Devil a Daughter, 2, 94, 99–100, 107, 139, 149, 150, 166
Toho, 11, 108, 111–18, 120, 121, 122, 124, 125, 126, 128, 132, 136, 138, 139, 140, 143
Top Gun: Maverick, 3
Trevelyan, John, 45, 46, 47, 48, 50, 54, 55, 56, 57, 69
Tsutski, W., 112
Twins of Evil, 69, 97, 179
Tyburn, 60

Universal, 19, 20, 21, 22, 23, 24, 25, 29, 32, 33, 34, 35, 39, 169
University of Southern California (USC) Warner Bros. Archive, 6, 17, 173

Vampire Lovers, The, 69
Vampirella, 11, 87, 88, 92–104, 105, 106, 109, 113, 141, 142, 144, 174–80
Vampirella live script reading, 176–80
Variety, 1, 26, 43, 103, 114, 142, 143, 169, 171
Variety Club, the, 18, 108, 142
Vary, 171
Vaughan-Hughes, Gerald, 100
Victim of His Imagination, 65, 66, 84
Viking Queen, The, 111
Vlad Dracul, 147, 160, 161
Vlad the Impaler, 7, 11, 12, 87, 88–92, 98, 105, 109, 110, 111, 144, 147, 148–56, 157–66, 167, 168, 169, 170, 173
Von Ryan's Express, 118

Waggner, George, 33
Wake Wood, 169
Waldman, H., 4
Walker, Johnny, 2, 146, 148
Ward Baker, Roy, 64, 68, 69, 109, 122, 150, 165
Warner Bros./Warner International, 64, 65, 67, 66, 69, 70, 71, 72, 73, 77, 79, 80, 81, 82, 84, 85, 86, 94, 98, 108, 109, 157, 158, 159, 160, 161, 164, 167, 168, 170, 171
Warren Publishing, 92, 93, 97, 98–9
Warren, James, 92
Welch, Raquel, 95, 106
Welles, Orson, 99
Wesson, Penny, 130
Whale, James, 19, 20, 22
When Dinosaurs Ruled the Earth, 111, 112
Whispering Smith Hits London, 16

White, Gordon, 54
White, Henry, 102
Wicking, Christopher, 11, 71, 94, 95, 96, 98, 99, 100, 101, 105, 106, 107, 111, 113, 128, 132, 134, 137, 159, 177, 178, 179
Wild Geese, The, 138
Williams, Anthony, 130, 135–6, 137, 138
Williams, Linda Ruth, 174
Winchester Films, 158–9
Witch of Rose Hall, The, 154
Wolf Man, The, 33
Wolfshead: The Legend of Robin Hood, 97

Woodhouse, H., 27, 30, 31
Wragge, Martin/Martin Wragge Productions, 117, 137
Wreyford, Natalie, 174
Writers Guild of America, 140, 159
Wynorski, Jim, 104

X the Unknown, 16, 23
X-certificate, 16, 44, 48, 68, 69, 79, 52

Yesterday's Enemy, 46, 130
Young Riders, The, 161

Zaslav, David, 171
Zeppelins v Pterodactyls, 5, 176, 6

EU representative:
Easy Access System Europe
Mustamäe tee 50, 10621 Tallinn, Estonia
Gpsr.requests@easproject.com